THE BLACK MAN'S PRESIDENT

THE
BLACK MAN'S
PRESIDENT

Abraham Lincoln, African Americans,
& the Pursuit of Racial Equality

MICHAEL BURLINGAME

PEGASUS BOOKS
NEW YORK LONDON

THE BLACK MAN'S PRESIDENT

Pegasus Books, Ltd.
148 West 37th Street, 13th Floor
New York, NY 10018

Copyright © 2021 by Michael Burlingame

First Pegasus Books cloth edition November 2021

Interior design by Maria Fernandez

Library of Congress Cataloging-in-Publication Data is available.

ISBN: 978-1-64313-813-8

10 9 8 7 6 5 4 3 2 1

Printed in the United States of America
Distributed by Simon & Schuster
www.pegasusbooks.com

For Richard Hart,
who pioneered the way

CONTENTS

INTRODUCTION

O n June 1, 1865, Frederick Douglass strode into the Great Hall of New York's Cooper Union where an "immense mixed audience, people of color predominating," gathered to hear the famed African American orator eulogize Abraham Lincoln, assassinated six weeks earlier because he had, for the first time, publicly endorsed Black voting rights. "Every seat was filled, and several hundred persons were compelled to stand," according to the *New York Times*. On the extended platform sat scores of prominent citizens alongside "a select class of young ladies," students at the city's Black schools, who sang several numbers that evening. Presiding over the event was the Black abolitionist and educator Ransom F. Wake, who read a long statement condemning "in unmeasured terms" the New York City Council's order, issued in April, forbidding African Americans from participating in the funeral procession when the train bearing Lincoln's remains to Springfield passed through Manhattan. Incensed by the Council's action, Wake helped organize the Cooper Union meeting to protest the ban and allow African Americans to properly mourn Lincoln.

After reading the protest, Wake introduced Douglass, who began by further condemning the Council's action as "one of the most disgraceful and sickening manifestations of moral emptiness ever exhibited by any nation or people professing to be civilized." But, he asked, paraphrasing Hamlet's query about Queen Hecuba of Troy, "what was Lincoln to the colored people or they to him?" Answering his own question, he stated flatly that Lincoln was "emphatically the black man's President, the first to show any respect for the rights of a black man, or to acknowledge that he had any rights the white man ought to respect," the first chief executive to rise "above the prejudices of his times and country." Lincoln treated each African American "not as a patron, but as an equal."[1]

Months earlier, at the opposite end of the ideological spectrum, a Democratic newspaper which had been critical of Lincoln used some of that very language while asking with a sneer, "When did we ever have a President that made so much of the negro, or was ever [so] willing to take him into his private and social circles as Abraham Lincoln does? Mr. Lincoln is emphatically the black man's president and the white man's curse."[2]

The best evidence to support the contention that Lincoln was "emphatically the black man's president" is not just his policy decisions and public statements regarding emancipation, the enrollment of Black troops, and Black voting rights, but also his personal relations with African Americans. Because interactions speak louder than words, Lincoln's views on race are best understood through an examination of his dealings with Black Illinoisans and Black Washingtonians. His meetings with Frederick Douglass are well-known, but not his similarly revealing encounters with many other African Americans.

❦

As a racial egalitarian, Lincoln condemned the doctrine of White superiority. "Let us discard all this quibbling about this man and the other man—this race and that race and the other race being inferior, and therefore they must be placed in an inferior position," he boldly announced at the outset of his campaign for the Senate in 1858. "Let us discard all these things, and unite as one people throughout this land, until we shall once more stand up declaring that all men are created equal. . . . I leave you, hoping that the lamp of liberty will burn in your bosoms until there shall no longer be a doubt that all men are created free and equal."[3] The following year, while praising the Declaration of Independence, he referred scornfully to the belief that there were "superior races": "The principles of Jefferson are the definitions and axioms of free society. And yet they are denied and invaded, with no small show of success. One dashingly calls them 'glittering generalities'; another bluntly calls them 'self evident lies'; and still others insidiously argue that they apply only to 'superior races.'"[4] He warned White supporters of the enslavement of African Americans that they too might logically be enslaved: "You say A. is white, and B. is black. Is it *color*, then [that justifies enslaving people]; the lighter, having the right to enslave the darker? Take care. By this rule, you are to be slave to the first man you meet, with a fairer skin than your own."[5]

Historian David S. Reynolds observed that Lincoln's "public racial pronouncements were sometimes conservative," yet those "public racial pronouncements" made during his presidency were often far from conservative.[6] In 1864, for example, while accepting an honorary membership in the New York Workingmen's Democratic Republican Association, he declared, "None are so deeply interested to resist the present rebellion as the working people. *Let them beware of prejudice*, working division and hostility among themselves." Alluding to New York's murderous anti-Black draft riots of the previous year, he stated that the "most notable feature of a disturbance in your city last summer, was the hanging of some [Black] working people by other working people. It should never be so. The strongest bond of human sympathy, outside of the family relation, should be one uniting all working people, of all nations, and tongues, and kindreds." Lincoln reminded the

Workingmen's Association of what he had told Congress three years earlier: "The prudent, penniless beginner in the world, labors for wages awhile, saves a surplus with which to buy tools or land for himself; then labors on his own account another while, and at length hires another new beginner to help him. This is the just, and generous, and prosperous system, which opens the way to all—gives hope to all, and consequent energy, and progress, and improvement of condition to all."[7]

Lincoln believed that the chief aim of government was "to lift artificial weights from *all* shoulders—to clear the paths of laudable pursuit for *all*—to afford *all*, an unfettered start, and a fair chance, in the race of life."[8] The Declaration of Independence stated that "all *men* are created equal" and "endowed by their Creator with certain unalienable Rights." Individuals—not states, not regions, not identity groups—were endowed with rights. He rejected the "concurrent majority" theory of John C. Calhoun, who insisted that the two main regions—North and South—had equal rights, particularly to carry into the western territories whatever they wished, including slaves. Lincoln likewise rejected the notion that one race had rights that other races did not.

While Lincoln stressed that all people deserved "an unfettered start, and a fair chance, in the race of life," he did not believe that everyone would succeed equally. As he told a Connecticut audience in 1860, "I want every man to have the chance—and I believe a black man is entitled to it—in which he can better his condition." He added that "it is best for all to leave each man free to acquire property as fast as he can. Some will get wealthy. I don't believe in a law to prevent a man from getting rich." He and his fellow Republicans, he insisted, "wish to allow the humblest man an equal chance to get rich with everybody else."[9]

Lincoln thought that success in the race of life depended on resolute determination, industry, and dedication to self-improvement. To one young man who wished to become a lawyer, he suggested that "work, work, work, is the main thing."[10] To another, he wrote, "your own resolution to succeed, is more important than any other one thing." He added that if the would-be attorney was "resolutely determined to make a lawyer of yourself," then "the thing is more than half done already."[11] To his junior law partner, he explained that "the way for a young man to rise is to improve himself every way he can, never suspecting that any body wishes to hinder him."[12] When a friend of his eldest son was denied admission to college, Lincoln offered words of encouragement: "you *can* not fail, if you resolutely determine, that you *will* not."[13]

Lincoln's advice resembled that of Frederick Douglass, who declared that even people of "only ordinary ability and opportunity" can succeed in the race of life if they would make their watchwords "WORK! WORK!! WORK!!! WORK!!!!" Douglass elaborated: "Not transient and fitful effort, but patient, enduring, honest, unremitting and indefatigable work into which the whole heart is put."[14]

Lincoln championed equality of opportunity, not of results. Industrious, resolutely determined, self-improving, upwardly striving people of all races and religions would succeed if artificial weights were lifted from their shoulders and the paths of laudable pursuit were cleared. If some people failed, it was not the fault of the free labor system but rather "because of either a dependent nature which prefers it, or improvidence, folly, or singular misfortune."[15]

❧

Chapter 1 covers Lincoln's years in Springfield, where, as historian Kenneth J. Winkle noted, "Lincoln had extensive interaction with African Americans," living in a racially mixed neighborhood, representing African American clients, employing Black servants, knowing Black conductors on the Underground Railroad, befriending a leader of the Black community, and championing the antislavery cause.[16] Springfield's Black residents "were a significant part not only of the town's life, but of Abraham Lincoln's life and environment," according to historian and attorney Richard Hart.[17]

Lincoln did not meet with Black visitors during the first year of his presidency, but throughout his time in the White House he did interact with the mansion's Black staff members. Chapter 2 examines those interactions with African American employees, who found him a cordial, respectful, natural egalitarian. Among them was a leader of Washington's Black community, the impressive William Slade, who served as chief butler as well as a confidant to Lincoln. This chapter also describes Lincoln's interactions with African Americans outside the White House, including his memorable tour of Richmond soon after Union forces captured it, his visits to hospitals, and his inspection of United States Colored Troops.

In April 1862, the proverbial ice was broken when Lincoln met with two Black leaders whose visits are covered in Chapter 3. The first was Bishop Daniel Payne of the African Methodist Episcopal Church, a prominent educator with whom he discussed the abolition of slavery in Washington; the second was another prominent educator, Alexander Crummell, a philosopher who came seeking to promote colonization in Liberia, where he lived. This chapter also presents an overview of Lincoln's views on colonization, the subject of a controversial meeting he held with some leaders of Washington's Black community.

Chapter 4 describes and analyzes that event in depth, arguing that the president aimed his remarks not primarily at his five African American guests but at the millions of people in the lower north and border states who might disapprove of the Emancipation Proclamation that he was poised to issue. Those potential dissenters were willing to support the war as long as it was perceived as a struggle to restore the Union, but not if it were to become an abolitionist crusade. By letting them know that he was actively supporting the resettlement abroad of some African Americans, Lincoln believed he could sugarcoat the bitter pill of emancipation, reassuring conservative Northerners that a tsunami of freed slaves would not engulf their region. In addition to allaying those fears, he wanted to provide a haven for pessimistic African Americans who understandably despaired of achieving equality in the US.

In 1863, many more African Americans called at the White House, some to promote colonization and others to deal with a new matter: Black soldiers. The Emancipation Proclamation provided for the enlistment of Black men in the Union Army, reversing the administration's earlier policy. Chapter 5 describes how some African American visitors urged the president to accept an all-Black legion, others sought permission to preach to Black troops, and still others protested against the unequal treatment of such soldiers. The best known of these visitors was Frederick Douglass, whose well-documented interview established a remarkable partnership, each man moving toward the other's political position as they sought to promote both emancipation and military victory.

The year 1864, covered in Chapter 6, saw even more African Americans calling on the president. Lincoln summoned Frederick Douglass to help devise a plan to ensure that slaves *officially* freed by the Emancipation Proclamation could be liberated *in fact* if a Democrat should win that year's presidential election. One of the most important interviews the president ever held with African Americans took place in March, when two visitors from New Orleans submitted a petition calling for Black voting rights. They were so persuasive that Lincoln promptly urged the governor of Louisiana to have the state's constitutional convention enfranchise at least some African Americans.

Chapter 7 examines White House receptions where Black guests are known to have appeared. The most famous is the one held just after Lincoln's second inauguration on March 4, 1865, when Frederick Douglass was initially denied admittance. It is widely thought to be the first time that African Americans attended such a reception, but actually there had been at least four others, beginning on January 1, 1864. While the president was glad to receive African American guests, Democrats attacked him for doing so, and his wife was less than pleased.

Chapter 8 covers 1865, an annus mirabilis for African Americans during which they achieved many breakthroughs, some of which were facilitated by

Lincoln. Black soldiers and musicians participated in the inaugural parade; large numbers of African Americans attended the inauguration; a Black minister preached a sermon in the Capitol; a Black attorney argued a case before the Supreme Court; Illinois abolished most of its Black Laws; Congress established the Freedmen's Bureau, a social welfare agency whose main mission was to assist newly freed slaves; and Congress passed a constitutional amendment outlawing slavery throughout the land. Among Lincoln's Black guests was Martin R. Delany, the father of Black Nationalism, whose proposal for an all-Black army received the president's endorsement. To forward that plan, Delany was appointed a major, the first African American to serve as a line officer in the Union Army.

Chapter 9 compares Frederick Douglass's little-known 1865 eulogy for Lincoln, whom he deemed "emphatically the black man's president," with his well-known 1876 oration at the dedication of the Emancipation Memorial in Washington, in which he called Lincoln "preeminently the white man's president."

The Appendix examines evidence cited by critics of Lincoln's racial views.

A NOTE ON THE USAGE OF HISTORICAL LANGUAGE

One piece of evidence often cited as proof of Lincoln's racial prejudice is his occasional use of the word "nigger," most often while paraphrasing—and mocking—opponents, foremost among them the shameless racial demagogue, Senator Stephen A. Douglas. That taboo word is frequently quoted in this book, for while it was rarely spoken by Lincoln, it was widely employed by his political adversaries and critics as well as by some of his antislavery allies. The polite, socially acceptable terms for African Americans at the time were "Negro," "black," and "colored person."

As Professor Randall Kennedy of the Harvard Law School observed, "There is nothing necessarily wrong with a white person saying 'nigger,' just as there is nothing necessarily wrong with a black person saying it. What should matter is the context in which the word is spoken—the speaker's aims, effects, alternatives. The word '*nigger*' can mean many different things, depending upon, among other variables, intonation, the location of the interaction, and the relationship between the speaker and those to whom he is speaking." Moreover, "the N-word is not self-defining. Its actual meaning in any given instance always depends on surrounding circumstances. Deriving an understanding of *nigger* thus always requires interpretation," hence it cannot be automatically considered a slur. Professor Kennedy warned against "overeagerness to detect insult" and also advised that, considering "the power of 'nigger' to wound," historians should be careful "to provide a context within which presentation of that term can be properly understood." By the same token, it is "also imperative [to] permit present and future readers to see for themselves directly the full gamut of American cultural productions, the ugly as well as the beautiful, those that mirror the majestic features of American democracy and those that mirror America's most depressing failings." Historians should therefore present "politically sensitive nineteenth-century material" as it "appeared in historical context."[18]

By quoting the ugly N-word as it appeared in historical context, I feel an affinity for another scholar, the linguist John McWhorter, professor of English and comparative literature at Columbia University, who observed in his 2021 book *Nine Nasty Words: English in the Gutter*, "I sense myself as pushing the envelope—and feel a need to state that in this chapter ["Why Do We Call It 'The N-Word'?"] I will be writing the word [*nigger*] freely, rather than 'the N-word.' Am I taking advantage of the fact that I am Black, such that etiquette allows me a certain leverage? Yes indeed. I apologize for any discomfort it engenders but suspect that few readers or listeners would truly prefer that I . . . compose an entire chapter without naming what I am discussing, or write *the N-word* a hundred times. I will use it as sparingly as I can, but that will nevertheless leave a great many times when I do spell it out, love it though I shall not."[19]

Unlike Professor McWhorter, I am not Black, but much like him, I feel it necessary to apologize for any discomfort that quoting the N-word causes. I suspect that few readers or listeners would truly prefer that I compose a book involving nineteenth-century American racial politics with *N-word* written innumerable times. I do not love quoting it, but it is impossible to understand Lincoln's use of it without placing that usage in historical context, unpleasant as it may be to contemplate the use of a word that "mirrors America's most depressing failings."

On a related matter, I fear some readers may be made uncomfortable by language used by African Americans who greeted Lincoln on public occasions. That language was recorded in antislavery newspapers whose reporters evidently quoted the dialect not to belittle the speakers—though it was not uncommon for many Democratic journals, and even some Republican ones in the Midwest, to do so—but rather to accurately render what was said. Instead of paraphrasing or modernizing such language, I have reproduced it exactly as originally written in order to lend verisimilitude to those emotionally charged scenes. The dialect seems authentic, insofar as one can detect from recordings of former slaves made during the 1930s.[20] Moreover, the reporters whom I cite when quoting Black dialect, such as abolitionist Charles C. Coffin, supported African American freedom.

Some of the material in this volume first appeared in recent issues of the *Journal of the Abraham Lincoln Association* as well as in my earlier books, among them *Abraham Lincoln: A Life* and *The Inner World of Abraham Lincoln.*

THE BLACK MAN'S PRESIDENT

1

"Extensive Interaction with African Americans in Springfield"

The Illinois Years

L incoln's racial egalitarianism had roots in Illinois, as Arna Bontemps, the poet/novelist and prominent member of the Harlem Renaissance, noted many decades ago. In an essay titled "Lincoln and the Negro," Bontemps and co-author Robert Lucas asserted that "Lincoln's faith in the ability of the Negro to respond to education and opportunity can be traced to his contact with the Negroes he had known in Illinois," including "ordinary people who loved him as their country lawyer friend and later revered his memory as their martyred liberator."[1]

SPRINGFIELD'S BLACK COMMUNITY

During Lincoln's twenty-four years in Springfield, he lived in close proximity to members of the town's small Black population.[2] In 1860, about nine percent of the Illinois capital's African Americans resided within three blocks of the Lincolns' home at Eighth and Jackson Streets, including families who dwelt only a few houses away.[3]

Far from passively acquiescing to that era's racial order, Springfield's African Americans showed pluck and courage by actively trying to undermine slavery and improve the lot of their fellow Black Illinoisans. William H. K. Donnegan, Lincoln's bootmaker, helped runaway slaves to freedom via the Underground Railroad, as did Lincoln's near-neighbor Jameson Jenkins, a carter/drayman who lived half a block away with his wife, children, and mother-in-law, Jane Pellum, a laundress who worked for the Lincolns. Those men ran a grave risk in a city where antislavery sentiment was far from popular. In 1850, Jenkins boldly facilitated the northward flight of seven runaway slaves, creating an uproar in the local press.[4] That same year in Springfield, James Blanks and half a dozen other people of color who were "desirous of educating their children" denominated themselves trustees of "the Colored School" and publicly announced a fundraising effort. Two years later, Blanks joined with nineteen other Black men in signing a resolution calling for the establishment of a school for African American children. "We must speak in bold terms," they proclaimed. As "a portion of the colored population," they felt "a deep, very deep interest, in our schools, and think it the only sure way to redeem ourselves from the bondage we are now in." They pledged to "do everything that is in our power to educate our children by our exertions" without asking "aid from the people of the State."[5] In 1854, White public schools were first introduced in Springfield; four years later, a modest equivalent for Black children was established.

It is not known how personally acquainted Lincoln was with his Black neighbors, but when he departed Springfield for Washington in 1861, he and his luggage were taken to the train depot by his neighbor, Jameson Jenkins, an Underground Railroad conductor. That luggage had been packed with the help of Mariah Vance, a Black woman who worked off and on as a day servant in the Lincoln home during the 1850s.[6] Her purported memoirs are suspect, but other sources indicate that she regarded Lincoln highly.[7] She called him "one of the best men in the world," whom she knew "when he was a struggling young lawyer." His "treatment of her was always kind."[8] Born Maria Bartlett ca. 1819 near Springfield, she married Henry Vance in 1842 and had several children with him. In 1850, she began working in the Lincoln home as a cook. Many years later, Robert Todd Lincoln made a special effort to visit her in Danville, where she had moved after the Civil War, and recollected how he had enjoyed her cooking.[9]

Another African American woman, Ruth Stanton (née Burns) worked in the Lincolns' home ca. 1849–1851. As she told a journalist, her principal employer, Adeline Bradford, apparently took pity on the Lincolns, "who were poor then," and "sent me over to help Mrs. Lincoln every Saturday, for she had no servant and had to do her own housework. Then Mrs. Bradford sent me to live with the Lincolns." There she "scrubbed the floors and waited on the table," helped "to clean the dishes and do the washing," and tended to the children, young Robert and Eddy. An adolescent when employed at the Lincolns' home, she recalled that "Mr. Lincoln was a very good and kind man."[10]

Other African American servants also had positive memories of Lincoln. Among them was Henry Brown, a tall man who resembled Lincoln.[11] Born in North Carolina in 1823, he worked for the Lincolns from 1855 to 1861, performing a variety of jobs: calcimining and repairing the house's fences, gates, and outbuildings; tending the family's horse; digging in the garden; delivering messages; and serving as a valet for Lincoln and a chauffeur for his wife. Brown's spouse Mary was also employed by the Lincolns, milking their cow as well as helping with laundry, cleaning, and other household chores. Reportedly she "was a bright, intelligent, kindly woman" who "had been educated in a white school" in Paris, Illinois, "but after some color-line remonstrance" was "ousted from the school," thus ending her formal education. A physician who once treated her recalled that she said, "Mrs. Lincoln has been to my house a hundred times or more, and often talked with me perhaps an hour or more at a time."[12]

Henry Brown was a minister in the African Methodist Episcopal Church; he established a branch of that denomination in Quincy in 1858 while continuing to live in Springfield. Originally a Quaker, having resided as an adolescent with a Quaker family in Indiana, he became "famous for years as the Methodist preacher of the old school" and was known as Deacon Brown.[13] Like many other Quakers, he strove to undermine slavery and to protest against the second-class citizenship to which free African Americans were consigned. In 1853, while living in Edgar County, he served as a delegate to the first Convention of the Colored Citizens of the State of Illinois, held in Chicago. It adopted an address to the people of the Prairie State which asserted: "We have too long remained supinely inactive, and apparently indifferent to our oppressed and degraded condition. . . . But we have now resolved to come forward; and, like men, speak and act for ourselves." The delegates protested against the new Black Law which forbade African Americans to settle in the state: "Can such a monstrous injustice as this, be the will of the People? If so, would it not be more honorable in the Legislature of Illinois, to appoint a day upon which, every colored man, woman and child should be murdered and thus set the matters to rest?"[14]

(Another Black friend of Lincoln, the barber Spencer Donnegan, also served as a delegate to that convention. Like Brown, he was a minister in the African Methodist Episcopal Church; he founded a congregation in Springfield in 1843 and another in the nearby town of Lincoln in 1866.)

In both Springfield and Quincy, Deacon Brown aided passengers traveling to freedom along the Underground Railroad.[15] According to Brown's granddaughter, he "loved Mr. Lincoln, and the Lincolns felt the same way about him." When Brown "decided to combine his duties [at the Lincoln home] with the ministry, Mr. Lincoln was proud of him and encouraged him."[16] After Lincoln won the 1860 election, Brown asked if he could accompany him to Washington and continue serving as his body man. Lincoln at first agreed but eventually changed his mind. When the disappointed Brown asked why, Lincoln allegedly said, "Well, Brown, if the people of

Washington were to see us together around the White House they would not know which one was the president."[17] At Lincoln's funeral, Brown led the martyred president's horse in the procession to Oak Ridge Cemetery.

WILLIAM FLORVILLE, LINCOLN'S BEST BLACK FRIEND

The Black Springfielder closest to Lincoln was William Florville (also spelled Fleurville). Affectionately referred to as "Billy the Barber," he was born free in Haiti around 1806; during a revolution there fifteen years later, his god-mother took him to Baltimore and enrolled him in a Catholic school. When she died, a court apprenticed him to a barber. Having learned that trade and grown tired of Maryland's cold winters, he moved to New Orleans, where many Haitian refugees lived and he could speak his native French. Finding the social climate uncomfortable, he resettled in St. Louis. But as a freeborn African American, he lacked free papers and was thus vulnerable to kidnappers. So he crossed the Mississippi River to the free state of Illinois and headed for Springfield. In 1831, as he was making his way thither, he found himself near the village of New Salem. There he encountered Lincoln, who introduced him to friends and helped him find temporary work. Thus was planted the seed of what would become a friendship that transcended racial, class, and social boundaries.

After a brief stay in New Salem, Florville continued on to Springfield, where the following year he established a barbershop. By 1837, when Lincoln moved to that town, the industrious, business-savvy, gregarious barber had prospered. In 1849, a Springfield paper deemed him "one of the politest men in our city."[18] His shop became a popular social center where Lincoln not only received shaves and haircuts but also spent much time swapping stories with the humorous Florville and other customers. The barber won popular favor with his musical talent as well as his tonsorial skill; in the evenings he entertained townsfolk by playing one of the several instruments he had mastered. His granddaughter heard her father say that "Lincoln would come to the shop in the evening, to sprawl out in a chair and listen" to Florville play the violin.[19]

In time, Florville expanded his business horizons by setting up a dry cleaning establishment and profitably speculating in real estate. A generous philanthropist, he contributed liberally to local charities and churches, both Catholic and Protestant. When he died in 1868, his widow and five children inherited a substantial estate.[20] Lincoln helped him along, serving as his attorney in at least two cases.[21] When Florville acquired property in nearby Bloomington, Lincoln arranged to have the title to that land secured and the taxes paid.

Florville was more than Lincoln's barber and client; he was also a true friend. Nothing better illustrates the nature and depth of that friendship than a long letter he wrote to Lincoln in 1863, prompted by the warm wishes that the president had asked his friends Anson Henry and Illinois Governor Richard Yates to convey. Florville began by thanking Lincoln for those indirect verbal greetings, which made him think that it "might not be improper for one so humble in life and occupation, to address the President of the United States." Further justifying his decision to write was "our long acquaintance." He speculated that Lincoln might read his missive "with pleasure as a communication from Billy the Barber," for the president had shown that he esteemed "the poor, and downtrodden of the Nation" as highly as he did "those more favored in Color, position, and Franchise rights." For such egalitarianism, "I and my people feel greatful [sic] to you." He voiced special gratitude for the Emancipation Proclamation as well as the hope that it would be extended to cover the entire country, not just the Confederacy. "May God grant you health, and Strength, and wisdom, so to do, and so to act, as Shall redown[d] to his Glory, and the Good, peace, prosperity, Freedom, and hap[p]iness of this Nation." He hoped Lincoln would be reelected and prosecute the war to a successful conclusion, after which "the oppressed will Shout the name of their deliverer, and Generations to Come will rise up and call you blessed."

On a more personal note, Florville alluded to Lincoln's recent attack of varioloid, a mild form of smallpox: "I was Sorry to hear of your illness, and was glad when I learned that your health was improving. I hope by this time, you are able, or soon will be, to attend to your arduous buisness [sic]." He also offered belated condolences for "the death of your Son Willy. I thought him a Smart boy for his age, So Considerate, So Manly: his Knowledge and good Sence [sic], far exceeding most boys more advanced in years." He asked Lincoln to tell his younger son, Tad, "that his (and Willy[']s) Dog is alive and Kicking [and] doing well." Of further personal interest to Lincoln, Florville reported that "Your Residence here is Kept in good order" because the couple who rented it "has no children to ruin things." As for himself, "My family are all well. My son William is Married and in buisness [sic] for himself. I am occupying the Same place in Which I was at the time you left." Somewhat ominously, he added, "I should like verry [sic] much, to See you, and your family, but the priviledge [sic] of enjoying an interview, may not soon, if ever come." In closing, he asked Lincoln to "please accept my best wishes for yourself and family, and my daily desires for yourself that your Administration may be prosperous, Wise, and productive of Good results to this nation, and may the time Soon come, When the Rebellion Shall be put down; and Traitors, receive their just recompence of reward, and the People be at Peace, is the Sincere feelings of your obt [obedient] Servant William Florville the Barber."[22]

The warm personal tone, the domestic details, and the cordial sentiments expressed indicate that Florville and Lincoln were truly friends, not simply acquaintances or business associates. At Lincoln's funeral, Florville served as an honorary pallbearer. Decades later, Jacob C. Thompson, an authority on Springfield history, said, "There were just two men in Springfield who really knew Lincoln in those old days," William Herndon (his law partner for sixteen years) and William Florville.[23]

OTHER BLACK SPRINGFIELDERS

Lincoln's view of African Americans was shaped not only by those with whom he interacted in Springfield but also those whom he saw on the street and those about whom he read, like Florville's chief business competitor, the barber Samuel S. Ball. A leading supporter of African colonization (encouraging Black Americans to escape the prejudice they experienced in the US by resettling in Liberia), Ball probably attracted the attention of Lincoln, who shared his interest in the colonization movement. Though no evidence indicates that the two men interacted, Lincoln doubtless followed Ball's activities in the local press. In 1847, the Illinois Colored Baptist Association resolved to send "Elder S. S. Ball to Liberia, as an Agent to inquire into the condition of the aforesaid country, and to report to this Association on his return." The following year, a Springfield newspaper reported that "S. S. Ball, a very respectable colored man, late of this city, left Baltimore in a sch[oone]r on the 11th April for Liberia, for the purposes of examining that country as an asylum for free blacks."[24] Soon after returning home that summer, Ball published an impressive thirteen-page report, "Liberia, The Condition and Prospects of that Republic; Made from Actual Observation." In 1851, he told audiences in Springfield and St. Louis, "I am the warm friend and enthusiastic admirer of Liberia," which he depicted as "the brightest spot on this earth to the colored man. Liberia not only protects the colored man in the enjoyment of equal rights, but . . . its institutions fostered merit, developed the moral and intellectual faculties of its citizens, and produced great men."[25] In that same year, Ball drafted legislation authorizing the Illinois General Assembly to underwrite the expenses of any free African Americans who wished to resettle in Liberia. Though it enjoyed the support of Springfield's *Illinois State Journal* (a newspaper closely associated with Lincoln), the bill went nowhere in the legislature.[26]

An obituarist described Ball as "a man of good native talent, well cultivated for one in his circumstances" and "one of the most active, intelligent and useful colored Ministers in the State," best known for "his visit to the Colony of Liberia, in 1848, as an exploring agent of the Colored Baptist Association of Illinois." He "was affable in his deportment, respectable in scholarship, kind and affectionate in his social relations, [and] esteemed by all."[27] As president, Lincoln may have been willing to support colonization in part because of Ball's favorable report.

In all likelihood, Lincoln also followed news accounts indicating that many Black Springfielders did not share Ball's enthusiasm for colonization. In 1858, the following resolutions were adopted at a meeting of African Americans held to protest the Illinois Colonization Society's support for a bill like the one submitted by Ball seven years earlier:

> We have been unable to ascertain that any intelligent man of color either desires to remove to Africa, or requires aid for such an enterprise. We have no desire to exchange the broad prairies, fertile soil, healthful climate and Christian civilization of Illinois, for the dangerous navigation of the wide ocean, the tangled forests, savage beasts, heathen people and mismatic shores of Africa. We . . . believe that the operations of the Colonization Society are calculated to excite prejudices against us, and to impel ignorant or ill disposed persons to take measures for our expulsion from the land of our nativity, from our country and from our homes. We . . . most earnestly protest against the recent decision of the Supreme Court of the United States in the case of Dred Scott, which misrepresents, the great charter of American liberty, the Declaration of Independence and the spirit of the American people. . . . We take that Declaration as the Gospel of freedom; we believe in its great truth, "that all men are created equal, endowed with certain inalienable rights, among which are life, liberty and the pursuit of happiness." . . . We claim our rights . . . under this Declaration of the Old Thirteen.

We also claim the right of citizenship in this, the country of our birth. We were born here, and here we desire to die and to be buried. We are not African. The best blood of Virginia, Maryland, Kentucky and other States, where our brethren are still held in bondage by their brothers, flows in our veins. We are not, therefore, aliens, either in blood or in race, to the people of the country in which we were born. Why then should we be disfranchised and denied the rights of citizenship in the north, and those of human nature itself in the south?[28]

Lincoln interacted with many other Black Springfielders about whom little is known, including servants in his home (in addition to Ruth Stanton, Mariah Vance, and Jane Pellum), neighbors (in addition to the families of Jameson Jenkins and James Blanks), and passersby whom he encountered as he walked through his racially and ethnically diverse neighborhood en route to and from his office.

At that office Lincoln received Black callers, including the Rev. Mr. William J. Davis, pastor of the African Methodist Episcopal Church in Bloomington. He was described in the press as a native Kentuckian, "black as the ace of spades," from whom "religious zeal runs out at every pore." In 1863, Davis described his earlier interaction with the president: "I have been personally acquainted with him for eight years; I have heard him plead law in the bar in this city [Bloomington] often, and during the campaign of 1858 Stephen A. Douglas for United States Senator, I heard him speak to thousands of people. Mr. Lincoln is naturally a kind-hearted, sociable kind of man. In Feb. 1859, I was in Springfield, Ill. I called on him at his office and had quite a sociable talk with him. He asked me if I was ever a slave. I told him in reply that I had been one and was sold twice. 'Ah!' said he, 'Mr. Davis, this government is destined to fall under such a wretched system as American slavery.'"[29]

Lincoln also observed the activities of his African American fellow townspeople through the columns of Springfield newspapers, which he read closely. The local press reported that Black residents took an interest in public affairs related to their race. Aside from protesting against colonization, they celebrated Haiti's Independence Day and Emancipation Day, the anniversary of Britain's abolition of slavery in its West Indies colonies.

LINCOLN AND THE ILLINOIS BLACK LAWS

As noted above, two of Lincoln's Black friends (Henry Brown and Spencer Donnegan) attended the 1853 Chicago African American Convention called to protest against the Black Law passed that year by the Illinois General Assembly which forbade African Americans to settle in the state. Whether Brown and Donnegan discussed that legislation with Lincoln is unknown, but at least one attendee, H. Ford Douglas of Chicago, did so. In 1858, that twenty-seven-year-old Black abolitionist asked Lincoln to sign a petition calling for the repeal of Illinois' "testimony law" forbidding African Americans to testify against White people in court.[30] It was one of the Prairie State's most notorious Black Laws, which severely limited the rights of Black Illinoisans.

African Americans had been petitioning the state legislature to repeal the Black Laws since 1822, efforts which continued up to 1865 when those statutes were finally stricken from the books (except the ban on interracial marriage). Lincoln had nothing to say about those, but in 1839 he gave a hint of his feelings on the subject when a Democrat in the General Assembly introduced a resolution stating that "it is not only unconstitutional, but improper, inexpedient and unwise 'to repeal all laws existing on the statutes of the State, which graduate the right of the citizens by the color of the skin.'" Lincoln voted with the 44-36 majority to table and thus kill it.[31] Twenty-two years later, in his first inaugural address, he called for legislation outlawing prohibitions against Black resettlement in any state: "might it not be well . . . to provide by law for the enforcement of that clause in the Constitution which guaranties [sic] that 'The citizens of each State shall be entitled to all previleges [sic] and immunities of citizens in the several States.'"[32]

On July 4, 1860, H. Ford Douglas told an audience in Framingham, Massachusetts, that two years earlier, "I went to prominent Republicans, and among others, to Abraham Lincoln and Lyman Trumbull, and neither of them dared to sign that petition, to give me the right to testify in a court of justice! In the state of Illinois, they tax the colored people for every conceivable purpose. They tax the Negro's property to support schools for the education of the white man's children, but the colored people are not permitted to enjoy any of the benefits resulting from that taxation. We are compelled to impose upon ourselves additional taxes in order to educate our children. The state lays its iron hand upon the Negro, holds him down, and puts the other hand into his pocket and steals his hard earnings, to educate the children of white men; and if we sent our children to school, Abraham Lincoln would kick them out, in the name of Republicanism and antislavery!" He also mistakenly accused Lincoln of supporting the very policy that he strenuously and repeatedly opposed: "I do not believe in the antislavery of Abraham Lincoln, because he is on the side of this slave power of which I am speaking, that has possession of the federal government. What does he propose to do? Simply to let the people and the territories regulate their domestic institutions in their own way."[33] Soon thereafter, Douglas called Lincoln "worthless lumber" and told an Ohio audience, "I went to Abraham Lincoln, personally, with a petition for the repeal of this infamous [testimony] law, and asked him to sign it, and he refused to do it. I went also to Lyman Trumbull, with the same petition, and he also refused; and he told me, if I did not like the laws of Illinois, I had better leave the State!"[34]

Unlike Lincoln, Trumbull insisted in 1858 that the Republican party was "the white man's party. [Great applause.] We are for free white men, and for making white labor respectable and honorable, which it never can be when negro slave labor is brought into competition with it. [Great applause.] We wish to settle the Territories with free white men, and we are willing that this negro race should go anywhere that it can to better its condition, wishing them God speed wherever they go. We believe it is better for us that they should not be among us. I believe it will be better for them to go elsewhere." When asked "where?" he replied: Central America.[35]

A former slave, Douglas lectured widely throughout the country, lauding John Brown and championing the emigrationist movement, some of whose members encouraged African Americans to remove to Central America. In 1861, he abandoned his earlier focus on Africa, joined James Redpath's Haitian Emigration Bureau, and helped persuade Black Americans to immigrate to that Caribbean nation.

Lincoln left no record of his encounter with Douglas, nor did he speak or write about the Black Code of Illinois. When the provision of the 1848 constitution empowering the legislature to forbid Black immigration into the state was submitted for ratification, Lincoln did not cast a vote, for he was in Washington at the time serving in the House of Representatives. It seems likely that he would have opposed it, for many of his friends and fellow Whig leaders did so. They formed a distinct minority in Springfield, where the ban on Black settlement won the approval of 774 voters and the disapproval of only 148. (Statewide it was approved by a vote of 50,261 to 21,297.) Among that small minority in the Illinois capital was Stephen T. Logan, Lincoln's second law partner and strong political ally. As a delegate to the 1847 Illinois constitutional convention, Logan had opposed that provision, as did another of Lincoln's friends, Stephen A. Hurlbut. The husband of Mary Lincoln's sister Elizabeth, Ninian W. Edwards, also a delegate, tried to defeat the measure with a poison pill amendment. He had generously supported Lincoln when he was a fledgling lawyer and acted as Lincoln's political ally in the Illinois legislature. Other friends and associates of Lincoln who voted against Black exclusion were Ninian Edwards's brother Benjamin, a lawyer who studied with Stephen T. Logan and became a partner with John Todd Stuart, Lincoln's first partner; Anson G. Henry, a close friend and political ally of Lincoln as well as his family doctor; and

Simeon Francis, editor of Springfield's Whig newspaper, which published many of Lincoln's anonymous political writings. (Francis's wife, Eliza, helped facilitate the reconciliation and eventual marriage of Lincoln to Mary Todd.) Lincoln's friends who opposed Black exclusion also included James C. Conkling, the Whig mayor of Springfield and husband of Mary Lincoln's good friend Mercy Levering; James H. Matheny, one of the two groomsmen at Lincoln's wedding; and Albert Taylor Bledsoe, editorial writer for the Springfield Whig paper and a fellow party leader.[36] Many of these friends of Lincoln were members of the Colonization Society; in fact, sixty percent of that organization's Springfield chapter voted against the exclusion measure, indicating that they were not opposed to living in a biracial society.[37]

In 1845, when Anson S. Miller, an Illinois state legislator, vehemently denounced the state's original Black Code (especially the "testimony law"), Lincoln listened closely to his remarks. Miller recalled that Lincoln was "his most attentive auditor, leaning throughout the speech against a pillar in the [House of Representatives] chamber" and was "one of the first [auditors], and the warmest, to greet him when the speech was over."[38]

In 1857, Senator Stephen A. Douglas denounced Lincoln for implicitly criticizing the Black Code's provision that African Americans could not marry White people. According to the senator, whoever shared Lincoln's view that Black Americans were included in the Declaration of Independence's assertion that "all men are created equal" must necessarily "license him [the Black man] to marry a white woman."[39] Other Illinois Democrats expressed vehement opposition "to placing negroes on an equality with white men, by allowing them to vote and hold office, and serve on juries, and testify in the courts against white men, and marry white women, as advocated by those who claim that the Declaration of Independence asserts that white men and negroes were created equal by the Almighty."[40] A Democratic congressman who had represented Springfield said of Black people, "We wanted no intermixture of white blood with theirs."[41]

Lincoln had eloquently argued that indeed the signers of the Declaration meant to include African Americans when they asserted that "all men" were created equal. In 1858, he said of the signatories, "In their enlightened belief, nothing stamped with the divine image and likeness was sent into the world to be trodden on, and degraded, and imbruted by its fellows. They grasped not only the whole race of man then living, but they reached forward and seized upon the farthest posterity. They erected a beacon to guide their children and their children's children, and the countless myriads who should inhabit the earth in other ages. Wise statesmen as they were, they knew the tendency of prosperity to breed tyrants, and so they established these great self-evident truths, that when in the distant future some man, some faction, some interest, should set up the doctrine that none but rich men, *or none but white men*, were entitled to life, liberty and the pursuit of happiness, their posterity might look up again to the Declaration of Independence and take courage to renew the battle which their fathers began—so that truth, and justice, and mercy, and all the human and Christian virtues might not be extinguished from the land; so that no man would hereafter dare to limit and circumscribe the great principles on which the temple of liberty was being built."[42] Three years later, when Lincoln delivered a similarly impassioned paean to the Declaration, a Democratic journalist wrote disapprovingly that the Illinoisan had "declared he would 'rather be assassinated on the spot' than abandon his idea of negro independence and negro equality." As David S. Reynolds observed, what that reporter "recognized was the radical egalitarianism—a belief in the equality of *all* people, regardless of race or nationality—that Lincoln's reading of the Declaration implied."[43]

In response to Senator Douglas's taunts, Lincoln in 1858 suggested that, since the Black Laws had been passed by the Illinois General Assembly, Douglas should run for a seat in that body rather than the US Senate. Further, Lincoln declared, "I protest, now and forever, against that counterfeit logic which presumes that because I do not want a negro woman for a slave, I do necessarily want her for a wife. My understanding is that

I need not have her for either, but as God made us separate, we can leave one another alone and do one another much good thereby. There are white men enough to marry all the white women, and enough black men to marry all the black women, and in God's name let them be so married." Senator Douglas "regales us with the terrible enormities that take place by the mixture of races; that the inferior race bears the superior down." Lincoln told the Senator, "if we do not let them get together in the territories they won't mix there." He continued: "let us discard all this quibbling about this man and the other man—this race and that race and the other race being inferior, and therefore they must be placed in an inferior position. . . . Let us discard all these things, and unite as one people throughout this land, until we shall once more stand up declaring that all men are created equal."[44]

In 1859, when asked about his support for Illinois' ban on interracial marriage, Lincoln responded, "The law means nothing. I shall never marry a negress, but I have no objection to any one else doing so. If a white man wants to marry a negro woman, let him do it—*if the negro woman can stand it.*"[45]

Though disappointed by Lincoln's refusal to sign the petition advocating repeal of the "testimony law," H. Ford Douglas made speeches on his behalf in 1858, prompting the Democratic *Illinois State Register* of Springfield to observe: "he spoke in one of the Ottawa churches, much to the edification and delight of his abolition republican brethren, who seem in duty bound . . . to swallow every greasy nigger that comes along. They certainly need all the assistance, be it white or black, to bolster up the rapidly declining prospects of Abraham—hence it is perfectly right that he should take a nigger to his bosom."[46] The Ottawa *Little Giant* remarked: "We heard a prominent Republican tell another the other day that Mr. Schlosser should have been kicked out of the court house for presuming that a nigger was going to speak at the Free church, although the object of his address was to help Lincoln. Every fool knows that his speech would do Lincoln more harm than good."[47] In August 1858, Stephen A. Douglas evidently alluded to

H. Ford Douglas when he remarked during a debate with Lincoln: "I am told also that one of Fred Douglas' kinsmen, another rich black negro, is now traveling this part of the State making speeches for his friend Mr. Lincoln, who is the champion of the black man's party."[48] (Presumably he meant H. Ford Douglas, who was unrelated to Frederick Douglass.)

In 1860, H. Ford Douglas seemed to repent his earlier support for Lincoln. At Framingham, Massachusetts, he asked rhetorically, "if any man can tell me the difference between the anti-slavery of Abraham Lincoln, and the anti-slavery of the old Whig party, or the anti-slavery of Henry Clay," who "was just as odious to the anti-slavery cause and anti-slavery men as ever was John C. Calhoun." Douglas alleged that in 1849, Lincoln "introduced, on his own responsibility, a fugitive slave law for the District of Columbia."[49]

Rising from the audience in Framingham, Senator Henry Wilson—a dedicated champion of Black freedom and civil rights—challenged Douglas's version of Lincoln's proposed 1849 statute: "Mr. Lincoln was born in Kentucky, a slave State, and went to Illinois, and living in a portion of that State which did not entertain the sentiments of this State [Massachusetts], and with a constituency living under what he called the Black Laws of Illinois, he went into Congress and proposed to make the District of Columbia free. I think that he should be honored for that and not misrepresented." Passionately, Senator Wilson urged the assembled opponents of slavery to be more charitable: "When you undertake to arraign men who, in the halls of Congress, before dominating majorities, in a city where public sentiment is against them, where the sneer and the profane word meet them at every step in the streets, are true to the right, I ask you when you deal with such men that you shall do them justice, and that if they have done good deeds and brave deeds, that you say it." He declared that Lincoln was "ahead of the Anti-Slavery sentiment of the Republican party, rather than behind it."[50]

As the presidential campaign wore on, H. Ford Douglas came to regard Lincoln more favorably, reasoning that even if there may be little difference between the Republican standard bearer and Stephen A. Douglas, "there is in the Republican party a strong anti-slavery element. And though the party will do nothing for freedom now, that element will increase; and before long—I trust—springing up from the ruins of the Republican party will come a great anti-slavery party." So he somewhat grudgingly endorsed Lincoln: "I love everything the South hates, and since they have evidenced their dislike of Mr. Lincoln, I am bound to love you Republicans with all your faults," he told a Boston audience shortly before election day.[51] In doing so, he reflected the thinking of William Lloyd Garrison, who in 1859 had told his fellow abolitionists that the "Republican party has certainly been consistent in its efforts to prevent the extension of slavery; it has spent a vast amount of money for the purpose of enlightening the public sentiment so as to save Kansas and Nebraska, and the vast territories of the West, from the encroachments of the slave power. Let the party have the credit of it."[52]

During the Civil War, H. Ford Douglas joined the army, becoming a captain and one of the few Black officers to lead men into combat. In January 1863, he praised Lincoln for issuing the Emancipation Proclamation: "Abraham Lincoln has crossed the Rubicon and by one simple act of Justice links his memory with immortality."[53] Douglas died of malaria in November 1865.[54]

ATTORNEY LINCOLN'S DEALINGS WITH AFRICAN AMERICAN CLIENTS

As a lawyer, Lincoln represented some African Americans, including Mary Shelby, who in 1841 sued for divorce, and fifteen years later appealed for help to save her twenty-five-year-old son John, then languishing in a New Orleans jail. That incautious young man, a crew member aboard a steamship that docked at the Crescent City, had failed to take free papers with him when he went ashore. Soon after he debarked, police arrested him for violating the Louisiana law requiring African Americans to carry such documents. He was tried and given a fine that he could not pay. Faced with the prospect of being sold into slavery in order to raise the necessary money, he managed somehow to alert his mother, who turned to the same attorney she had hired years earlier when seeking a divorce. "Very much moved," Lincoln and his partner William Herndon visited the governor of Illinois, "who, after patient and thorough examination of the law, responded that he had no right or power to interfere," as Herndon recalled. After appealing in vain to the governor of Louisiana, the two law partners had a second interview with the Illinois governor which proved equally futile. Lincoln then erupted in anger: "By the Almighty! I'll have that negro back soon, or I'll have a twenty years' excitement in Illinois until the Governor does have a legal and constitutional right to do something in the premises!"[55]

Finally, Lincoln and Herndon resolved to hire a New Orleans attorney. "Lincoln drew up a subscription-list, which I circulated, collecting funds enough to purchase the young man's liberty," Herndon remembered. With the money thus raised—supplemented with Lincoln's own personal funds—they retained Benjamin F. Jonas (son of Lincoln's good friend and political ally, Abraham Jonas of Quincy), who secured Shelby's freedom. His mother was "overjoyed" to have her son back.[56]

The rescue of young Shelby from prison occurred near the end of Lincoln's twenty-four-year law career; at its beginning, he may well have performed a similar service. While a member of the Illinois General Assembly, which met in Vandalia (the state capital from 1819 to 1839), he evidently helped a young Black indentured servant/slave escape from her indentures. The details are lost to history, but in an obituary of Mary Turner (1822–1897), wife of the Rev. Mr. John Turner, there appears the following statement: "She was an indentured slave under the Illinois laws, until she was eighteen years old; but was freed much sooner through the instrumentality of Abraham Lincoln, then a struggling young lawyer, boarding at her mother's house in Vandalia, Ill."[57] Marriage records indicate that Mrs. Turner's maiden name was Mary Duncan; her mother apparently worked as a slave at a Vandalia boardinghouse owned by Matthew Duncan, brother of Governor Joseph Duncan (1834–1838). Lincoln may have lodged there during at least some sessions of the legislature. It is not clear just what steps had to be taken in order to liberate Mary Duncan from her indenture before 1840, when it was scheduled to expire. She would have needed a "free paper" similar to one issued in 1833 by a Kentucky official and registered six years later by the county clerk in Vandalia. It stated: "Dinah Free Paper: Let the bearer Dinah pass and repass to Vandalia in the State of Illinois without molestation." The clerk noted "that this foregoing free paper, belonging to Dinah (color[ed]) has been this day truly recorded in my said office."[58] Alas, the records of the county clerk for the 1830s, which may have contained such a document for Mary Duncan, are incomplete.

Lincoln officially began his law career in September 1836 when the Illinois Supreme Court licensed him to practice throughout the state. He may well have informed Mary Duncan about a recent Illinois Supreme Court decision that was relevant to her situation. Meeting in Vandalia from December 1836 to March 1837, when the legislature was in session (with Lincoln in attendance), the justices ruled in the case of *Boon v. Juliet* that indentures made before Illinois became a state in 1818 were constitutional, but that any children born thereafter to an indentured servant/slave could not be held to indentures. Therefore, Mary may have been eligible to be freed before reaching the age of eighteen.[59]

In 1841, Lincoln helped another young African American servant/slave, Nance Legins-Costley, solidify her freedom.[60] In the case of *Bailey v. Cromwell*, Lincoln represented David Bailey, who in 1836 had bought Nance from Nathan Cromwell with a promissory note containing the proviso that Cromwell would submit proof that she was in fact a slave and could therefore be legally sold. When no such proof was forthcoming, Bailey refused to honor the note. In the meantime, Cromwell had died, and the administrators of his estate sued for payment, prompting Bailey to hire Lincoln, who maintained that Cromwell had not fulfilled his contractual obligation to submit evidence proving that Nance was actually a slave. In

1839, a trial court ruled in favor of Cromwell, but two years later the Illinois Supreme Court overturned that verdict. In arguing for his client, Lincoln cited precedents that in turn cited the Northwest Ordinance of 1787 and Illinois' state constitution of 1818, both of which banned slavery and "involuntary servitude" in the Prairie State. Referring to earlier relevant cases, the court ruled against Cromwell: "With us the presumption is in favor of liberty," and therefore "the sale of a free person is illegal, and that being the consideration for the note, that is illegal also, and consequently, no recovery can be had upon the note."[61] As a result, not only did David Bailey win his case but Nance gained her freedom *de jure*, which she had been exercising *de facto* for several months as the "property" of Bailey, an abolitionist. She continued living free in the town of Pekin with her husband, Benjamin, and their children.

Six years later, Lincoln apparently did a volte-face, representing a slaveholder, Robert Matson, who employed his legal services to help recover a slave family being sheltered by abolitionists.[62] Matson, a Kentucky resident, cultivated a farm near Charleston, Illinois, with slaves he temporarily imported from the Bluegrass State. That practice was legal in Illinois, where slaveholders were forbidden to domicile bondsmen but could import them seasonally. Anthony Bryant, a free Black man, was married to Jane, with whom he had four children. In 1847, Matson seemed ready to sell Jane and the children, who had settled in Illinois more than two years earlier. To prevent Matson from making that sale, Anthony Bryant enlisted the help of an abolitionist, Gideon Ashmore, who in turn obtained the assistance of a fellow abolitionist, Dr. Hiram Rutherford; the former provided Bryant's wife and children asylum at his home. After Matson failed to persuade Jane to return, he sued Ashmore and Rutherford for damages and filed a complaint against them for violating the state's Black Laws; the court ruled that Jane and her offspring should be committed to the custody of the local sheriff, who jailed them. The abolitionists then filed for a writ of habeas corpus on behalf of the Bryants.

Such was the situation when Lincoln, then traveling the legal circuit, arrived in Charleston. Usher Linder and Thomas Marshall, attorneys for Matson, sought his help in suing Rutherford and Ashmore. Soon thereafter, Rutherford also solicited his assistance, which Lincoln said he could not provide because he had already been approached by somebody acting "in Matson's interest," presumably his counsel. At that time, lawyers felt obliged to abide by the so-called "cab-rank" rule: attorneys must accept the first client who hails them. But, Lincoln added, he would try to get Usher and Marshall to release him. Those two agreed, but when Lincoln told Rutherford he was now free to represent him, the hotheaded abolitionist angrily replied that he had already retained another attorney. If Rutherford had been less petulant, Lincoln would have defended him. But he defended Matson instead.

However reluctant Lincoln may have been to act on Matson's behalf, he forcefully if unsuccessfully argued his client's case. Jane Bryant had been living in Illinois for over two years and was clearly not just a seasonal worker, so the court ruled against Matson. Though it failed to decide that any slave whose foot trod Illinois soil was automatically freed, it did decide that slaveholders' claims—that they were merely taking their slaves through the state or using them as seasonal workers—must be bona fide. Matson dropped his case against Ashmore and Rutherford, who then helped the Bryant family immigrate to Liberia.

Historians have deemed Lincoln's participation in the Matson case "one of the greatest enigmas of his career," the "most profound mystery ever to confound Lincoln specialists," and "one of the strangest episodes in Lincoln's career at the bar."[63] Lincoln was following not only the cab-rank rule but also the widely honored advice of Judge George Sharswood, a celebrated nineteenth-century American commentator on legal ethics, who urged attorneys "not to pass moral judgments on potential clients, but to rely on the legal process itself to determine the merits of the claim." Sharswood held that a lawyer "is not morally responsible for the act of the party in maintaining an unjust cause, nor for the error of the court, if they fall into error, in deciding in his favor." An attorney "who refuses his professional assistance because in his judgment the case is unjust and indefensible, usurps the function of both judge and jury."[64]

Of course, Lincoln could have refused to assist Usher and Marshall, and he may well have been tempted to do so, but those men were personal friends and political allies whom he probably did not wish to disappoint.[65] (The affable Lincoln once quipped that he was glad he had not been born female because he couldn't say "no."[66]) Marshall, a nephew of Henry Clay, may have had a special claim on the respect of Lincoln, who called Clay his "beau ideal of a statesman."[67] An attorney representing the Bryants said that "Lincoln took a hand in the case" at the "earnest solicitation" of Marshall.[68]

According to a close friend, Lincoln avoided runaway slave cases "because of his unwillingness to be a party to a violation of the Fugitive Slave Law," a statute which he wanted modified so that African Americans accused of being runaway slaves would enjoy, as he put it in his first inaugural address, "all the safeguards of liberty known in civilized and humane jurisprudence" to ensure "that a free man be not, in any case, surrendered as a slave." Apropos of reforms to be made to the Fugitive Slave Act, he added, "might it not be well, at the same time, to provide by law for the enforcement of that clause in the Constitution which guarranties [sic] that 'The citizens of each State shall be entitled to all previleges [sic] and immunities of citizens in the several States?'"[69] As historian Kate Masur observed, this appeal indicated unmistakably that from "the outset of his presidency, Lincoln hoped that Congress would take action to affirm African-American citizenship."[70] (Though Lincoln did not represent fugitive slaves in court, he did defend some abolitionists accused of aiding runaway bondsmen.[71])

⚬⚬

This record of Lincoln's interaction with Black Illinoisans, both direct and indirect, belies historian Benjamin Quarles's assertion that before 1861,

Lincoln knew only "the Negro of dialect story, minstrel stage, and the sea chantey" and "little of Negro life, of the Negro's hopes, and of his efforts to move into the mainstream of American life."[72] In fact, he knew many capable, self-respecting Black Illinoisans and their abilities, character, hopes, and "efforts to move into the mainstream of American life." He interacted with them for over two decades before moving to Washington. As he departed the Prairie State for the nation's capital, he memorably said, "To this place, and the kindness of these people, I owe everything." Those people included William Florville, Henry Brown, Mary Brown, Mariah Vance, Ruth Stanton, Mary Shelby, John Shelby, Jameson Jenkins, James Blanks, Jane Pellum, William H. Johnson, William Donnegan, and Spencer Donnegan—African Americans whom he knew and respected, and who in turn knew and respected him.

2

"Blinded by No Prejudices Against Race or Color"

*Lincoln and African Americans
on the White House Staff*

African Americans did not start to call on President Lincoln until 1862, but he began interacting with Black Washingtonians as soon as he occupied the White House in March 1861. Rosetta Wells, a seamstress who did some sewing and mending for the First Family, recalled that "he treated the servants like 'people,' and would laugh and say kind things to them."[1] Echoing her was another seamstress, the former slave Elizabeth Keckly (Mrs. Lincoln's dressmaker and confidante), who told a journalist, "I loved him [the president] for his kind manner towards me." He "was as kind and considerate in his treatment of me as he was of any of the white people about the white house."[2] Peter Brown, a Black waiter, had a young son who spent much time at the Executive Mansion (as the residence was then called) during the Civil War and remembered that Lincoln "was kind to everybody" and "sympathized with us colored folks, and we loved him."[3] The daughter of William Slade, head butler at the White House, reported that the president "never treated [the employees there] as servants, but always was polite and requested service, rather than demand it of them."[4] Presidential secretary William O. Stoddard recalled that in Lincoln's dealings with both Black and White employees, he "took their presence and the performance of their duties so utterly for granted" that none "of them was ever made to feel, unpleasantly, the fact of his [or her] inferior position by reason of any look or word of the President."[5]

LINCOLN AND WILLIAM H. JOHNSON

The best example of Lincoln's solicitude for Black staff members was his treatment of William H. Johnson, a servant who accompanied the First Family on their journey from Springfield to Washington in 1861. Little is known about Johnson's time in Springfield other than that he began working at the Lincoln home in early 1860. He may have been the African American who in May of that year helped set up refreshments for the visiting Republican delegation which informed Lincoln of his nomination.[6] Johnson may also have been the one to whom Lincoln assigned the task of procuring the family's daily bread from a local bakery.[7] In addition, he may have helped tend to the Lincolns' young sons, Willie and Tad. In June 1861, Mrs. Lincoln described him to a friend: "We brought a man, with us, who takes care of them [the children], most of the time."[8]

Johnson enters the historical record while on the rail journey from Springfield to Washington in February 1861. A journalist aboard the train described him as "a very useful member" of the entourage whose "untiring vigilance" as "he took care of the Presidential party" was "entitled to high credit."[9]

Shortly after arriving in Washington, Johnson began working at the Executive Mansion as a porter and presidential valet, much to the consternation of other African American employees. According to John E. Washington, who interviewed Black Washingtonians who had worked in Lincoln's White House, the appointment of Johnson "almost caused an open rebellion, because of a social distinction. Johnson's color was very dark and White House servants were always light. He was mistreated in such a way that it became necessary for the president to look elsewhere for employment for him."[10] A historian of intra-racial prejudice in antebellum Washington asserted that "the tradition of complexion-based elitism among blacks was formal, well organized, and of dire social consequences."[11]

Such intra-racial prejudice has recently been denominated "colorism," similar to the nineteenth-century term "colorphobia," a synonym for Negrophobia. In 2007, sociologist Margaret Hunter noted that many "African Americans feel that discussions of colorism 'air our dirty laundry' for all to see and judge" and that most "people of color agree that colorism is an 'in house' issue, a personal one that is a tragedy within communities of color. It is at minimum, embarrassing, and at its worst, a sign of racial self-hatred."[12] Such intra-racial prejudice was not confined to the nation's capital. In 1837, the abolitionist Sarah Grimké expressed dismay at the social stratification within Philadelphia's Black community: "I mourn the aristocracy that prevails among our colored brethren. I cherished the hope that suffering had humbled them and prepared them to perform a glorious part in the reformation of our country, but the more I mingle with them the fainter are my hopes. They have as much caste among themselves as we have and despise the poor as much as I fear as [do] their pale brethren."[13]

Three days after his inauguration, Lincoln gave Johnson a letter of recommendation: "Whom it may concern. William Johnson, a colored boy, and bearer of this, has been with me about twelve months; and has been, so far, as I believe, honest, faithful, sober, industrious, and handy as a servant."[14] Soon thereafter, the president wrote to Navy Secretary Gideon Welles: "The bearer (William) is a servant who has been with me for some time & in whom I have confidence as to his integrity and faithfulness. He wishes to enter your service. The difference of color between him & the other servants is the cause of our seperation [sic]. If you can give him employment you will confer a favour on yours truly."[15]

When nothing came of those overtures, Lincoln temporarily reassigned Johnson as a White House furnace keeper. Rather than have him remain in that lowly job, the president kept trying to find him employment in some government department. Finally, in November 1861, he successfully appealed to Treasury Secretary Salmon P. Chase: "You remember kindly asking me, some time ago whether I really desired you to find a place for William Johnson, a colored boy who came from Illinois with me. If you can find him the place [I] shall really be obliged."[16] In response, Chase appointed Johnson to a $600-per-year job in his department, evidently as an assistant and messenger for the librarian of the treasury, Samuel Yorke Atlee. To enable Johnson to earn extra money, the president facilitated his efforts to moonlight for others, and Johnson continued to work part-time at the White House as Lincoln's barber, valet, and body man.[17] Occasionally Lincoln gave him checks for small amounts to supplement his modest salary.[18]

In October 1862, Lincoln again provided a recommendation for Johnson: "The bearer of this, William Johnson (colored), came with me from Illinois; and is a worthy man, as I believe."[19] Two months later, the president wrote a memo, referring to Johnson's request for permission to visit Norfolk. It was in reply to a letter that a White House secretary had drafted for Lincoln's signature and addressed to General John A. Dix: "I decline to sign the within [letter], because it does not state the thing quite to my liking. The colored man William Johnson came with me from Illinois, and I would be glad for him to be obliged, if he can be, consistently with the public service; but I can not make an order about it, nor a request which might, in some sort, be construed as an order."[20]

In November 1863, Lincoln asked that Johnson be given time off from his treasury department job to accompany him on his trip to Gettysburg. Soon after they returned to Washington from Pennsylvania, Johnson, like

Lincoln, was laid low by smallpox, which sidelined the president for three weeks and which killed Johnson in January 1864. One day that month, as Johnson lay in his hospital sickbed, a journalist discovered Lincoln counting out greenbacks and placing them in envelopes. He explained that such activity "is something out of my usual line; but a President of the United States has a multiplicity of duties not specified in the Constitution or acts of Congress. This is one of them. This money belongs to a poor negro [Johnson] who is a porter in one of the departments and who is at present very bad with the smallpox. He did not catch it from me, however; at least I think not. He is now in hospital, and could not draw his pay because he could not sign his name. I have been at considerable trouble to overcome the difficulty and get it for him, and have at length succeeded in cutting red tape. . . . I am now dividing the money and putting by a portion labeled, in an envelope, with my own hands, according to his wish."[21]

To purchase a house, Johnson had borrowed money from the First National Bank of Washington, using Lincoln as an endorser. After Johnson's death, the bank's cashier, William J. Huntington, happened to mention the outstanding notes to Lincoln: "The barber who used to shave you, I hear, is dead."

"'Oh, yes,' interrupted the President, with feeling; 'William is gone. I bought a coffin for the poor fellow, and have had to help his family.'"

When Huntington said the bank would forgive the loan, Lincoln replied emphatically, "No you don't. I endorsed the notes, and am bound to pay them; and it is your duty to make me pay them."

"Yes," said the banker, "but it has long been our custom to devote a portion of our profits to charitable objects; and this seems to be a most deserving one."

When the president rejected that argument, Huntington said, "Well, Mr. Lincoln, I will tell you how we can arrange this. The loan to William was a joint one between you and the bank. You stand half of the loss, and I will cancel the other."

After thinking it over, Lincoln said, "Mr. Huntington, that sounds fair, but it is insidious; you are going to get ahead of me; you are going to give me the smallest note to pay. There must be a fair divide over poor William. Reckon up the interest on both notes, and chop the whole right straight through the middle, so that my half shall be as big as yours. That's the way we will fix it."

Huntington agreed, saying, "After this, Mr. President, you can never deny that you indorse [sic] the negro."

"That's a fact!" Lincoln exclaimed with a laugh, "but I don't intend to deny it."[22]

It is not clear just where William Johnson's grave is located. Some claim that Lincoln had him interred at Arlington Cemetery, but the evidence is inconclusive. A headstone there is marked "William H. Johnson, Citizen," but it is not certain that this refers to the same Johnson; he could well have been interred in a long-since destroyed graveyard for Black smallpox victims. With a similar lack of evidence, some also assert that Lincoln paid for his gravestone. If in fact the stone in Arlington Cemetery marks Johnson's final resting place, some have assumed that the designation "Citizen" indicates that Lincoln regarded African Americans as citizens. But the designation "Citizen" is found on many gravestones in the area where Johnson is purportedly buried; that word was simply the equivalent of "civilian," as opposed to military veteran, so it lacks the greater significance sometimes attributed to it.

The story of Lincoln's relationship with William Johnson does, however, shed light on the president's humanity and his racial egalitarianism. Some might object that Lincoln, by referring to him on two occasions as a "boy," demonstrated something less than full respect for Johnson.[23] But the president also referred to him twice as a "man," indicating that, in his mind at least, "boy" did not have the pejorative meaning it later acquired.[24] Moreover, as John E. Washington wrote in 1942, "Lincoln's constant interest in William Johnson shows us, even more than do some of his greatest public deeds and much heralded acts, the great heart of this man. He had induced Johnson to leave Springfield and accompany him to Washington on a most perilous journey and thereafter never ceased to be interested in him, but continued to assist him in every manner possible. Lincoln was not like many employers who bring servants to strange cities and then dispense with their services and leave them stranded in a strange place without home or employment. Although he deemed it undiplomatic to force Johnson's presence upon the resentful servants of the White House, Lincoln felt it a bounden duty to look out for him."[25]

Just as he had helped William H. Johnson obtain a government job, so too did Lincoln assist Samuel Williams, the twenty-one-year-old son of a White House cook, "Aunt Mary" Williams.[26] The young man was working as a barber in the Executive Mansion when the president wrote to Treasury Secretary Chase in July 1862: "The bearer of this, son of our cook, is a good barber, and a good boy generally, I believe. He had a position during the session of Congress, in which he gave entire satisfaction as I understand, but which came to an end by the adjournment. Please see him a moment, & do something for him if you can."[27] According to Williams, Lincoln's "high regard" for his mother prompted him to write that recommendation.[28] On September 10, 1862, Chase appointed Williams to a position in the treasury department, where he remained employed for the next two decades.

To fill the treasury department post that William H. Johnson had held, Lincoln suggested his twenty-two-year-old Black barber/attendant, Solomon J. Johnson. A year later, he recommended Johnson for a promotion. Eventually Johnson became one of the first African Americans to hold a white-collar position in the federal government.[29] Historian Eric Yellin noted that "Solomon Johnson led the way" for Black civil servants: "During his career, 620 black men and women joined him in Washington's various department offices, laying the foundation for black civil service for the next quarter century."[30]

The cases of Solomon Johnson, Samuel Williams, and William H. Johnson reflected a trend established by the Lincoln administration: the federal government would appoint African Americans to clerkships and other jobs that were more than menial.[31] In 1863, William J. Wilson, a Black schoolteacher and journalist based in Brooklyn, visited Washington, where he was surprised to find "responsible colored men, by scores, employed here, in the Capitol, in the Treasury, in the State Department; in fine, in all the Departments of government." To Wilson, such employment represented "an acknowledgement of a capacity, but more, an evidence of political recognition." He marveled that the "individual colored man may rise as he pleases. I speak for the great masses."[32] Two years later, Lincoln signed a bill overturning the rule that the Post Office could only hire White applicants.[33] This was no small matter, for at the time more than seventy-five percent of all federal government civilian workers, White and Black, were employed in that department.

WILLIAM SLADE: BUTLER, COMMUNITY LEADER, AND PRESIDENTIAL CONFIDANT

To replace William H. Johnson as his valet, Lincoln appointed William Slade, a forty-seven-year-old, light-skinned African American who was serving as a treasury department messenger. A native of Washington and son of a prominent White citizen, Slade had worked for many years as the head porter at the Indian Queen Hotel. In the late 1850s, he moved to Cleveland so that his children might obtain a better education than they could in the District of Columbia.[34] Upon Lincoln's election, Slade returned to the capital, where he had established a reputation as a leader of the Black community. He was widely liked and respected for his industry, reliability, and amiable personality.[35] One of Lincoln's assistant personal secretaries described Slade as "faithful, prudent and dignified," and a journalist who had known him in both Cleveland and Washington reported him to be "honest and brave," a man "whom all were bound to respect."[36]

Slade acted as the chief White House servant (referred to as the usher or steward, equivalent to the head butler at an English manor house). In addition to his manifold duties—among them supervising the African American staff, conveying messages, making arrangements for small dinner parties, and serving as a presidential valet—he became a confidant to Lincoln. According to John E. Washington, who interviewed Slade's daughter Katherine and others who knew him, he "had a wonderful disposition, never became excited, always could see the bright side of things, even when Lincoln was downcast and needed a cheering, hopeful friend." Slade "was really a confidential and constant companion, and was treated by Lincoln with the greatest intimacy." The two "would talk sometimes nearly all night about matters of grave concern. Lincoln just had to have somebody to loosen up on and in Slade he found the right person." Like his boss, Slade was a humorist with a large fund of jokes and stories. According to his cousin Hannah Brooks, Slade was "much beloved" by Lincoln.[37]

Further bonding the two men were Slade's children (Katherine, Andrew, and Jessie), who played with Tad after his brother Willie died in 1862. The young Slades would sometimes come to the Executive Mansion and "spend the entire day playing with Tad in the basement, in the White House grounds, or any other part of the house that the little son of the President wanted to use." On occasion, Tad would visit the Slades' nearby home, a boardinghouse on Massachusetts Avenue. Residents of that neighborhood "said that Tad played with all the children and he was a real boy in the midst of real boys and girls, white and colored."[38]

Lincoln was doubtless aware of Slade's status as a leader of Washington's African Americans and a champion of their rights. A near-relative recalled that Slade was "always ready to join any effort for the elevation of his people."[39] In addition to being an elder in the elite Fifteenth Street Presbyterian Church (near the White House), he served as president of the

Social, Civil, and Statistical Association, some of whose members met with Lincoln in 1862 to discuss colonization. That same year, Slade established an evening school for African Americans, staffed by government clerks. Slade and his wife, Josephine, also participated actively in the affairs of the National Freedmen's Relief Association.[40] Slade was a prominent member of both a Masonic lodge and the Columbian Harmony Society, an organization founded by Washington's Black community "to aid each other in infirmity, sickness, disease, or accident, and to provide burial for them after death."[41] Lincoln's views on race were surely affected by his close relationship with such an impressive figure.

ENCOUNTERS WITH AFRICAN AMERICANS OUTSIDE THE WHITE HOUSE

When away from the White House, Lincoln treated African Americans as respectfully as he did the Black employees at the Executive Mansion. In May 1862, he visited Washington's Columbia College Hospital, where nurse Rebecca Pomroy presented him first to officers on the staff and then to members of the Black kitchen crew.

"And who are these?" he asked in a kindly voice as three African American cooks came forward.

"This is Lucy, formerly a slave from Kentucky. She cooks the nurses' food."

"How do you do, Lucy?" he asked as he extended his hand to shake hers. "And who are these on your left?"

"This is Garner, and this Brown. They are serving their country by cooking the low diet for our sickest boys."

"How do you do, Garner? How do you do, Brown?" he asked as he shook their hands.

Lucy, Garner, and Brown were amazed and joyful; the White staff was also amazed but not joyful. Nurse Pomroy quickly "became aware of a feeling of intense disapprobation and disgust among the officers, who a moment before had been all graciousness and suavity. Their conversation was afterwards reported to her. 'Anybody would know she was a Massachusetts woman,' they said, 'for no one else would do such a mean, contemptible trick as to introduce those d[amned] niggers to the President.'

"'Yes,' said the surgeon in charge, 'it was in Massachusetts that the first abolition egg was laid.'"

Even the hospital's patients felt insulted by the president's unusual cordiality to African Americans. Later, when Pomroy asked him if he had been hurt by those introductions, he replied: "Hurt? No, indeed! it did my soul good. I'm glad to do them honor."[42]

Lincoln exhibited similar egalitarianism in his relations with Black crew members of the *River Queen*, the ship that had taken him to the Virginia front near the close of the war. On April 7, 1865, he accompanied his wife and some friends on a rail trip to Petersburg, recently abandoned by the Confederates. One member of the party, Charles Adolphe Pineton (Marquis de Chambrun), recalled that their railcar "was an ordinary American car, and we took seats in its centre, grouping ourselves around Mr. Lincoln. In spite of the car's being devoted to Mr. Lincoln's special use, several officers also took their places in it without attracting any remark. Curiosity, it seems, also had induced the negro waiters of the *River Queen* to accompany us." Lincoln "had not what can be termed false dignity" and "allowed them to sit quietly with us." The president, wrote Chambrun, "was blinded by no prejudices against race or color."[43]

Earlier in the war, Lincoln visited a Washington camp housing so-called "contrabands" (refugee slaves). Mary Dines, a former slave who cooked for the Lincolns at the Soldiers' Home, recalled that when at that camp, the president "was very fond of the hymns of the slaves and loved to hear them and even knew most of them by heart." One Saturday, he and the First Lady attended a camp concert. As the Black residents intoned hymns and patriotic airs, Lincoln wiped tears from his eyes. During the final number—"John Brown's Body"—he "joined in the chorus and sang as loud as anyone there." Once or twice he choked up. On another visit, he asked to hear "some more good old hymns." When the camp residents obliged, he sang along with them. Mary Dines reported that "he was so tenderhearted that he filled-up [i.e., his eyes teared up] when he went over to bid the real old folks good-by." He was, she said, "no President when he came to camp. He just stood and sang and prayed just like all the rest of the people." Whenever the older contrabands got carried away and began shouting and yelling during prayers, "he didn't laugh at them, but stood like a stone and bowed his head." Mary Dines "said she really believed that the Holy Ghost was working on him."[44]

On April 4, 1865, two days after the Union Army captured Richmond, Lincoln toured the Confederate capital.[45] While doing so, he was wildly cheered by throngs of African Americans. When the president and his companions first arrived, the abolitionist reporter Charles C. Coffin pointed them out to some nearby Black workers, who shouted "Hallelujah!" and "Glory! Glory! Glory!" Dozens of them raced to the landing site, yelling and screaming, "Hurrah! Hurrah! President Linkum hab come!" Hearing the commotion, more Black men, women, and children poured into the streets. Coffin reported the scene:

> They gathered round the President, ran ahead, hovered upon
> the flanks of the little company, and hung like a dark cloud
> upon the rear. Men, women, and children joined the constantly

increasing throng. They came from all the by-streets, running in breathless haste, shouting and hallooing and dancing with delight. The men threw up their hats, the women waved their bonnets and handkerchiefs, clapped their hands, and saying, "Glory to God! glory! glory! glory!"—rendering all the praise to God, who had heard their wailings in the past, their moanings for wives, husbands, children, and friends sold out of their sight, had given them freedom, and, after long years of waiting, had permitted them thus unexpectedly to behold the face of their great benefactor. "I thank you, dear Jesus, that I behold President Linkum!" was the exclamation of a woman who stood upon the threshold of her humble home, and with streaming eyes and clasped hands gave thanks aloud to the Savior of men. Another, more demonstrative in her joy, was jumping and striking her hands with all her might, crying—"Bless de Lord! Bless de Lord! Bless de Lord!" as if there could be no end of her Thanksgiving.[46]

A few White celebrants also joined the throng. Coffin informed readers of the *Boston Journal* that "no written page or illuminated canvas can give the reality of the event—the blacks and poor whites who have suffered untold horrors during the war, their demonstrations of pleasure, the shouting, dancing, the thanksgiving to God, the mention of the name of Jesus—as if President Lincoln were next to the son of God in their affections—the jubilant cries, the countenances beaming with unspeakable joy, the tossing up of caps, the swinging of arms of a motley crowd—some in rags, some barefoot, some wearing pants of Union blue and coats of Confederate gray, ragamuffins in dress through the hardships of war, but yet of stately bearing."[47]

A Black newsman reported that as soon as Lincoln landed, some African Americans, "feeling themselves free to act like men, shouted that the President had arrived." Others, mistakenly assuming that this was an allusion to Jefferson Davis, cried out: "Hang him!" "Hang him!" "Show him no quarter!" Upon realizing it was Lincoln, "their joy knew no bounds."[48] When some of them knelt before him, he said: "Don't kneel to me. That is not right. You must kneel to God only, and thank him for the liberty you will hereafter enjoy."[49]

When Lincoln asked directions to General Godfrey Weitzel's headquarters, a Black man offered to show the way.[50] Half a dozen sailors, armed with carbines, led the presidential party; another six brought up the rear. The Black crowd enveloped the little entourage, shouting, clapping, dancing, throwing hats into the air, waving bonnets and handkerchiefs, and applauding loudly. They stirred up great clouds of dust which, combined with the smoke from smoldering buildings set ablaze by the retreating Confederates, made the warm atmosphere oppressive. Lincoln, wearing a long overcoat, was perspiring freely and fanning himself to cool off.[51] In a letter written that day, one member of the military escort reported that "we had a hard road to travel as the crowd was getting more dense at every moment, almost impossible to get through as it was not an ordinary task to keep the people back or prevent them from enveloping us entirely—whilst there was one incessant roar of cheering: from the almost frantic population, and at every corner it was augmented and the streets on all sides were filled with people running to get a glimpse of Old Abe."[52]

Because of the heat, and since Tad had trouble keeping up, the little party stopped to rest. At that point, according to Coffin, "an old negro, wearing a few rags, whose white, crisp hair appeared through his crownless straw hat, lifted the hat from his head, kneeled upon the ground, clasped his hands, and said, 'May de good Lord bress and keep you safe, Massa President Linkum.'" The President "lifted his own hat and bowed to the old man."[53] Lincoln's gesture was, Coffin thought, "a bow which upset the forms, laws, customs, and ceremonies of centuries. It was a death-shock to chivalry, and a mortal wound to caste." A White woman observing this scene turned away "with unspeakable contempt."[54] Many other White observers resented Lincoln's presence, for not only were they mortified by the Confederate defeat, but "worst of all, that plain, honest-hearted man was recognizing the 'niggers' as human beings by returning their salutations!"[55] To Coffin, the most impressive feature of the day "was the respect which Lincoln showed to the poor creatures when he removed his hat, while the old negro prayed God to bless him."[56] Coffin added that "tears almost came" to the president's eyes "as he heard the thanksgivings to God and Jesus, and the blessings uttered for him from thankful hearts."[57]

Lincoln then entered a carriage and toured Richmond with some military leaders. As they rode along, hundreds of African Americans, in a frenzy of exultation, shouted out expressions of gratitude and joy, sang songs of deliverance, wept, and threw their hands in the air.[58] A Black correspondent told readers of the *Philadelphia Press* that there was "no describing the scene along the route. The colored population was wild with enthusiasm. Old men thanked God in a very boisterous manner, and old women shouted upon the pavement as high as they had ever done at religious revival."[59] One celebrant declared, "Jeff Davis did not wait to see his master but he had come at last."[60] Others exclaimed, "thank God, Jesus Christ has come at last" and "God Bless Abum Linkum, bless his heart, I give him the last thing I got in the world."[61] The president "looked at it all attentively, with a face expressive only of a sort of pathetic [i.e., emotional] wonder."[62]

At Capitol Square, Lincoln reportedly addressed a huge, mostly Black crowd. According to Admiral David Dixon Porter, the president said, "My poor friends, you are free—free as air. You can cast off the name of slave and trample upon it; it will come to you no more. Liberty is your birthright. God gave it to you as he gave it to others, and it is a sin that you have been deprived of it for so many years. But you must try to deserve this priceless boon. Let the world see that you merit it, and are able to maintain it by your good works. Don't let your joy carry you into excesses. Learn the laws and obey them; obey God's commandments and thank him for giving you liberty, for to him you owe all things. There, now, let me pass on; I have but little time to spare. I want to see the capital, and must return at once to Washington to secure to you that liberty which you seem to prize so highly."[63]

Some sources indicate that Lincoln did not address the crowd, but seventeen-year-old Lelian Cook, living at the home of the Rev. Mr. Moses D. Hoge, recorded in her diary on April 4 that after visiting Jefferson Davis's residence, "Lincoln appeared on the square, accompanied by an escort of colored troops. He was in a carriage-and-four. I heard he made an address to the colored people, telling them they were free, and had no master now but God."[64]

That address resembles the one Lincoln made in November 1864 to several hundred Black Washingtonians who descended on the White House to celebrate the adoption of Maryland's new constitution abolishing slavery. The president told them, "It is no secret that I have wished, and still do wish, mankind everywhere to be free. [Great cheering and cries of 'God bless Abraham Lincoln.'] And in the State of Maryland how great an advance has been made in this direction. It is difficult to realize that in that State, where human slavery has existed for ages, ever since a period long before any here were born—by the action of her own citizens—the soil is made forever free. [Loud and long cheering.] I have no feeling of triumph over those who were opposed to this measure and who voted against it, but I do believe that it will result in good in the white race as well as to those who have been made free by this action of emancipation, and I hope that the time will soon come when all will see that the perpetuation of freedom for all in Maryland is best for the interests of all, though some may thereby be made to suffer temporary pecuniary loss. And I hope that you, colored people, who have been emancipated, will use this great boon which had been given you to improve yourselves, both morally and intellectually."[65]

As historian Michael Vorenberg observed, this speech showed that "the president was willing to entertain a biracial vision of the country, a vision that depended on Blacks maintaining an appetite for education."[66] When presenting a reconstruction scheme to Union authorities in New Orleans,

Lincoln instructed General Nathaniel P. Banks: "Education for young blacks should be included in the plan."[67] In his first political campaign three decades earlier, Lincoln had emphasized the importance of education: "I view it as the most important subject which we as a people can be engaged in" and expressed a "desire to see the time when education, and by its means, morality, sobriety, enterprise and industry, shall become much more general than at present."[68]

The reception Lincoln received from the Black population of Richmond may well have reminded him of the similar reception he experienced in June 1864 when he visited the Virginia front. After inspecting some White army units there, he took General U. S. Grant's suggestion that he "see the colored troops, who behaved so handsomely in [General William F.] Smith's attack on the works of Petersburg last week." The president expressed keen interest in doing so, for he had not yet reviewed any of the United States Colored Troops: "I had fully intended to go out and take a look at the brave fellows who have fought their way down to Petersburg in this wonderful campaign, and I am ready to start at any time." He was delighted by reports of their gallantry, which vindicated his controversial decision to authorize the enlistment of Black soldiers. "I think[,] general," he told Grant, "we can say of the black boys what a country fellow who was an old-time abolitionist in Illinois said when he went to a theater in Chicago and saw Forrest playing *Othello*. He was not very well up in Shakespeare, and didn't know that the tragedian was a white man who had blacked up for the purpose. After the play was over the folks who had invited him to go to the show wanted to know what he thought of the actors, and he said: 'Waal, layin' aside all sectional prejudices and any partiality I may have for the race, darned ef I don't think the nigger held his own with any on 'em.'" Reflecting on the decision to allow Black men to serve in the army, Lincoln added: "I was opposed on nearly every side when I first favored the raising of colored regiments, but they have proved their efficiency, and I am glad they have kept pace with the white troops in the recent assaults."[69]

When Lincoln reached the camp of the Eighteenth Corps, hundreds of Black troops, "wild with excitement and delight," rushed to see him, hurrahing and cheering. A journalist reported that it "was a spontaneous outburst of love and affection for the man they looked upon as their deliverer from bondage."[70] They "received him most enthusiastically, grinning from ear to ear," Colonel Horace Porter wrote his wife. With "much fervor," they shouted:

> "God bress Massa Linkum!"
> "De Lord save Fader Abraham!"
> "De day ob jubilee am come, shuah."[71]

They swarmed about Lincoln, kissing his hands, patting his horse, and reverently touching his dust-covered black suit. Grant's aide Adam Badeau wrote a friend that the Black troops "had never seemed so to realize the reality of their freedom as when they saw this incarnation or representative of it."[72] As he rode bare-headed with tears in his eyes, Lincoln bowed left and right and tried to acknowledge the plaudits, but his voice was, according to Porter, "so broken by emotion that he could scarcely articulate the words of thanks and congratulation which he tried to speak to the humble and devoted men through whose ranks he rode. The scene was affecting in the extreme, and no one could have witnessed it unmoved."[73]

Earlier that year, when the Eighteenth Corps marched past the White House, African American soldiers waved their caps and heartily cheered "Hurrah for Massa Linkum!" and "Three cheers for the President!"[74] With tears in his eyes, Lincoln bowed to them, exclaiming in a low voice, "It'll do! It'll do!"[75]

While it is commonly acknowledged that the service of those Black troops—who eventually comprised nine percent of the Union's armed forces—helped persuade Lincoln that African Americans deserved full citizenship rights, the similar role played by his interaction with Black civilians is not so widely appreciated.

Lincoln's informal interactions with Black men and women described in this chapter illustrate his instinctive racial egalitarianism. That same egalitarianism characterized his formal encounters with Black visitors to the Executive Mansion. As Michael Vorenberg observed, the "president's position exposed him to black ministers, black educators, and even officials from the newly recognized republics of Haiti and Liberia."[76] Such educated, sophisticated callers helped deepen Lincoln's egalitarian faith and enlarge his frame of reference as he thought about the future of African Americans. In addition to such guests, Lincoln also met with ordinary Black men and women, some in his office and others at White House receptions.

While Black civilian visitors expanded Lincoln's knowledge of African Americans well beyond what he had known in Illinois and disposed him to look favorably on extending citizenship rights to them, his willingness to receive them respectfully and cordially, and to take their concerns seriously, represented an important milestone on the long road to racial equality, for it symbolized a dramatic change in the country's racial climate.[77]

3

"Expressing a Hearty Wish for the Welfare of the Colored Race"

Initial Meetings with African American Leaders

APRIL 1862

In 1862, Lincoln spoke with several African Americans about colonization, a program encouraging some of their race to emigrate. For decades it had been championed by Thomas Jefferson and other national leaders as well as some Black emigrationists. The term "colonization" is often regarded as synonymous with "White supremacy," but many anti-racists at the time—including Black Americans—supported it as part of a strategy to abolish slavery.[1] In its compulsory form, it has been likened to a kind of "ethnic cleansing."[2] While it is true that some supporters of colonization (especially in the South) were Negrophobes who sought to buttress slavery by deporting all free African Americans, many other colonizationists were humanitarians who endorsed a program of voluntary resettlement for various benign reasons: to combat the Atlantic slave trade, to help Africa modernize and prosper, to spread Christianity to that continent, to facilitate emancipation, and to provide a refuge for Black pessimists who feared that they would never attain full citizenship status in the US.[3]

LINCOLN AND COLONIZATION

Lincoln favored colonization for the last two of those reasons. He did not support it as a mass measure constituting a panacea for all the challenges of racial adjustment that would attend emancipation. As historian Eric Foner put it, Lincoln "saw voluntary emigration as a kind of safety valve for individual blacks dissatisfied with their condition in the United States."[4] The president told his cabinet that it was "essential to provide an asylum for a race which we had emancipated," a race that, thanks to deep-seated and widespread Negrophobia, "could never be recognized or admitted to be our equals."[5] While Lincoln understood that colonization on a massive scale was impracticable, he also believed that by publicly endorsing such a policy, he could not only help some African Americans find an overseas sanctuary but also allay the fears of the many White Northerners who opposed emancipation because they feared liberated slaves would swarm into their states.

Lincoln's support for colonization was not "ardent," as some have alleged, but rather lukewarm.[6] He backed it "fitfully and inconsistently," as James Oakes put it.[7] Moreover, he was a latecomer to the movement. During the 1830s and 1840s, he failed to join any of the three colonization societies that emerged in and around Springfield, even though John Todd Stuart (his political mentor and first law partner) did so. As a congressman in 1849, he framed a bill abolishing slavery in the District of Columbia that lacked a colonization clause. Earlier in the 1840s, several Whig lawyers, but not Lincoln, helped found the Illinois Colonization Society, a group that Lincoln addressed in 1853 and 1855 and for which he served as one of its eleven "managers," a post more honorary than functional. In an

1855 speech to the society, he was, according to a reporter, "emphatically non-committal," stating that colonization "was a subject entered into by men of all parties and schools of thought." He said he "would be in favor of the project" only "if it could be accomplished without trouble, without confusion."[8] (In 1860, he told a promoter of Haitian colonization that he would favor that scheme "provided as he himself expressed it, 'it could be brought about fairly and voluntarily.'"[9]) Lincoln's notes for his 1855 address indicate that it was probably a rather dry history lecture, one which Springfield's Whig paper failed to mention.[10] Nor did Lincoln arrange to have that speech published, as he did some of the other addresses he gave at that time. In 1856, he joined the American Colonization Society but did little more than pay dues; unlike Stephen A. Douglas, the egregious race-baiting senator, he never held office in that organization.[11] During his 1858 senatorial campaign against Douglas, Lincoln named three criteria for the successful abolition of slavery in Washington; colonization was not one of them. (In fact, the subject hardly came up during that epic contest.) Moreover, the Illinois Republican party platforms of 1856 and 1858, both of which Lincoln helped draft, contained no mention of colonization, nor did the 1860 Republican national party platform.[12]

In 1852, at the age of forty-three, while eulogizing Henry Clay, Lincoln for the first time spoke publicly about colonization: "If as the friends of colonization hope, the present and coming generations of our countrymen shall by any means, succeed in freeing our land from the dangerous presence of slavery; and, at the same time, in restoring a captive people to their long-lost father-land, with bright prospects for the future; and this too, so gradually, that neither races nor individuals shall have suffered by the change, it will indeed be a glorious consummation."[13] In a passage that foreshadowed the inaugural address he was to deliver thirteen years later, he expressed the insisted that colonization must be voluntary and without expense to those who availed themselves of the opportunity. In addition, the host countries must provide African American immigrants "conditions which shall be equal, just, and humane."[14]

In his first major antislavery speech, delivered in 1854, Lincoln seemed to offer support for colonization with one hand and take it away with the other. Though colonization might seem appealing in theory, it was not so in practice, he told his audience: "If all earthly power were given me, I should not know what to do, as to the existing institution [of slavery]. My first impulse would be to free all the slaves, and send them to Liberia, to their own native land. But a moment's reflection would convince me, that whatever of high hope, (as I think there is) there may be in this, in the long run, its sudden execution is impossible. If they were all landed there in a day, they would all perish in the next ten days; and there are not surplus shipping and surplus money enough in the world to carry them there in many times ten days."[15] (In the nineteenth century, the mortality rate among African American immigrants to Liberia was extraordinarily high.[16]) He went on to say, apropos of White Americans' unwillingness "to make blacks politically and socially our equals," that a "universal feeling, whether well or ill-founded, can not be safely disregarded."[17] This is a classic example of what historian David S. Reynolds referred to as a "racist sounding pronouncement" that was "cunningly surrounded with phrases that pointed in a radically abolitionist direction," for Lincoln implied broadly that such White prejudice was "ill-founded."[18]

Three years later, Lincoln noted that neither political party formally addressed colonization, but insofar as they did so informally, their approaches were strikingly dissimilar: "How differently the respective courses of the Democratic and Republican parties incidentally bear on the question of forming a will—a public sentiment—for colonization, is easy to see." Immediately thereafter, he delivered one of his most passionate denunciations of slavery and racism: "The Republicans inculcate, with whatever of ability they can, that the negro is a man; that his bondage is cruelly wrong, and that the field of his oppression ought not to be enlarged. The Democrats deny his manhood; deny, or dwarf to insignificance, the wrong of his bondage; so far as possible, crush all sympathy for him, and cultivate and excite hatred and disgust against him; compliment themselves as Union-savers for doing so; and call the indefinite outspreading of his bondage 'a sacred right of self-government.'"[19]

In Lincoln's view, support for voluntary colonization was part of a humanitarian project, rooted in concern for the well-being of African Americans, for it facilitated emancipation and provided a haven for Black racial pessimists. In the notes for his 1855 lecture to the Illinois Colonization Society, he wrote apropos of the emergence of the colonization movement: "*All the while*—Individual conscience [was] at work."[20]

As president, Lincoln first mentioned colonization publicly in December 1861, when he told Congress that slaves who had fled to Union lines should "be at once deemed free" and that steps should "be taken for colonizing" them "at some place, or places, in a climate congenial to them." He added that it "might be well to consider, too, whether the free colored people already in the United States could not, so far as individuals may desire, be included in such colonization." To implement such a plan "may involve the acquiring of territory" as well as "the appropriation of money beyond that to be expended in the territorial acquisition."[21]

The previous month, he had worked behind the scenes to develop a compensated emancipation plan for submission to the Delaware state legislature; it contained similar language about colonization. In March 1862, however, when he went public with an expanded version of that plan, proposing that Congress compensate any state which abolished slavery, his message said nothing about colonization.

Soon thereafter, Congress twice appropriated funds for colonization. In April, it abolished slavery in Washington and simultaneously authorized the president to spend as much as $100,000 "to aid in the colonization and settlement of such persons of African descent now residing in said District, including those to be liberated by this act, as may desire to emigrate to the

Republic of Haiti or Liberia, or such other country beyond the limits of the United States as the President may determine." Three months later, Congress appropriated another $500,000 as part of the Second Confiscation Act, money that the president was authorized to spend on colonizing slaves who wanted to resettle "in some tropical country beyond the limits of the United States" but only after the administration had obtained "the consent of the Government of said country to their protection and settlement within the same, with all the rights and privileges of freemen."[22]

A supporter of Liberian immigration described that money as "the *carcass* over which the turkey buzzards are gathered together!"[23] Champions of Liberia, Haiti, and Central America hastened to feast on that carcass. In April, some Black residents of Washington had submitted a memorial to Congress asking to be colonized in Central America: "Send us—our prayer is *send us*—to that country we have indicated, that we may not be wholly excluded from you, that we may aid in bringing to you that great commerce of the Pacific, which will still further increase the wealth and power of your country."[24]

Apropos of this appeal, an English journalist observed that even though Black Washingtonians "will not voluntarily live in the North," nonetheless a "fear has arisen among the laboring classes of the Free States that if there was a general act of emancipation the negroes would begin a stampede north. But this fear is groundless. Still it has taken a deep hold on the Northern mind, and politicians with pro-slavery tendencies skillfully make use of this general belief to induce people to oppose emancipation."[25] That fear had indeed taken a deep hold on the public mind, especially in the Midwest. During a debate on abolition in the District of Columbia, Indiana Senator Joseph Wright declared that he and other legislators representing the Hoosier State as well as its neighbors Ohio and Illinois "tell you that the black population shall not mingle with the white population in our States. We tell you in your zeal for emancipation you must ingraft colonization upon your measure. We intend that our children shall be raised where their equals are;

and not in a population partly white and partly black; and we know that equality never can exist between the two races."[26]

In his December 1862 annual message to Congress, Lincoln addressed that common anti-emancipation argument. In doing so, he supported colonization while simultaneously denying the need for it: "I cannot make it better known than it already is, that I strongly favor colonization." (Here Lincoln stretched the truth for political purposes.) "And yet I wish to say there is an objection urged against free colored persons remaining in the country, which is largely imaginary, if not sometimes malicious. It is insisted that their presence would injure, and displace white labor and white laborers." He sternly scolded those who raised such an objection: "If there ever could be a proper time for mere catch arguments, that time surely is not now. In times like the present, men should utter nothing for which they would not willingly be responsible through time and in eternity." Using arguments that opponents of slavery had been deploying for years, he asked why was it "dreaded that the freed people will swarm forth, and cover the whole land? Are they not already in the land? Will liberation make them any more numerous? Equally distributed among the whites of the whole country, and there would be but one colored to seven whites. Could the one, in any way, greatly disturb the seven? There are many communities now, having more than one free colored person, to seven whites; and this, without any apparent consciousness of evil from it."[27] As one historian noted, this passage represented a "courageous appeal for tolerance."[28] By rebutting those "catch arguments," he implicitly made the case that White and Black Americans could peacefully coexist.

But Lincoln went on to cite an argument that seemed to endorse steps taken by Northern states to forbid Black immigration: "And, in any event, cannot the north decide for itself, whether to receive them?" The previous month, Illinois Republicans had suffered at the polls because the War Department had sent refugee slaves into the Prairie State to help with the harvest.[29] That same month, skittish Republican leaders in Massachusetts, including abolitionist governor John A. Andrew, assured constituents they were fighting government plans to have refugee slaves settled in their midst.[30] Lincoln may well have been indirectly tweaking the voters of those states rather than justifying their Negrophobia.

BISHOP DANIEL PAYNE CALLS ON LINCOLN

As president, Lincoln welcomed African American callers, listening courteously and respectfully to their concerns. Such hospitality was exceedingly rare: there are only two known precedents. The first occurred in 1812, when James Madison met with Paul Cuffe, a wealthy Black merchant and ship builder. The cargo aboard one of his vessels had been seized by American customs authorities, and Cuffe successfully appealed to the president to overrule their decision. Thirty years later, John Tyler invited the minister Daniel Payne to preach a funeral sermon for the president's body servant.[31]

Two decades thereafter, Payne (by then a bishop) was again a Black caller at the White House. Writing at that time, the radical abolitionist James Redpath described him as "probably the most influential and respected colored American in this country."[32] Educated at the Lutheran Seminary in Gettysburg, Pennsylvania, Payne helped found Wilberforce University in 1856 and eventually served as its president. His good friend Booker T. Washington called Payne "one of the leading spirits in the establishment of the African-American Methodist Episcopal Church," as well as "a great man, a man of character, a man of vision."[33] The bishop conferred with Lincoln on the evening of April 14, 1862, two days after Congress passed legislation abolishing slavery in the District of Columbia. That bill was sitting unsigned on the president's desk when Payne called.

Lincoln had hesitated to affix his signature to the statute, even though as a congressman in 1849 he had framed a bill liberating slaves in the nation's capital. In March 1862, he publicly urged Congress to facilitate emancipation by providing funds to compensate slaveholders in any state that freed its slaves. Though the loyal Border Slave States resisted that offer, his message encouraged antislavery senators and congressmen to outlaw human bondage in Washington. There the federal government could do so legally, for the Constitution granted Congress plenary power over the District of Columbia. Lincoln had reservations, as he told Horace Greeley in late March: "I am a little uneasy about the abolishment of slavery in this District, not but I would be glad to see it abolished, but as to the time and manner of doing it. If some one or more of the border-states would move fast, I should greatly prefer it; but if this can not be [done] in a reasonable time, I would like the bill [abolishing slavery in the District] to have the three main features—gradual—compensation—and vote of the people."[34] He did not include colonization in his list of desiderata.

Some in Congress favored a more radical approach than Lincoln's. In December 1861, Massachusetts Senator Henry Wilson had introduced a bill not entirely to the president's liking, for though it incorporated compensation to slave owners, it did not provide for a referendum by the voters of Washington and it mandated immediate rather than gradual emancipation. Four months later, lawmakers heatedly debated Wilson's measure, adding a provision for voluntary colonization to be funded by Congress.[35] On March 24, the senate deadlocked on an amendment providing that slaves emancipated by the bill *must* be resettled abroad. Vice President Hannibal Hamlin broke the tie by voting no.[36]

Maryland Unionists denounced the proposed statute as "an act of bad faith on the part of Congress."[37] When a congressman from that state, John A. Crisfield, called at the White House to protest, Lincoln "said he greatly objected to the time, and terms of the bill, and saw the trouble it would cause," but "he also saw the troubles to arise on its rejection." He "could not say it was unconstitutional, and he had come to the conclusion, after full consideration of all the pros & cons, that he would do less mischief by approving than by rejecting it; and he hoped that the people of Maryland, would see the difficulties of his position, and treat him with forbearance."[38]

To his good friend, Illinois Senator Orville H. Browning, Lincoln expressed concern that if the legislation as written were implemented, "families would at once be deprived of cooks, stable boys &c and they [would be deprived] of their protectors without any provision for them." He delayed signing the bill in order to allow Kentucky Congressman Charles Wickliffe time to remove from Washington two sick slaves who, in the president's view, "would not be benefited by freedom."[39] Lincoln also hesitated to approve the bill even though he "never doubted" Congress's authority "to abolish slavery in this District" and had "ever desired to see the national capital freed from the institution in some satisfactory way." The only problem was "the one of expediency, arising in view of all the circumstances."[40] Referring to the legislation he had written as a congressman more than a decade earlier, he told a friend: "Little did I dream in 1849, when . . . I proposed to abolish slavery at this capital, and could scarcely get a hearing for the proposition, that it would be so soon accomplished."[41] In his 1858 debates with Stephen A. Douglas, Lincoln declared that he "would be exceedingly glad to see Congress abolish slavery in the District of Columbia, and, in the language of Henry Clay, 'sweep from our Capital that foul blot upon our nation.'"[42]

As the bill lay on Lincoln's desk without his signature, some slaves in the Washington area were hiding, fearful that their owners might remove them from the District in anticipation of the president's action.[43] Lincoln, who had been conversing with Illinois Congressman Elihu Washburne when Payne sent in his card, met the bishop at the office door, shook his hand, and led him to a seat by the fireplace, near Washburne. They were soon joined by Carl Schurz, recently arrived from Madrid, where he had been serving as America's minister to the Spanish court.

After a few pleasantries, the bishop said to Lincoln, "I am here to learn whether or not you intend to sign the bill of emancipation."

The president replied, "There was a company of gentlemen here to-day requesting me by no means to sign it."

Schurz interjected, "But, Mr. President, there will be a committee to beg that you fail not to sign it; for all Europe is looking to see that you fail not."

The bishop continued, "Mr. President, you will remember that on the eve of your departure from Springfield, you begged the citizens of the republic to pray for you."

"Yes."

"From that moment we, the colored citizens of the republic, have been praying: 'O Lord just as thou didst cause the throne of David to wax stronger and stronger, while that of Saul should wax weaker and weaker, so we beseech thee [to] cause the power at Washington to grow stronger and stronger, while that at Richmond shall grow weaker and weaker.'"

Lincoln's response was evasive: "Well, I must believe that God has led me thus far, for I am conscious that I never would have accomplished what has been done if he had not been with me to counsel and to shield."

Frustrated by the president's failure to answer his question directly, Payne decided that since he had been in the White House for about forty-five minutes, it was time to withdraw. He presented his host with a copy of his denomination's monthly magazine and a recent issue of its weekly newspaper to give the president some idea of what the church was "doing to improve the character and condition of our people in the republic," and departed.

In his memoirs, the bishop wrote that there "was nothing stiff or formal in the air and manner of His Excellency—nothing egotistic." Lincoln "received and conversed with me as though I had been one of his intimate acquaintances or one of his friendly neighbors. I left him with a profound sense of his real greatness and of his fitness to rule a nation composed of almost all the races on the face of the globe."[44]

A few days later, an account of this meeting appeared in *The Christian Recorder* (perhaps written by Payne himself) stating that "Bishop Payne had quite a long and profitable interview with President Lincoln." The bishop had assured his host that he was in "the prayers of the colored people." The president in turn spoke "of his reliance on Divine Providence" and expressed "a hearty wish for the welfare of the colored race."[45]

When Lincoln finally signed the law on April 16, Black Washingtonians were jubilant.[46] In New York, the eminent preacher and colonizationist Henry Highland Garnet told a rejoicing Black crowd that he believed that the president's "mind was made up to sign the bill long before it was passed" and that the president was "one of the first statesmen and rulers in the nation, whose tardiness he belikened to a hostler with a vicious horse, who first cautiously slicks down the animal and then takes him with a master's hand by the mane."[47] Alluding to Proverbs 14:34, Frederick Douglass hailed the new law as "that first great step towards that righteousness which exalts a nation." The New York *Anglo-African* said, "Americans abroad can now hold up their heads when interrogated as to what the Federal Government is fighting for, and answer, 'There, look at our capital and see what we have fought for.'" The president's action, it observed, "marks the grandest revolution of the ages, a revolution from barbarism to civilization" and among African Americans won for him a "confidence and admiration . . . such as no man has enjoyed in the present era."[48]

ALEXANDER CRUMMELL AND JOHN D. JOHNSON CALL ON LINCOLN

The day after hosting Bishop Payne, Lincoln met with the prominent Black abolitionist Alexander Crummell, a philosophy professor and Episcopal priest visiting from his home in Liberia, whose government he was representing as a "commissioner of emigration." A native of New York and an alumnus of Queen's College, Cambridge, Crummell spent the 1850s and 1860s in Monrovia teaching English and philosophy at Liberia College. He championed nationalism and rationalism, the former as a Pan-Africanist and the latter as a moral philosopher. In 1862, the New York publisher Charles Scribner and Co.

issued his book, *The Future of Africa.* Regarded as "the most prominent rationalist of the black American enlightenment thinkers in the nineteenth-century," Crummell eventually became a mentor to W. E. B. Dubois.[49]

Accompanying Crummell was another such commissioner, John D. Johnson, a Monrovia merchant and former barber/saloonkeeper in Brooklyn.[50] Both were lobbying the president, who had just been authorized by Congress to spend $100,000 on efforts to colonize any Black Washingtonians who wished to emigrate. The only press account of that conversation erroneously stated that the visitors "urged the compulsory transportation of freed slaves to Liberia." When Crummell and Johnson asked Lincoln to correct that mistake, he wrote them stating "that neither you nor any one else have ever advocated in my presence the compulsory transportation of freed slaves to Liberia, or elsewhere."[51] (In fact, two cabinet members—Montgomery Blair and Edward Bates—favored involuntary colonization, as did many US senators.)

Crummell and Johnson had been charged by the Liberian authorities to press "the claims which the government and people of Liberia have upon the sympathy of the civilized world" and provide Lincoln with "the necessary information preparatory to a formal recognition of the Liberian republic." They were to convey the desire of Liberia's government "to make arrange-ments for the comfortable settlement in Liberia of such of the free blacks" in the US "as choose to emigrate thither." Further, they were to explain that their government "offers to all men who choose to immigrate to that country a free passage for themselves and families, six months support and medical attendance free after arrival in the country, and sufficient farmlands—say one hundred acres to each family; and the migrants are not bound to remain in the country unless they are pleased with it."[52]

This meeting escaped the attention of Benjamin Quarles, who stated that Crummell and Johnson did not meet with Lincoln.[53] The historian's mistake is understandable, for the press ignored it. But four months later, newspapers did cover extensively Lincoln's meeting with five prominent Black Washingtonians.

4

"A Sop to Conservatives"

A Meeting with Leaders of Washington's African American Community

AUGUST 14, 1862

Lincoln's discussion with Alexander Crummell and John D. Johnson was a prelude to his most extensive remarks on colonization, delivered in August to a deputation of Black Washingtonians. Unlike previous presidents, Lincoln invited African Americans to the White House to discuss public affairs. The first such occasion was his August 1862 meeting with five leaders of the capital's Black community whose support he enlisted for a voluntary colonization project in Central America.[1] This proved to be one of the more controversial steps he took during his administration, for some abolitionists denounced his remarks at that meeting as proof he was a bigot who wished to deport all African Americans, a view endorsed by some later writers.[2] But such an interpretation is profoundly misguided.[3]

ARRANGING THE MEETING

As advocates of various colonization schemes flocked to Washington in search of financial support for their projects, Lincoln decided to invite leaders from the capital's Black community to discuss how best to spend the funds that Congress placed at his disposal. He assigned the task of arranging such a meeting to James Mitchell, a Methodist minister and former agent of the American Colonization Society who had helped found chapters of that organization in Illinois and his home state of Indiana.[4] Lincoln met him in Springfield in 1853, and they corresponded during the 1860 presidential campaign.[5] In May 1862, Interior Secretary Caleb B. Smith recommended that Lincoln hire Mitchell as "an efficient agent familiar with the subject" of colonization.[6] That same month, Mitchell published a report he had written for the president on the "necessity of colonization," an expansion of a long letter he sent Lincoln in December 1861.[7] The president liked him well enough to have him appointed on August 4, 1862, as "Agent for Emigration" (alternatively "Commissioner for Emigration") whose duties were "to organize and locate colonies, superintend the immigration, settlement, or colonization of colored people of African descent under the direction of the President, who, by their own free consent may desire to migrate to countries beyond the limits of the United States, and such other general duties as may be directed by the President, on the subject of migration."[8]

On Sunday, August 10, ministers of several Black churches in Washington read from their pulpits Mitchell's announcement that Lincoln wanted to meet with some African Americans on an important matter. In response, several congregants of Black parishes met later that day in Union Bethel African Methodist Episcopal Church, where Mitchell informed them "that it was the express wish of the President, as trustee of the $500,000 [that Congress had appropriated the previous month to facilitate colonization], for colored men to confer with him as to its disposition" and "urged the appointment of a Committee to wait upon his Excellency, and hear what he desired to say in this matter." They agreed to meet again on August 14 at the same church.

Colonization had long been a controversial subject within antislavery ranks.[9] Black Washingtonians were so sharply divided over it that violence erupted that July when a lobbyist for resettlement in Central America, Joseph Enoch Williams, "was waited on by a party of young men" opposed to emigration. They "gave him a severe beating, and kicked him from the National Hotel, and afterwards treated him to a few buckets of cold water." About the same time, a member of the Liberian delegation visiting Washington, John D. Johnson, was assaulted by two members of an anti-emigration organization, the Social, Civil, and Statistical Association. The assailants were fined and given jail sentences.[10] (In May 1863, Lincoln commuted the latter punishment but retained the former.)

When African Americans reassembled at Union Bethel Church on August 14 in response to Mitchell's appeal, they were inclined to regard the president's request skeptically. Mitchell "stated that the call had been made by himself, seconded by the Rev. H[enry] M[cNeal] Turner, pastor of the Israel M. E. Church, who had sought an interview on his own responsibility with the President in relation to the $600,000 emigration fund." (Turner was a young, highly respected Washington pastor who favored immigration to Haiti.) Mitchell "also stated that the President wished an interview with the meeting as a body, or [rather] with a delegation from it, as his time was so entirely engrossed that he could not attend the meeting in person."

Mitchell's audience debated the request at length, expressing some concern about "whether it was the voluntary action of the President, or forced upon his consideration by the selfish interest of non-resident parties," like lobbyists touting Liberia, Haiti, and Central America. Their curiosity was understandable, for in April 1862, the president had not summoned local Black residents to discuss the $100,000 that Congress appropriated for colonizing Black Washingtonians. So why now? To be sure, Congress in mid-July had appropriated another $500,000 for colonization, but why hadn't he sought African Americans' opinion regarding the earlier appropriation?

LINCOLN'S MOTIVE FOR SUPPORTING COLONIZATION

The reason is doubtless that in August 1862, Lincoln was worried about public reaction to the Emancipation Proclamation he had read to his cabinet the previous month, which he planned to announce as soon as Union arms won a significant victory. (Such a victory would occur in the following month.) He knew many Northerners who gladly supported a war to preserve the Union would not back a war to free the slaves. In order to prepare the country for that epochal proclamation and to help weaken resistance to it, Lincoln took various steps, among them writing a public letter to Horace Greeley the week after meeting with the African American deputation, a document in which he explained that whatever emancipation measures he adopted would be designed to help win the war, whose *aim* would still be the preservation the Union; emancipation, if it were to come, would simply be a *means* to help achieve that end.[11] Similarly, as noted in the previous chapter, he forcefully and at length rebutted the widely shared belief that freed slaves would flood the North and take jobs from workers there.[12] As part of the strategy to defuse hostility to emancipation, Lincoln not only invited Black community leaders to an unprecedented White House meeting but also made sure a stenographic reporter was present to record his words.

At that time it was widely assumed that the public, especially in the loyal Border Slave States (Missouri, Delaware, Kentucky, and Maryland) as well as in the adjacent Free States (Iowa, Kansas, Illinois, Indiana, Ohio, Pennsylvania, and New Jersey), would accept emancipation *only* if it were coupled with colonization. Lincoln's close friend, Kentuckian Joshua Speed, warned him, "So fixed is public sentiment in this state against freeing negroes &

allowing negroes to be emancipated & remain among us—That you had as well attack the freedom of worship in the north or the right of a parent to teach his child to read—as to wage war in a slave state on such a principle."[13] Another Kentuckian, Senator Garrett Davis, assured the president that unionists in the Bluegrass State "would not resist his gradual emancipation scheme if he would only conjoin with it his colonization plan." (To Kansas Senator Samuel Pomeroy, Lincoln at the very time cited this statement to explain his support for colonization.[14])

In July 1862, the president appealed to the Border States' congressional delegations, saying, "I do not speak of emancipation *at once*, but of a *decision at once* to emancipate *gradually*. Room in South America for colonization, can be obtained cheaply, and in abundance; and when numbers shall be large enough to be company and encouragement for one another, the freed people will not be so reluctant to go."[15] An Indiana politician told Lincoln that colonization "will, if adopted, relieve the free states of the apprehension now prevailing, and fostered by the disloyal, that they are to be overrun by negroes made free by war."[16] Wisconsin Senator James R. Doolittle similarly remarked that "every man, woman, and child who comes from these [Slave] States, tells me that it is utterly impossible for them to talk of emancipation within any slave State without connecting it with the idea of colonization."[17] Pennsylvania Representative Edward McPherson received a like message from a Democratic constituent: "If you can only send the whole [Black] race out of the country, I think all loyal democrats would be willing to see slavery abolished at once, regardless of any other consideration. . . . If the black race is once removed, we will have repose—not sooner."[18] New York Democrats at a Tammany meeting declared they were "opposed to emancipating negro slaves, unless on some plan of colonization."[19] A former resident of the South told Ohio Senator John Sherman how essential it was "that colonization should be held out in order to win the nonslaveholding and especially the poor whites of the South," who "are the men who must uphold the United States rule in the slave states." Ninety percent of them "when they once understand it will hail manumission and colonization as God's blessing. The slaveholders rule them by creating a horror of what the negroes would do if freed among them, but with all this there is a strong though secret hatred of slavery."[20] In early 1862, a Treasury official in St. Louis, appalled by the discrimination that African Americans endured in the Free States, exclaimed that if emancipation were not accompanied by colonization, then "God pity the poor Negro!" for many Northern states would outlaw Black settlement within their borders.[21]

In January 1860, Radical Republican Senator Ben Wade of Ohio declared that in the US there was "a race of men who are poor, weak, uninfluential, incapable of taking care of themselves. I mean the free negroes, who are despised by all, repudiated by all." It was "perfectly impossible that these two races can inhabit the same place and be prosperous and happy. I see that this species of the population are just as repugnant to the southern states, and perhaps more so, than to the north." Therefore it was necessary to create "a separation of the races. Let them go into the tropics. . . . let them be separated; it is easy to do it. I understand that negotiations may easily be effected with many of the Central American states by which they will take these people and confer upon them homesteads, confer upon them great privileges if they will settle there. They are so easy of access that a nucleus being formed, they will go with themselves and relieve us of the burden." He hoped "after that is done, to hear no more about negro equality or anything of that kind," he told his colleagues. Republicans "shall be as glad to rid ourselves of these people, if we can do it consistently with justice, as any one else."[22]

In response to Wade's speech, a constituent wrote him expressing thoughts shared by many reticent White citizens: "I like this new touch of colonizing the Niggers. I believe it is a d[am]n humbug. But it will take with the people. If we are to have no more slave states what the devil do we do with surplus niggers? Your plan will help us out on this point. But I have not much faith in it[.] You could not raise twenty five cents from a Yankee to transport a nigger to South America."[23]

A few months later, Francis P. Blair Sr. of Maryland urged Lincoln to endorse colonization, for it "might ward off the attacks made upon us about negro equality &c &c."[24] In June 1862, Democratic Congressman Charles John Biddle of Pennsylvania predicted that alarm about emancipation "would spread to every man of my constituents who loves his country and his race, if the public mind was not lulled and put to sleep with the word 'colonization.' I say the *word*, not the thing; for no practicable and adequate scheme for it has ever been presented or devised. The word is sung to us as a sort of 'lullaby.'"[25] His fellow lawmakers evidently agreed, for when in April 1862 they passed the District of Columbia Emancipation Act, they also tacked on a $100,000 appropriation to facilitate the colonization of both free African Americans and the slaves to be liberated. Englishman Frederick Milnes Edge, a correspondent for the London *Star,* interpreted that statute for his readers: one clause "is likely to meet with misconstruction in Europe—namely, the appropriation for colonising the freed slaves. This was adopted to silence the weak-nerved, whose name is legion, and to enable any of the slaves who see fit to migrate to more congenial climes."[26]

Frederick Edge was not the only observer to suggest that Republican support for colonization was intended to prepare the public mind for emancipation and "ward off the attacks" made against Republicans "about negro equality," as Francis P. Blair noted. In late September 1862, a few days after the Emancipation Proclamation was announced, the Black abolitionist minister Henry McNeal Turner wrote, "Mr. Lincoln is not half such a stickler for colored expatriation as he has been pronounced." The president "loves freedom as well as any one on earth," and the colonization proposal he made was less a practical plan than a "strategetic [sic] move upon his part in contemplation of this emancipatory proclamation just delivered. He knows as well as any one, that it is a thing morally impracticable, ever to rid this country of colored people unless God does it miraculously, but it was a preparatory nucleus around which he intended to cluster the raid [rain?]

of objections while the proclamation went forth." To assuage the fears of anxious voters, "the President stood in need of a place to *point to*," a place where African Americans could, with government support, resettle if they wished to do so.[27]

Turner's analysis seems based on what the president told him. As noted above, James Mitchell stated that Turner "had sought an interview on his own responsibility with the President in relation to the $600,000 emigration fund." Presumably he was granted that interview, though it is not documented. The meaning of Turner's account is somewhat difficult to glean from his rather opaque language, but he hinted broadly that he was *reporting* Lincoln's views rather than merely *speculating* about them. After Turner stated "Mr. Lincoln is not half such a stickler for colored expatriation as has been pronounced," he immediately added, "I am responsible for the assertion," by which he evidently meant, *"I know whereof I speak."* Turner provided a similar hint after his statement: "He knows as well as any one, that it is a thing morally impracticable, ever to rid this country of colored people unless God does it miraculously, but it was a preparatory nucleus around which he intended to cluster the raid [rain?] of objections while the proclamation went forth in the strength of God and executed its mission." Immediately after this interpretation of the president's thinking, Turner added, "I do not wish to trespass upon the key that unlocks a private door for fear that I might lose it, but all I will say is that the President stood in need of a place to *point to*." The reference to the key and private door apparently meant, *"I enjoy access to the president which I do not want to jeopardize by revealing too much of what he told me, but I will at least say this."*

Thus, when Lincoln in 1862 welcomed the Black deputation to the White House, along with a stenographic reporter to take down his words, he in all likelihood did so to silence the legions of "weak-nerved" voters who might object to the Emancipation Proclamation and also to "ward off attacks about Negro equality." His main audience was not those five African American guests but the millions of conservatives in the Lower North and

Border Slave States. As David S. Reynolds observed, Lincoln's speech to the deputation "was mainly a sop to conservatives," especially "of the Monty Blair stripe for whom colonization was *the* solution to slavery."[28]

This is not to suggest that the president's endorsement of voluntary colonization was insincere or that he thought attempts to make African Americans equal citizens were hopeless, but rather that he believed Negrophobia was so deeply ingrained that at least some African Americans might reasonably agree with Black abolitionist John Russwurm, a Bowdoin College graduate and editor of the country's first African American newspaper, who considered it a "waste of words to talk of ever enjoying citizenship in this country; it is utterly impossible in the nature of things; all, therefore, who pant for this, must cast their eyes elsewhere."[29] Such pessimists deserved a sanctuary abroad where they could enjoy full-fledged citizenship.

That included two of Frederick Douglass's three sons, twenty-one-year-old Lewis and his eighteen-year-old brother Charles, both of whom signed up for Lincoln's colonization project, much to the dismay of their father. "To see my children usefully and happily settled in this, the land of their birth and ancestors," Douglass wrote to the official in charge of implementing that project, "has been the hope and ambition of my manhood," but forces too powerful for him to overcome had persuaded his sons to join the colonization movement that he had so long and so fiercely denounced.[30]

Thus, Lincoln's support of voluntary colonization (and his attempt to publicize that support) was not rooted in a desire to banish the country's Black population. As historian James Oakes speculated, "Lincoln's support for colonization probably had less to do with racism than with racial pessimism."[31] It might also encourage the loyal Border Slave States to liberate their bondsmen by sugarcoating the bitter pill of emancipation.[32] Lincoln preferred state emancipation, for it was definitely constitutional, unlike military emancipation, which might be successfully challenged in court. During the war, Maryland, Missouri, Arkansas, Tennessee, and West Virginia would in fact abolish slavery. Lincoln's respect for constitutional constraints led him to restrain his antislavery instincts, but as time went by, he came to see ever more clearly that his belief that all men were created equal not only justified abolition but also the extension of citizenship rights to African Americans.[33]

Lincoln's assumption that Negrophobia might prove intractable was common. According to English journalist Edward Dicey, then-Secretary of State William Henry Seward "obviously shared the ordinary American opinion as to the impossibility of the black and white races associating on equal terms."[34] When Secretary of War Edwin Stanton asked liberated slaves in Georgia if they preferred to live in racially segregated or integrated areas, they replied that they wished to reside "in colonies by ourselves" because there was "a prejudice against us in the South that will take years to get over."[35] James Redpath, a strong ally of John Brown, declared that "pride of race, self-respect, social ambition, parental love, madness of the South, and the meanness of the North, the inhumanity of the Union, and the inclemency of Canada—all say to the Black and the man of color, Seek elsewhere a home and a nationality."[36]

In his 1852 book, *The Condition, Elevation, and Destiny of the Colored People of the United States*, Martin Delany similarly urged African Americans to resettle in order to escape discrimination in the US: "freemen even in the non-slaveholding States, occupy the very same position politically, religiously, civilly and socially (with but few exceptions,) as the bondsman occupies in the slave States." Delany favored Central America as the preferred site for a colony.[37]

Negrophobia was widespread in the North, where seventy-five percent of the voters were antislavery and ninety percent anti-Black, according to Orestes Brownson.[38] Black codes existed not only in the South and Illinois, but also in Michigan, California, Rhode Island, and Indiana. Even in progressive New England, African Americans suffered discrimination. As a prominent Massachusetts newspaper observed two days after Lincoln met with Black leaders in Washington, the Bay State might be "an anti-slavery state" with "a kind feeling toward the negroes who are in bondage," but nonetheless it was "neither a negro loving nor a negro respecting state." In "our anti-slavery sympathies and our inhuman prejudices against the black, we are guilty of an inconsistency which is a crime in itself sufficient to evoke the vengeance of Heaven."[39] Discrimination was common in Boston, as Black abolitionist John Rock explained in a speech published on the same day that newspapers reported Lincoln's remarks to the five Black Washingtonians. Rock, who in 1865 became the first African American to argue a case before the US Supreme Court, said: "The position of the colored people in Massachusetts is far from being an enviable one." There, the "educated colored man meets, on the one hand, the embittered prejudices of the whites, and on the other the jealousies of his own race." Nowhere in the US "is the colored man of talent appreciated. Even in Boston, which has a great reputation for being anti-slavery, he has no field for his talent." Black Bostonians "are proscribed in some of the eating-houses, many of the hotels, and all the theatres but one" as well as in "some of the churches." Such "proscription is carried even to the grave-yards. This is Boston—by far the best, or at least the most liberal large city in the United States."[40] In the fall of 1862, the abolitionist governor of Massachusetts, John A. Andrew, strongly objected to a proposal that 2,000 refugee slaves living in overcrowded, squalid contraband camps in Virginia be relocated to his state (population 1,231,000). In doing so, Governor Andrew was reflecting the opinion of his constituents who dreaded the prospect of Black immigration.[41]

In 1865, Jacob D. Cox, elected that year as governor of Ohio, wrote that White Southerners' fierce resistance to African American citizenship "would be no different if you exchanged populations & sent the New Englanders down there in place of the Southerners."[42] That same year, Cox received a letter from a fellow Buckeye, Radical Republican Congressman (and future president) James A. Garfield, admitting that he felt a "strong feeling of repugnance when I think of the Negro being made our political equal.

And I would be glad if they could be colonized. Sent to heaven, or got rid of in any decent way it would delight me."[43]

In explaining why colonization was desirable, John W. Forney, editor of a paper widely regarded as an administration organ, stressed an argument Lincoln had made: African Americans suffered badly from intractable Negrophobia. (Months earlier, Lincoln had urged Forney to prepare public opinion for a decision he knew would be unpopular: the release of two Confederate diplomats whom the Union Navy had unlawfully seized while they were en route to Europe.)[44] The president may well have inspired the following piece by Forney. "Our people do not like the negro," Forney wrote disapprovingly three days after Lincoln met with African American leaders in Washington. "He is not [regarded as] a congenial companion, nor an acceptable fellow-citizen. There must forever be an antagonism of race. The blue-eyed Saxon, with his fair hair, projecting chin, and overhanging forehead, his pride of country, ancestry, religion, and literature, must always be an exclusive and despotic race. He eats his own corn and the corn of his neighbor. Justice is nothing [compared] to expediency. Instinct governs conscience—passion controls principle. There can be nothing like an equality of race where the blue-veined Saxon exists. The tawny East Indians are crouching at his feet—the Chinaman cowers in dismay— the Indian proudly and submissively moves on to oblivion and the setting sun, while the negro tills his fields, grows his cotton, digs his entrenchments, and gathers his food and raiment." Forney lamented that the Black man "cannot eat at my table, or sit in my parlor, or ride in my carriage, or lounge in my opera-box; he cannot be my partner in business, the friend of my social life, or the husband of my kinswomen. He is forever an inferior being, and all he can hope for is a dollar when I am generous, or the half-worn garments in my wardrobe." Regretting that such prejudice was "deep-seated" and "ineradicable," Forney added, "I am anxious that this should no longer be, and I find in President Lincoln's wise, humane, and practical address the best remedy for this wrong of a race to a race." African Americans could flourish abroad, but not at home: "Place the negro in Central America or Africa, in any equatorial country, and we may hope to see again the spirit of the Moor when he occupied Spain, and the enterprise of the Ethiopian when he bartered and sold in the markets of Tyre and Sidon."[45]

Lincoln shared Forney's belief that the Negrophobia of the "exclusive and despotic" White race was so "deep-seated" and "ineradicable" that African Americans could reasonably fear they would never enjoy equal treatment in the US. The president's pessimism was doubtless shaped by his three decades' residence in Illinois, arguably the most Negrophobic of the Free States.[46] There, in 1858, Lincoln lost a senate race to Stephen A. Douglas, who blatantly appealed to race prejudice throughout the campaign. A decade earlier, Prairie State voters overwhelmingly approved a new constitution forbidding African Americans to settle there. They voted the same way again in 1862. Moreover, Black Illinoisans could not legally vote, hold office, serve on juries or in the militia, testify against White people in court, or intermarry. (According to a journalist writing from Springfield in 1855, any Black man in Illinois, even if born in the state, was "an alien, nay worse—almost a beast. He has no rights, except the right of being taxed; he has no privileges, except the privilege of paying. His children are booted out of public schools, while no provision is made for their separate education; his testimony is not received in a Court of justice; his accounts, though he may be an honest hard-working mechanic, are worth nothing in evidence; his friends, if they remove hither from any other State, though perchance just redeemed from the thrall of chattel Slavery, are liable to be thrust into prison and thence sold into bondage."[47]) Similar bigotry prevailed in other Midwestern states. Color prejudice was so widespread that it even infected the Black community, as Lincoln observed firsthand when the light-skinned African Americans on the White House staff refused to accept as a colleague the dark-skinned William H. Johnson.

If, as Eric Foner has argued, Lincoln in 1862 "overestimated the intractability of northern racism as an obstacle to ending slavery," historians have overestimated and misinterpreted Lincoln's support for colonization.[48] After 1862, the president made no further public reference to that subject. In 1864, William Henry Seward suggested that Lincoln had earlier supported such a policy not because he was personally enthusiastic about it but rather because he was acceding to public pressure: "The American people have advanced to a new position in regard to slavery and the African class since [the time when] the President *in obedience to their prevailing wishes* accepted the policy of colonization."[49]

Indeed, public attitudes had changed with the passage of time. As Lincoln observed in his second inaugural address, truly astonishing developments occurred between 1861 and 1865: "Neither party expected for the war, the magnitude, or the duration, which it has already attained. Neither anticipated that the *cause* of the conflict [slavery] might cease with, or even before, the conflict itself should cease. Each looked for an easier triumph, and a result less fundamental and astounding."[50] What the public had opposed in 1862 was not what it would oppose in 1865; similarly, what Lincoln thought necessary in August 1862, when he so dramatically recommended colonization, was not what he would think necessary in April 1865, when he publicly (and fatally) endorsed Black voting rights.

As James Russell Lowell put it, "time makes ancient good uncouth." What was enlightened in one era often looks retrograde in later ones.

CHOOSING THE DEPUTATION TO VISIT THE WHITE HOUSE

Returning to the events of August 14, 1862: on that day, James Mitchell assured his skeptical Black audience at Washington's Union Bethel AME Church that Lincoln wished to share with their representatives his thoughts about colonization. While those African Americans agreed to send a deputation to the White House that day, they had reservations which they expressed in instructions for the group: "Resolved, That in the present condition of the public affairs of this country, we, the few assembled, deem it inexpedient, inauspicious, and impolitic to agitate the subject of emigration of the colored people of this country anywhere, believing that time, the great arbiter of events and movements, will adjust the matter of so infinitely vital interest to the colored people of these United States. And furthermore, that we judge it unauthorized and unjust for us to compromise the interests of over four-and-a-half millions of our race by precipitate action on our part."[51]

In light of such strong reservations about the propriety of sending a deputation to the White House, it is hard to understand why the African Americans at the Union Bethel AME Church did so anyway. They were evidently swayed by the argument of a White man in attendance, Jacob R. S. Van Vleet, a firm supporter of African American rights as well as associate editor of the pro-administration Washington *National Republican*. He was also acting as an agent for Bernard Kock, promotor of a colonization effort in Haiti. Van Vleet "urged the propriety of waiting on the President, as it would be by his own special request." To reject that invitation "might be considered as treating him discourteously, and his request with contempt." Convinced by Van Fleet's entreaties, the men at Bethel Church approved a motion to appoint a committee, evidently as a gesture of respect for the president.

The deputation consisted of Edward M. Thomas, John F. Cook, Cornelius C. Clark, John T. Costin, and Benjamin McCoy. They promptly headed for 1600 Pennsylvania Avenue, where Lincoln received them "with great kindness, shaking hands very cordially with each one," according to a detailed report in the *National Republican*.[52] The quintet enjoyed high standing in the African American community.[53] Its chairman, forty-two-year-old Edward M. Thomas, had long served as a messenger for the US House of Representatives, a post in which he "gained the respect and confidence of every member of Congress and habitue of the House." An affable, philanthropic, religious, civic-minded leader, he headed the Anglo African Institute for the Encouragement of Industry and Art and served as an agent of the National Freedman's Relief Association.[54] When he died in 1863, a newspaper described him hyperbolically as "the most prominent colored man in the country."[55] John T. Costin, a Freemason Grand Master, also worked at the Capitol and, like Henry McNeal Turner, moved to Georgia after the Civil War and became a Republican party leader. Benjamin M. McCoy, a teacher who helped found Washington's Asbury African Methodist Episcopal Church, was elected to Washington's common council during Reconstruction and headed the Colored Order of Odd Fellows. Along with John F. Cook Jr., he established the first Sunday school for Black Washingtonians.[56]

The twenty-nine-year-old Cook, who also set up a weekday school for the capital's African American children, had attended Oberlin College before returning to run the seminary that his recently deceased father had established. (In 1841, John F. Cook Sr. founded the Fifteenth Street Presbyterian Church, one of the most prominent and politically active Black houses of worship in Washington.) After the war, he played a leading role in Washington's political, philanthropic, and social life. As the first African American elected to a citywide office (city registrar), he championed efforts to overturn Jim Crow laws. In 1869, a Virginia newspaper identified him as a leader of Washington's African American "aristocracy."[57] Thanks in part to shrewd real estate investments, he became the city's wealthiest Black man.[58]

Cornelius C. Clark, like Cook and Thomas, was a member of the Social, Civil, and Statistical Association, which opposed emigration and sought to demonstrate that African Americans could thrive in the US. Headed by William Slade, that organization enjoyed the support of Washington's Black elite. Slade may have suggested to the president that he invite members of the Association to a White House meeting.

Lincoln treated those five gentlemen respectfully, though he did not do much listening. As one paper noted: "It is true the negro has had his first admission to the White House,—audience it was not. He went, not to receive a hearing but a lecture."[59] That lecture would focus on the so-called Chiriquí plan.

THE CHIRIQUÍ PLAN

The Chiriquí scheme was the brainchild of wealthy Philadelphia businessman Ambrose W. Thompson, who said he controlled over 2,000,000 acres in Chiriquí Province, then part of Colombia and today a province in Panama.[60] In the 1850s, he had established the Chiriquí Improvement Company and vainly tried to persuade the Navy Department to purchase coal that could be mined there by his company. To sweeten the offer, in August 1861 he proposed to sell coal at half-price if African Americans were colonized there to work the mines. That offer caught the attention of Congress and the president.[61] Lincoln appointed a commission to assess Thompson's proposal and had his wife's brother-in-law, attorney Ninian Edwards, scrutinize the contract.[62] Strengthening the president's favorable view of the Chiriquí project may well have been the lobbying effort of an old friend from his days as a congressman, Richard W. Thompson of Indiana, who served as an attorney for the Chiriquí Improvement Company.[63] That Hoosier was not only a personal friend of the president but also an influential conservative Republican whose backing Lincoln had solicited in 1860.

In November 1861, Francis P. Blair Sr. presented Lincoln an elaborate brief arguing that Ambrose Thompson's plan could facilitate "the acquisition of safe and well fortified Harbors on each side of the Isthmus" of Panama as well as "a good and sufficient Railway transportation between them" and "a command of the coal-fields to afford adequate supply for our Navy." In addition, it would provide a million acres "for the colonization of American Freeman in Homesteads and freeholds."[64] Treasury Secretary Salmon P. Chase told Lincoln he was "much impressed with the prospects" Thompson's contract held.[65] In mid-November, Thompson wrote that "Lincoln is willing to make a contract for coal, at one dollar less per ton than the Govt now pays."[66] A few days later, the president recommended that Chase endorse the contract if he could do so "consistently with the public interest."[67] The following month, Assistant Secretary of the Interior John P. Usher explained to Thompson that Lincoln "is quite anxious to make the arrangement but is held back by the objection of Seward," who "thinks that the Government had better make the arrangements direct with the New Grenadian [i.e., Colombian] Government," and also by the objection of Chase, "who complains on account of the money."[68] And so Lincoln canceled the contract.

Several months later, in the spring of 1862, when Congress appropriated money to facilitate the resettlement of the newly freed slaves of Washington, Lincoln enjoined Secretaries Chase and Smith to reevaluate Ambrose Thompson's scheme.[69] Chase appointed Treasury Solicitor Edward Jordan, who agreed with Interior Secretary Smith that the Chiriquí Improvement Company should be contracted to supply coal to the navy and that African Americans should be colonized in the region.[70] Usher enthusiastically concurred.[71]

By mid-July 1862, when Congress appropriated $500,000 more to support colonization efforts, Lincoln was predisposed to favor Chiriquí rather than Haiti or Africa as the best resettlement location for Black emigrants. He seems to have been thinking of people like Henry Highland Garnet and the other signers of Joseph Enoch Williams's petition (in favor of immigration to Central America) when he expressed support for Chiriquí, which he did at length during his meeting with the African American deputation the following month. Lincoln may also have been thinking of James Mitchell's remark that Black Washingtonians resisted colonization because they "are to a great extent satisfied with their new liberties and franchises, with hopes of further enlargement." Mitchell predicted that "it will require time . . . before they will feel that an escape from their present relation to the American people is a duty and a privilege."[72]

THE MEETING ON AUGUST 14, 1862

The president began the August 14 meeting by explaining to his five Black guests that he wanted to consult with them about how he should spend the

$600,000 Congress had provided. To justify colonization, he remarked, "You and we are different races. We have between us a broader difference than exists between almost any other two races. Whether it is right or wrong I need not discuss, but this physical difference is a great disadvantage to us both, as I think your race suffer very greatly, many of them by living among us, while ours suffer from your presence. In a word we suffer on each side. If this is admitted, it affords a reason at least why we should be separated." (In earlier years, Lincoln had explained that though Black and White people could obviously coexist, they could not do so on the basis of equal political and social rights, thanks to widespread Negrophobia, especially in the South and Lower North. Now he strongly intimated that he might think it wrong to so believe, otherwise he would not have alluded to the possibility that it could, after all, be wrong.)

Lincoln frankly acknowledged that American slaves were the victims of a uniquely cruel form of oppression: "Your race are suffering, in my judgment, the greatest wrong inflicted on any people." That comment applied to free African Americans as well as slaves: "even when you cease to be slaves, you are yet far removed from being placed on an equality with the white race. You are cut off from many of the advantages which the other race enjoy. The aspiration of men is to enjoy equality with the best when free, but on this broad continent, not a single man of your race is made the equal of a single man of ours." Lincoln does not state that African Americans *are* inherently unequal to White people but that they are *made* unequal by law and custom. "Go where you are treated the best, and the ban is still upon you. I do not propose to discuss this, but to present it as a fact with which we have to deal. I cannot alter it if I would. It is a fact, about which we all think and feel alike, I and you."[73]

This was a remarkably empathic statement, for obviously African Americans hated the discrimination they suffered; Lincoln was saying he felt the same way. A member of Congress, upon reading Lincoln's accurate description of Northern Negrophobia, exclaimed, "What a stigma it casts upon our Country! . . . What a humiliating confession to be quoted by the aristocrats of Europe!"[74]

Lincoln continued, "We look to our condition, owing to the existence of the two races on this continent. I need not recount to you the effects upon white men, growing out of the institution of Slavery. I believe in its general evil effects on the white race. See our present condition—the country engaged in war!—our white men cutting one another's throats, none knowing how far it will extend; and then consider what we know to be the truth. But for your race among us there could not be war, although many men engaged on either side do not care for you one way or the other. Nevertheless, I repeat, without the institution of Slavery and the colored race as a basis, the war could not have an existence."

Lincoln was stating an obvious truth: the Civil War was caused by the South's desire to maintain slavery and White supremacy at all costs. If no African Americans had been in the country, no fierce devotion to White supremacy would exist and hence no war would have occurred.

From these hard realities Lincoln concluded that it "is better for us both, therefore, to be separated." Colonization as he envisioned it would be voluntary. But how to persuade freeborn African Americans and newly liberated slaves to leave the country? To this problem Lincoln now turned. Slavery, he argued, could be more easily abolished if some Black Americans agreed to emigrate. Those already free owed it to their enslaved brothers and sisters to spearhead a colonization effort: "I know that there are free men among you, who even if they could better their condition are not as much inclined to go out of the country as those, who being slaves could obtain their freedom on this condition." (Some slaveholders—and slave states—might well agree to liberate their slaves if only they agreed to be resettled abroad.) "I suppose one of the principal difficulties in the way of colonization is that the free colored man cannot see that his comfort would be advanced by it. You may believe you can live in Washington or elsewhere in the United States the remainder of your life [comfortably], perhaps more so than you can in any foreign country, and hence you may come to the conclusion that you have nothing to do with the idea of going to a foreign country. This is (I speak in no unkind sense) an extremely selfish view of the case."

What about those slaves whose masters might liberate them only if they were to be resettled abroad? "But you ought to do something to help those who are not so fortunate as yourselves. There is an unwillingness on the part of our people, harsh as it may be, for you free colored people to remain with us." Even as Lincoln proposed the establishment of a colony abroad where African Americans who despaired of ever enjoying equal treatment in the US might find refuge, he implicitly criticized the "harsh" prejudice underlying that sentiment.

Lincoln said that educated free African Americans should take the lead by volunteering to emigrate, for they would serve as role models for slaves who might eventually be liberated. "If we deal with those who are not free at the beginning, and whose intellects are clouded by Slavery, we have very poor materials to start with. If intelligent colored men, such as are before me, would move in this matter, much might be accomplished. It is exceedingly important that we have men at the beginning capable of thinking as white men, and not those who have been systematically oppressed." (Similarly, Frederick Douglass insisted that if the government resettled any African American volunteers abroad, "intelligent colored men" must accompany them for "the purpose of counselling the emigrants, and aiding in the direction of their future movements."[75])

These observations have been misinterpreted as evidence of Lincoln's purported racism, but he was suggesting to his callers that, insofar as African Americans lagged behind White people intellectually, it was because they were oppressed, not because they were biologically inferior. He clearly implied that African Americans were capable of thinking "as white men" once they were no longer oppressed.[76]

Lincoln appealed to his guests' altruism. "There is much to encourage you. For the sake of your race you should sacrifice something of your present comfort for the purpose of being as grand in that respect as the white people. It is a cheering thought throughout life that something can be done to ameliorate the condition of those who have been subject to the hard usage of the world. It is difficult to make a man miserable while he feels he is worthy of himself, and claims kindred to the great God who made him. In the American Revolutionary war sacrifices were made by men engaged in it; but they were cheered by the future. Gen. Washington himself endured greater physical hardships than if he had remained a British subject. Yet he was a happy man, because he was engaged in benefiting his race—something for the children of his neighbors, having none of his own."

To the practical question of just where Black Americans might resettle, Lincoln at first pointed to Africa. "The colony of Liberia has been in existence a long time. In a certain sense it is a success. The old President of Liberia, [Joseph Jenkins] Roberts, has just been with me—the first time I ever saw him. He says they have within the bounds of that colony between 300,000 and 400,000 people. . . . The question is if the colored people [of the US] are persuaded to go anywhere, why not there? One reason for an unwillingness to do so is that some of you would rather remain within reach of the country of your nativity. I do not know how much attachment you may have toward our race. It does not strike me that you have the greatest reason to love them. But still you are attached to them at all events." Lincoln once again expresses empathy for African Americans, especially if they do not love White Americans—for good reason.

Indeed, most Black Americans resisted the appeal of colonization, including several Philadelphians who told Lincoln, "Many of us . . . have our own houses and other property, amounting, in the aggregate, to millions of dollars. Shall we sacrifice this, leave our homes, forsake our birth-place, and flee to a strange land, to appease the anger and prejudice of the traitors now in arms against the Government, or their aiders and abettors in this or in foreign lands?"[77] These protestors failed to understand that Lincoln was not forcing anyone to emigrate but rather suggesting a program that would provide Black pessimists an overseas refuge.

Another possible relocation site would be the Chiriquí province. Early proponents of colonization, including Thomas Jefferson, James Madison, and Benjamin Lundy, had favored the Western Hemisphere. In more recent times, the Blair family had championed colonization there. In 1861 and early 1862, Mexico and lightly populated Central American nations expressed interest in such schemes.[78]

In urging his Black guests to support colonization in the province of Chiriquí, Lincoln pointed out that it "is nearer to us than Liberia—not much more than one-fourth as far as Liberia, and within seven days' run by steamers. Unlike Liberia it is on a great line of travel—it is a highway. The country is a very excellent one for any people, and with great natural resources and advantages, and especially because of the similarity of climate with your native land—thus being suited to your physical condition. The particular place I have in view is to be a great highway from the Atlantic or Caribbean Sea to the Pacific Ocean, and this particular place has all the advantages for a colony. On both sides there are harbors among the finest in the world. Again, there is evidence of very rich coal mines. A certain amount of coal is valuable in any country, and there may be more than enough for the wants of the country." Mining coal "will afford an opportunity to the inhabitants for immediate employment till they get ready to settle permanently in their homes. If you take colonists where there is no good landing, there is a bad show; and so where there is nothing to cultivate, and of which to make a farm. But if something is started so that you can get your daily bread as soon as you reach there, it is a great advantage. Coal land is the best thing I know of with which to commence an enterprise."

Lincoln also tried to convince the Black deputation that the Chiriquí project was not a corrupt scheme designed to enrich a few greedy swindlers: "you have been talked to upon this subject, and told that a speculation is intended by gentlemen, who have an interest in the country, including the coal mines." But that consideration was irrelevant. "We have been mistaken all our lives if we do not know whites as well as blacks look to their self-interest. Unless among those deficient of intellect everybody you trade with makes something. You meet with these things here as elsewhere. If such persons have what will be an advantage to them, the question is whether it cannot be made of advantage to you. You are intelligent, and know that success does not as much depend on external help as on self-reliance. Much, therefore, depends upon yourselves. As to the coal mines, I think I see the means available for your self-reliance. I shall, if I get a sufficient number of you engaged, have provisions made that you shall not be wronged. If you will engage in the enterprise I will spend some of the money intrusted [sic] to me."

African Americans' suspicion that backers of the Chiriquí scheme were corrupt speculators was justified. In 1862, Navy Secretary Gideon Welles alleged "that there was fraud and cheat" in the Chiriquí affair, that it "appeared to be a swindling speculation," and that the entire project "was a rotten remnant of an intrigue of the last [Buchanan] administration."[79] In fact, Lincoln would scuttle the plan when he learned more about the financial shenanigans of those backers.[80]

The president frankly warned his Black guests there was no guarantee they would prosper in Chiriquí: "I am not sure you will succeed. The Government may lose the money, but we cannot succeed unless we try; but we think, with care, we can succeed. The political affairs in Central America are not in quite as satisfactory condition as I wish. There are contending factions in that quarter; but it is true all the factions are agreed alike on the subject of colonization, and want it, and are more generous than we are here. To your colored race they have no objection." (One commentator found it truly remarkable that the president made the "humiliating statement" that "the semi-civilized States of South America 'are more generous' than the great model Republic."[81])

The "political affairs" were indeed a problem. Both Costa Rica and Colombia (New Grenada) laid claim to Chiriquí. In addition, their governments, along with those of El Salvador, Guatemala, Honduras, and Nicaragua, justifiably feared the US might infringe their sovereignty. Lincoln expressed a keen desire to make sure African Americans would not become second-class citizens in that province. He promised his guests he "would endeavor to have you made equals, and have the best assurance that you should be the equals of the best." That insistence might eventually become an excuse for US intervention in the region. (Four decades later, Theodore Roosevelt's meddling in Panamanian affairs showed that their anxiety was reasonable, as did the experience of Mexico, whose government in the 1820s had fatefully invited Americans to settle in their northern province, which had a low population at the time. That paved the way for the US to annex a large portion of that country.)

Moreover, Central American nations were reluctant to accept former slaves, preferring instead White settlers, belying Lincoln's assertion that they had no objection to Black immigrants. The American minister to Nicaragua reported that people there "feel indignant at the idea of being ranked with the North American negro," and deeply resent "their assumed equality with the African race."[82] Guatemala and El Salvador desired colonists "who may have had a more liberal education than can be acquired in a state of slavery."[83] The president of Honduras told an American diplomat that his government "is anxious for an immigration of industrious whites, especially of *German* emigrants, who have, by their establishment in Costa Rica, done so much to develop the resources and add to the wealth of that country." But "an immigration of enfranchised slaves from the United States is not at all desirable. We have a great deal of trouble . . . from the free negroes . . . who do not obey the orders of the government, and engage in contraband trade constantly."[84]

Secretary of State Seward therefore objected to the Chiriquí scheme and helped kill it.[85] He disagreed with colonizationists (according to an English journalist who interviewed him) for he "obviously looked to the solution of the negro question by the gradual dying out of the black race, as soon as emancipation had really begun to work."[86] Many Whites shared that view.

After laying out these particulars to his Black guests, Lincoln finally posed a question: "The practical thing I want to ascertain is whether I can get a number of able-bodied men, with their wives and children, who are willing to go, when I present evidence of encouragement and protection. Could I get a hundred tolerably intelligent men, with their wives and children, to 'cut their own fodder,' so to speak? Can I have fifty? If I could find twenty-five able-bodied men, with a mixture of women and children, good things in the family relation, I think I could make a successful commencement. I want you to let me know whether this can be done or not. This is the practical part of my wish to see you."

Lincoln acknowledged that his guests could hardly be ready to answer right away. "These are subjects of very great importance, worthy of a month's study, [instead] of a speech delivered in an hour. I ask you then to consider seriously not pertaining to yourselves merely, nor for your race, and ours, for the present time, but as one of the things, if successfully managed, for the good of mankind—not confined to the present generation, but as

'From age to age descends the lay,
To millions yet to be,
Till far its echoes roll away,
Into eternity.'"

Lincoln closed by urging the deputation to take as much time as it needed to answer his question.[87]

(Earlier that day, Lincoln had told Liberia's former President Joseph Jenkins Roberts and William McLain, a financial agent for the American Colonization Society, that he believed Liberia would be a suitable locale for African American emigrants. Angry at Lincoln's inconsistency in praising Liberia as a venue for colonization then criticizing it later that same day, McLain denounced both the president and the Central America plan: "Out upon all such men and such schemes!"[88])

THE CLIMATE OF RACIAL OPINION

To place Lincoln's remarks in context, it should be noted that some of his cabinet members (Montgomery Blair, Caleb B. Smith, and Edward Bates) and congressional Republicans (notably Frank Blair, Lyman Trumbull, James R. Doolittle, and Preston King) were colonizationists, and that during the antebellum era, many White humanitarians who strongly opposed slavery also supported colonization (among them Theodore Parker, Horace Greeley, Gerrit Smith, Salmon P. Chase, Leonard Bacon, Harriet Beecher Stowe, Thaddeus Stevens, James G. Birney, Eli Thayer, Benjamin Lundy, and James Lane).

So too did several Black antislavery champions, including such luminaries as John Russwurm, Samuel Cornish, Alexander Crummell, James McCune Smith, James T. Holly, Martin Delany, Henry Highland Garnet, and Paul Cuffe. Moreover, in the 1850s, delegates to Black emigration conventions had endorsed a large-scale exodus.[89] Other African Americans took more active steps: Martin Delany inspected sites in the Niger Valley for the relocation of African Americans; James Whitefield did the same in Central America; and James Theodore Holly followed suit in the West Indies.[90] In 1858, Black colonizationists under the leadership of Garnet founded the African Civilization Society to encourage Black immigration to Yoruba (modern Nigeria).

Some light-skinned African Americans would agree to emigrate but not to a location where they would have to coexist with their dark-skinned compatriots. In 1855, the abolitionist Owen Lovejoy, brother of the martyred Elijah Lovejoy, introduced into the Illinois legislature "a remonstrance from the colored people of the State against their colonization in Africa, until they are all able to read and write, and unless separate colonies be assigned to those of different shades of color. The reason assigned for the latter objection is, that blacks and mulattoes cannot live in harmony together."[91] Similarly, people of mixed race in Cincinnati favored colonization but only if they could settle somewhere apart from full-blooded African Americans.[92]

Several thousand Black Americans fled the US between 1830 and 1861, especially during the 1850s.[93] According to historian Ira Berlin, "emigration found an increasingly large following" among African Americans in that decade: "Reluctantly, some free Negroes looked for a new home where they might find a modicum of freedom, new opportunities, and a taste of manhood. '[I] cannot be a man heare and . . . I am ready to go [even] if I [have to] live on bread and warter or die the never [very?] day I get there,' declared a Liberia-bound black."[94] Lott Cary, a free African American in Virginia, explained why he would immigrate to Africa: "In this country, however meritorious my conduct and respectable my character, I cannot receive the credit due to either. I wish to go to a country where I shall be esteemed by my merits—not by my complexion."[95] After moving to Liberia, he taunted his Black former countrymen: "You will never know whether you are men or monkies so long as you remain in America," for there, they suffered from what later generations would call the soft bigotry of low expectations: "You will get Praise—although your best writings be mixt with a great deal of error." He challenged America's Black community: "I shall believe you to be men when I see you conducting the affairs of your own Government; and not before but so long as you are in your present state of subserveance [sic] we cannot view you as on a level with us."[96]

Even during the Civil War, when the prospects for emancipation improved dramatically, some African Americans wished to emigrate; between 1860 and 1862, around 2,000 removed to Haiti.[97] In December 1862, Lincoln told Congress, "Applications have been made to me by many free Americans of African descent to favor their emigration, with a view to such colonization as was contemplated in recent acts of Congress."[98] Months earlier, Congress received a petition from 242 Black Californians expressing their desire to be colonized in a "country in which their color will not be a badge of degradation." The following April, sixty Black Washingtonians submitted another such appeal, asking to be resettled in Central America.[99] The latter petition was circulated by Joseph Enoch Williams, a Black emigrationist who had earlier promoted a resettlement program sponsored by the government of Haiti.[100]

Many African Americans had looked favorably on that country's invitation, among them Frederick Douglass, who in January 1861 wrote, "We think this movement one of the most important in connection with the colored people which has come under our notice. Isolated, and oppressed, and degraded, by a base prejudice which yet cannot be removed, it seems to us that a large class of the intelligent free people of African origin in the Northern States, and more especially in the Southern States, whose inhuman legislation tends to trample out all the few rights the free colored population have hitherto enjoyed in these communities; will avail themselves of this comprehensive offer of their Haytian brethren in the fraternal spirit which prompts the movement."[101] That winter, Douglass became a "qualified emigrationist," declaring that he was "in favor of emigration as a colored man," at least for those "who have no foothold here." He wished a dozen families well who were immigrating thither from his town of Rochester. The Caribbean nation could provide a sanctuary for the many African Americans who feared that their condition would soon deteriorate: "The apprehension is general, that proscription, persecution and hardships are to wax more and more rigorous and more grievous with every year." And so Black Americans "are now, as never before, looking out into the world for a place of retreat, an asylum from the apprehended storm which is about to beat pitilessly upon them." Douglass clearly implied that Haiti could be their "place of retreat," their "asylum." To inspect it firsthand, he accepted an invitation from the Haitian government to spend a few weeks there that spring, at its expense. When the Civil War broke out in April, however, he canceled those plans.[102]

Many Black supporters of the Haitian project soon became disillusioned, including Douglass and his close ally, William Watkins, along with the

Black novelist William Wells Brown.[103] Most of the African Americans who immigrated to Haiti in the early 1860s returned to the US, frustrated by the local government's failure to provide all that it had promised. Haitian prejudice against African Americans led Joseph Enoch Williams to fear that they "were to hold inferior positions, to become mere slaves, 'hewers of wood and drawers of water' for men of our own color."[104] Instead of Haiti, Williams urged his compatriots to resettle in the Chiriquí province.

A month before Lincoln hosted the five Black Washingtonians, the House Special Committee on Emancipation endorsed a scheme that coupled emancipation with colonization, recommended an appropriation of $20,000,000 to facilitate the voluntary emigration of African Americans, and noted that the most serious objections to emancipation arose "from the opposition of a large portion of our people to the intermixture of the races, and from the association of white and black labor." The committee stated that "the presence of a race among us who cannot, and ought not to, be admitted to our social and political privileges, will be a perpetual source of injury and inquietude to both. This is a question of color, and is unaffected by the relation of master and slave." The "most formidable difficulty which lies in the way of emancipation," the committee maintained, was "the belief, which obtains especially among those who own no slaves, that if the negroes shall become free, they must still continue in our midst, and, so remaining after their liberation, they may in some measure be made equal to the Anglo-Saxon race." The "Anglo-American will never give his consent that the negro, no matter how free, shall be elevated to such equality. It matters not how wealthy, how intelligent, or how morally meritorious the negro may become, so long as he remains among us the recollection of the former relation of master and slave will be perpetuated by the changeless color of the Ethiop's skin, and that color will alike will be perpetuated by the degrading tradition of his former bondage." The "highest interests of the white race, whether Anglo-Saxon, Celt, or Scandinavian, require that the whole country should be held and occupied by those races alone."

Therefore, a home "must be sought for the African [American] beyond our own limits and in those warmer regions to which his constitution is better adapted than to our own climate, and which doubtless the Almighty intended the colored race should inhabit and cultivate."[105]

It was in this environment that Lincoln made his August 14 remarks, in part intended to satisfy the broad support for colonization in the US and in part designed to mollify opponents of his forthcoming Emancipation Proclamation.

AFRICAN AMERICANS' REACTION TO LINCOLN'S REMARKS

Many of the African American elite denounced Lincoln's remarks. Robert Purvis, a well-to-do Philadelphian, wrote the president a stinging public letter: "It is in vain you talk to me about 'two races' and their 'mutual antagonism.' In the matter of rights, there is but one race, and that is the human race. God has made of one blood all nations, to dwell on the face of the earth. . . . Sir, this is our country as much as it is yours, and we will not leave it."[106] Frederick Douglass was Lincoln's harshest critic. He excoriated the president for appearing "silly and ridiculous" by uttering remarks that revealed "his pride of race and blood, his contempt for negroes and his canting hypocrisy." Douglass scouted the administration's entire record on slavery: "Illogical and unfair as Mr. Lincoln's statements are, they are nevertheless quite in keeping with his whole course from the beginning of his administration to this day, and confirms the painful conviction that though elected as an anti-slavery man by Republican and Abolitionist voters, Mr. Lincoln is quite a genuine representative of American prejudice and negro hatred and far more concerned for the preservation of slavery, and the favor of the Border States, than for any sentiment of magnanimity or principle of justice and humanity." Lincoln, in Douglass's view, was saying to Black Americans, "I don't like you, you must clear out of the country." The polite tone of the president's self-described "speech" is "too thin a mask not to be seen through," for it lacked the "genuine spark of humanity" and a "sincere wish to improve the condition of the oppressed."[107] Hyperbolically, Douglass declared that "the nation was never more completely in the hands of the Slave power."[108]

(For a man whose sons wanted to participate in the Chiriquí project, Douglass's vehemence seems excessive. If two of his adult children agreed to take part in it, why assume that Lincoln was a Negrophobe for supporting it?)

Other abolitionists and historians have echoed Frederick Douglass's denunciation, finding Lincoln's remarks to his Black visitors patronizing at best and hateful at worst. The conventional wisdom holds that the president's "dictatorial and condescending" appeal constituted an embarrassing, tactless blunder that purportedly exposed his true racist colors.[109]

The Radical Republican editor John W. Forney, however, described the meeting as a historic occasion: "The negro may well say that under President Lincoln he has had his first hearing in the White House. Other presidents have bought and sold him, and driven him from the territories, and closed their eyes to the nefarious system under which he was captured in Africa and dragged over the ocean in chains. But President Lincoln has listened to his story and given him counsel and advice."[110] Another journalist called Lincoln's remarks to the Black delegation "very sympathetic," manifesting "his sincere and earnest desire to see them [African Americans] invested with the rights and privileges of real freemen."[111] The historian Phillip Shaw Paludan pointed out that "Lincoln did not treat these delegates with contempt, and he did not reveal the 'soft racism' of addressing them in a tone different from one he would use to a white delegation. He did not act as though they should be treated with kid gloves." Moreover, "almost everything he said was true."[112]

Some African American leaders defended Lincoln, among them the abolitionist minister Henry McNeal Turner. Reporting from Washington, he hastened to alleviate fears that the president was calling for the mass deportation of Black Americans. On August 25, Turner wrote: "This has been one of the most excitable weeks with our people, I suppose, ever known in their history." Lincoln's desire "to have an interview with a committee of colored men, and a compliance with that desire on the part of our people, very nearly made some of our citizens frantic with excitement," for they "seemed to have thought that it was in the voluntary [discretionary] power of the President to transport at his option all the colored people out of the country." Such mistaken fears "seemed to have gained a respectable idea of currency in the mind of some class of thinkers." In fact, there was "no need of such wild excitements," for the president lacked the power to deport the Black population, and "I don't believe that he would use it if he had." Turner denied that he himself had supported mass deportation, insisting that he "hated the infamous scheme of compulsory colonization."[113]

Henry Highland Garnet, a leading Presbyterian minister based in New York, also defended the president. He had a radical reputation stemming from a speech he had made in 1843, when he urged slaves to "arise, arise! Strike for your lives and liberties. Now is the day and the hour. Let every slave throughout the land do this, and the days of slavery are numbered. You cannot be more oppressed than you have been—you cannot suffer greater cruelties than you have already. *Rather die freemen than live to be slaves.*"[114]

A colonization supporter, Garnet had long championed Africa as the most appropriate place for Black Americans to resettle, though lately he had backed Haiti as an alternative. Now he deemed Lincoln's plan to establish a haven for African Americans in Central America "the most humane, and merciful movement which this or any other administration has proposed for the benefit of the enslaved." Garnet considered "the free and voluntary emigration of our people to any portion of the globe" to be "among the most sacred of human rights" and believed "this is one of God's ways by which the families of the earth are improved and advanced in national character." Rhetorically, he asked, "Where are the freed people of the South to seek a refuge? Neither the North, the West, nor the East will receive them. Nay—even our colored people of the North do not want them here. They all say, [both] white and black—'these Southern negroes if they come here, *will reduce the price of labor, and take the bread out of our mouths.*'" Garnet feared that newly emancipated slaves might be captured by Confederates and re-enslaved (which did happen to some African Americans during the war): "if Jeff Davis does not emancipate [the slaves of the Confederacy], and our government does not provide a territory on this continent as a refuge for those who have been freed by our armies, then the condition of these people will be worse than ever it was before. When they again fall into the hands of their tormentors, they will be tortured as human beings never were in this world." (Confederate forces did indeed torture, murder, and mutilate some African American troops who had surrendered, and in liberated areas of Mississippi and Louisiana, Confederate raiders slaughtered hundreds of former slaves who were working on plantations as hired hands without adequate military protection.[115]) But if Lincoln's plan was adopted, Garnet said, "hundreds of thousands of men will be saved, and the Northern bugbear 'they will all come here' [will] be removed."[116] Garnet supported emigration only for those who wanted to relocate and who also "had the means to prosper." He told fellow Black countrymen: "We are planted here, and we cannot as a whole people be re-colonized back to the fatherland."[117]

Garnet "and other colored men of influence at the North" reportedly wrote to James Mitchell "warmly seconding the plan of the president for the colonization of the free negroes in Central America."[118] Mitchell claimed that he had received "hundreds of letters from colored men in all parts of the country."[119] Garnet evidently met with Lincoln after the president's interview with the five Black Washingtonians. In a letter to the editor of the New York *Anglo-African*, Garnet criticized two passages in Lincoln's statement to those men: "The declaration of President Lincoln that '*we* (the colored people) *are the cause of the war*' is a fallacy, and is freighted with mischief to us, inasmuch as it gives encouragement to our persecutors in the free

States, who are eager to lap our blood. The other statement of the President that we cannot live with the white race is equally fallacious, as the history of this country for the last two centuries proves. These opinions I stated in plain terms to the Chief Magistrate, and I hold them still."[120] Garnet may have made these points to Lincoln in writing, but no such document is to be found in the president's papers or is known to exist in government archives. More likely, Garnet said this to Lincoln in person, though no account of such a conversation has come to light.

Another serious objection was voiced by an African American who signed his protest "Cerebrus": "We did and do still consider voluntary emigration as simply the stepping-stone to *compulsory* expatriation."[121] Responding to that objection, a Black Rhode Island resident who identified himself as W. C. D. echoed Henry McNeal Turner's remarks. Writing from Newport, he assured readers of *The Christian Recorder* that "there will be no compulsion in the matter," for "the President only wishes those to go that are willing," people who "are the proper persons to found a colony," including "men that have become tired of being footballs for the white man," men "who have become weary of working for other people, and feel like doing something for themselves," and finally "those who feel themselves degraded, and are sick of hearing their wives and daughters slandered and insulted on the highways, and feel their position; those who are willing to sacrifice their lives for a better home, if such can be found." Those "are the kind of men to found a colony in a foreign land, and if successful in their under-taking, will be treasured in the hearts of their countrymen as a Columbus or a Washington." He lamented that free African Americans like himself were "not even respected by our own people; let us try and make ourselves respected." Respect was, unlike mere courtesy and toleration, something to be earned, and the best way to earn it was "to lay hold of this colonization scheme and carry it through to the end, and see what we can accomplish through the means offered to us. Let the people see we have the energy to accomplish the work set before us. Will we let Congress give us $5000, and make no effort to see what benefit can be derived from it? They say, what will be done with the negroes? Let them go where there will be equality, and they will act for themselves; and if every man of color feels the same as I do upon the subject, they will join heart and hands in building up a country where we can enjoy liberty to the utmost extent."[122]

LINCOLN'S EMPATHY FOR AFRICAN AMERICANS

Substantial evidence shows Lincoln favored colonization because he empathized with African Americans like that Rhode Islander. The president's empathy for people in general was unusually sensitive, one of the hallmarks of his character. After his early years as a "slasher-gaff politician" who excelled at ridiculing political opponents, he "came to be unusually respectful in his personal conduct of the dignity and independence of the human beings with whom he dealt," as William Lee Miller observed.[123]

Lincoln articulated his compassion for African Americans to his best friend, Joshua Speed. In an 1855 private letter to that Kentuckian, he described himself as someone "who abhors the oppression of negroes" and expressed revulsion for the way that escaping slaves were treated: "I hate to see the poor creatures hunted down, and caught, and carried back to their stripes, and unrewarded toils." Lincoln reminded Speed of a river journey they had taken: "In 1841 you and I had together a tedious low-water trip, on a Steam Boat from Louisville to St. Louis. You may remember, as I well do, that from Louisville to the mouth of the Ohio there were, on board, ten or a dozen slaves, shackled together with irons. That sight was a continual torment to me; and I see something like it every time I touch the Ohio, or any other slave-border. It is hardly fair for you to assume, that I have no interest in a thing which has, and continually exercises, the power of making me miserable."[124]

In 1857, while condemning the Supreme Court's *Dred Scott* decision, Lincoln vividly described the plight of Black Americans. He insisted that the justices had misread history: "It is grossly incorrect to say or assume that the public estimate of the negro is more favorable now than it was at the origin of the government." On the contrary, he declared, "in this country, the change between then and now is decidedly the other way," and the "ultimate destiny" of African Americans "has never appeared so hopeless as in the last three or four years." Since the Revolution, he noted, some states that had once allowed Black men to vote had rescinded that right; legal restraints on slave owners who wished to emancipate their slaves had grown tighter; the power of state legislatures to emancipate slaves had been curtailed; and millions of acres in the western territories once set aside for freedom were now open to slavery. In former times, "our Declaration of Independence was held sacred by all, and thought to include all; but now, to aid in making the bondage of the negro universal and eternal, it is assailed, and sneered at, and construed, and hawked at, and torn, till, if its framers could rise from their graves, they could not at all recognize it."

Now Black Americans were hounded worse than ever: "All the powers of earth seem rapidly combining against him. Mammon is after him; ambition follows, and philosophy follows, and the Theology of the day is fast joining the cry. They have him in his prison house; they have searched his person, and left no prying instrument with him. One after another they have closed the heavy iron doors upon him, and now they have him, as it were, bolted in with a lock of a hundred keys, which can never be unlocked without the concurrence of every key; the keys in the hands of a hundred different men, and they scattered to a hundred different and distant places; and they stand musing as to what invention, in all the dominions of mind and matter, can be produced to make the impossibility of his escape more complete than it is."[125]

The following year, Lincoln criticized the tendency of Stephen A. Douglas's "popular sovereignty" doctrine "to dehumanize the negro—to take away from him the right of ever striving to be a man."[126] In 1859, he upbraided Democrats like Douglas for bringing "the public mind to the conclusion that when men are spoken of, the negro is not meant; that when negroes are spoken of, brutes alone are contemplated. That change in public sentiment has already degraded the black man in the estimation of Douglas and his followers from the condition of a man of some sort, and assigned him to the condition of a brute."[127]

In November 1862, Lincoln said that the problem most troubling him "is to provide for the blacks" who were soon to be liberated by the Emancipation Proclamation.[128] That concern led him to authorize the establishment of the American Freedmen's Inquiry Commission, whose members—antislavery stalwarts James McKaye, Robert Dale Owen, and Samuel Gridley Howe—investigated the conditions of newly freed slaves, ascertained their concerns, and made recommendations to promote their well-being. In 1865, those efforts culminated in the passage of the Freedmen's Bureau Bill, which Lincoln signed into law.[129]

Some critics have alleged that Lincoln callously disregarded the plight of African Americans in the South, for in February 1865 he purportedly told three leading Confederate officials that the former slaves must fend for themselves without government assistance or else die. At Hampton Roads, Virginia, Lincoln met with Vice President of the Confederacy Alexander Stephens, a leader of the Confederate senate, Robert M. T. Hunter, and a member of the Confederate cabinet, Secretary of War John A. Campbell, to discuss surrender terms. In the course of their conversation, Hunter said that with the abolition of slavery, the eleven states that had seceded would face starvation, for their newly freed slaves would no longer plant, tend, and harvest crops. Hunter reportedly was most concerned that elderly and very young African Americans would suffer. Lincoln replied with a story about an Illinois farmer named Case who sought to feed his swine by planting potatoes which the porkers would unearth with their snouts and devour. When asked what the poor creatures would do when the ground froze,

Case admitted that winter conditions would pose a problem, but that the swine would simply have to "root hog, or die." Stephens alleged that Lincoln meant that the liberated slaves would starve and that he did not care if they did so. But according to a well-connected Northern journalist, David W. Bartlett, Lincoln clearly implied that *White Southerners* would starve unless they went to work now that they could no longer force the Black population to toil for them without compensation. "The moral was this: the southern people can go to work like honest people or starve," Bartlett reported. He closed his article saying, "every word I have written is true. Very little has been divulged regarding the four hours interview [at Hampton Roads], but Mr. Lincoln has spoken of a few things that took place to some of his intimate friends."[130] Those friends were doubtless Bartlett's source. Throughout the war he reported more of Lincoln's conversations than any other correspondent, and his accounts seem reliable.

Moreover, the first paper to report the Hampton Roads conversation, the *New York Herald*, indicated that Lincoln's hog story applied to White plantation owners, not the slaves. One of the Confederate emissaries remarked that the abolition of slavery "might complicate affairs a little with the South. The heavy planters insisted upon maintaining that institution and defending it, and asked Mr. Lincoln if he thought he could get around that fact. Old Abe was ready for them with one of his stories" and told the tale of farmer Case and his hogs.[131]

Lincoln was doubtless far more solicitous of the welfare of former slaves than Stephens, Hunter, and Campbell; to believe that Hunter was deeply concerned about the well-being of Black elders and children strains credulity. The president was almost certainly referring to the indolence of White slave owners, for he derided the lazy White Southerners' exploitation of Black labor. When he teased Ward Hill Lamon about indolence in Dixie, his Virginia-born-and-bred friend protested, causing Lincoln to reply, "Oh, yes; you Virginians shed barrels of perspiration while standing off at a distance and superintending the work your slaves do for you."[132]

Similarly, Lincoln ridiculed a proslavery theologian, Frederick Ross, author of *Slavery Ordained of God:* "The sum of pro-slavery theology seems to be this: 'Slavery is not universally *right*, nor yet universally *wrong*; it is better for *some* people to be slaves; and, in such cases, it is the Will of God that they be such.' Certainly there is no contending against the Will of God; but still there is some difficulty in ascertaining, and applying it, to particular cases. For instance we will suppose the Rev. Dr. Ross has a slave named Sambo, and the question is 'Is it the Will of God that Sambo shall remain a slave, or be set free?' The Almighty gives no audable [sic] answer to the question, and his revelation—the Bible—gives none—or, at most, none but such as admits of a squabble, as to it's [sic] meaning. No one thinks of asking Sambo's opinion on it. So, at last, it comes to this, that *Dr. Ross* is to decide the question. And while he consider[s] it, he sits in the shade, with gloves on his hands, and subsists on the bread that Sambo is earning in the burning sun. If he decides that God Wills Sambo to continue a slave, he thereby retains his own comfortable position; but if he decides that God will's [sic] Sambo to be free, he thereby has to walk out of the shade, throw off his gloves, and delve for his own bread. Will Dr. Ross be actuated by that perfect impartiality, which has ever been considered most favorable to correct decisions? But, slavery is good for some people!!! As a *good* thing, slavery is strikingly perculiar [sic], in this, that it is the only good thing which no man ever seeks the good of, *for himself.* Nonsense! Wolves devouring lambs, not because it is good for their own greedy maws, but because it [is] good for the lambs!!!"[133]

Musing on the argument that African Americans were biologically inferior, Lincoln once wrote, "Suppose it is true, that the negro is inferior to the white, in the gifts of nature; is it not the exact reverse justice that the white should, for that reason, take from the negro, any part of the little which has been given him? *'Give* to him that is needy' is the Christian rule of charity; but 'Take from him that is needy' is the rule of slavery."[134] (He clearly implied that it was equally possible to suppose that Black

Americans were *not* "inferior to the white, in the gifts of nature.") Lincoln hated slavery in part because it represented the systematic robbery of Black workers by White owners. It outraged his sense of justice that some people worked hard in the hot sun all day and others reaped all the profits.

⋘⋙

Lincoln was appalled not only by slavery but also by discrimination in Free States, though before 1861 he felt politically compelled to at least pay lip service to Illinois' Black Laws. During his August 1862 meeting with the African American delegation, as noted above, he alluded disapprovingly to the mistreatment that Northern Blacks faced: "on this broad continent, not a single man of your race is made the equal of a single man of ours. Go where you are treated the best, and the ban is still upon you." In that meeting, he told his visitors that he would establish a refuge only where Black settlers were able to enjoy full-fledged citizenship, in keeping with the provision of the Second Confiscation Act stipulating that "the President of the United States is hereby authorized to make provision for the transportation, colonization, and settlement, in some tropical country beyond the limits of the United States, of such persons of the African race, made free by the provisions of this act, as may be willing to emigrate, *having first obtained the consent of the government of said country to their protection and settlement within the same, with all the rights and privileges of freemen.*"[135] Secretary of State Seward notified European colonial powers that the US would agree to facilitate the voluntary immigration of African Americans to those nations' colonies *only* if they guaranteed that "such immigrants and their posterity shall forever remain free, and in no case be reduced to bondage, slavery, or involuntary servitude, except for crime; and they shall specially enjoy liberty of conscience, and the right to acquire, hold, and transmit property, and all other privileges of person, common to inhabitants of the country in which they reside."[136]

Soon after the 1863 New York draft riots, during which mobs viciously attacked African Americans, lynching many and burning down an orphanage, Lincoln remarked that "it would have been much better to separate the races than to have such scenes as those in New York the other day."[137] In March 1864, he alluded to those riots when he warned a New York workingmen's organization to "beware of prejudice," the kind that had led some workingmen to hang others. White workers, he said, should feel a bond of solidarity with Black workers.[138]

THE DEPUTATION'S REACTION TO LINCOLN'S SPEECH

The five Black Washingtonians did not respond formally to Lincoln's appeal to spearhead a colonization effort in Chiriquí, though two days after the meeting the chairman, Edward Thomas, wrote the president offering to sample opinion among African Americans in other cities. Evidently speaking for the entire deputation but signing only his own name, he said, "We would respectfully Suggest that it is necessary that we Should confer with leading colored men in Phila[delphia] New York and Boston upon this movement of emigration to the point recommended in your address. We were entirely hostile to the movement until all the advantages were so ably brought to our views by you and we believe that our friends and co-laborers for our race in those cities will when the Subject is explained by us to them join heartily in Sustaining Such a movement. It is therefore Suggested in addition to what is Stated that you authorize two of us to proceed to those cities and place your views before them to facilitate and promote the object. We desire no appointment only a letter from your hand Saying you wish us to consult with our leading friends. As this is part of the movement to obtain a proper plan of colonization we would respectfully Suggest to your Excellency that the necessary expenses of the two (or more if you desire) be paid from the fund appropriated. It is our belief that Such a conference will lead to an active and zealous Support of this measure by the leading minds of our people and that this Support will lead to the realization of the fullest Success, within the Short time of two weeks from our departure the assurance can be Sent you of the results of our mission and that a Success."[139]

Just after writing this missive, Thomas evidently called on Lincoln bearing a letter of introduction from Jacob R. S. Van Vleet, an editor of the Washington *National Republican*, as well as Bernard Kock's "home agent" and chaplain-designate for the prospective settlers on Haiti's Île-à-Vache.[140] "Mr. Thomas is an intelligent & highly respectable man, and as a mark of the estimation in which he is held by the men of color in all parts of the country, you will see that he has been selected as President of an important Institution recently established. Mr. Thomas believes he can be of great service in forwarding your great scheme of colonization, by confer[r]ing with the leading men of his color in the Northern cities, and for that purpose he desires to go, together with one of the other members of the delegation. In conclusion, permit me to say, that he is entirely worthy of your confidence, and I trust, will bring you a favorable report from his Northern friends."[141] Van Vleet offered to pay for the proposed trip, which did not take place, perhaps indicating the Lincoln failed to take the Chiriquí project seriously.

Curiously, Thomas did not report back to the group that had gathered at the Union Bethel Church on August 14 and sent the delegation to the White House. A week after that meeting with the president, some forty of those men reassembled to hear the deputation's report but were disappointed when only one of its members, John T. Costin, appeared. The assembly rejected his offer to provide a minority report, "severely criticised" the deputation's members for having "overstepped their instructions," expressed disapproval of the Chiriquí plan, and decided to "adjourn, until they could receive information as to the committee's whereabouts, at which time they will again convene" to hear its report.[142]

That never happened; instead, Thomas reported to the Social, Civil, and Statistical Association, a group so critical of his endorsement of the Chiriquí scheme that they put him on trial in absentia. Ultimately, they decided not to expel him.[143]

IMPLEMENTING THE CHIRIQUÍ PLAN

The anger of the Social, Civil, and Statistical Association's elite was not universally shared by ordinary Black Washingtonians.[144] According to a journalist, "quite a number of colored people" in the District of Columbia "have agreed to emigrate to the settlement in Central America about to be founded by the President of the United States." Those would-be emigrants "say that confiding in his generosity and the power of the government to negotiate with the authorities of Central America, they thus enroll themselves as candidates for places amongst the first settlers."[145] They did so in large numbers, including "some parties who were very recently much opposed to the Central American project" but who "have become its converts, and are going out in the first ship."[146] In late August, when Kansas Senator Samuel Pomeroy, at Lincoln's behest, announced that he was organizing transportation to Chiriquí for African Americans who wished to emigrate, around 4,000 quickly signed up. Of those, the senator, with the help of William Watkins, chose 500 to make the initial voyage, scheduled to depart in early October. (Pomeroy estimated that the number of applicants eventually reached 14,000.)

Those would-be pioneers sold their homes and possessions in anticipation of the move, but when Central American governments objected strongly to the colonization project, it was shelved on September 24, leaving the volunteers destitute. Among them was J. Willis Menard, a twenty-year-old poet, journalist, and ardent colonization supporter from Illinois whose complexion was so light that in 1860 he was allowed to vote. Two years later, he worked in Washington as a hospital steward.[147] The following year he was appointed a clerk in James Mitchell's Office of Emigration, one of the first Black Americans to hold such a post in the federal civil service. Among his duties was inspecting British Honduras as a possible resettlement site.[148] Menard wrote a report about his travels thither and offered it to Lincoln.[149] His tenure at the Emigration Office did not last long, for "prejudice against color was so intense in the department, that after a few months' service he was forced to resign."[150] Five years later, he became the first African American elected to Congress when Louisiana voters sent him to Washington, where the House of Representatives refused to seat him.[151]

In October, Menard and others wrote Lincoln, pointing out that many of their number "have sold our furniture" and "given up our little homes to go on the first voyage." The delay was "reducing our scanty means, until fears are being created that these means are being exhausted." And so "[p]overty in a still worse form than has yet met us may be our winter prospect." Menard and his fellow petitioners expressed their unwillingness "to believe that your Excellency would make arrangements [for us] to go—would tell us that we could not live prosperously here—would create hopes within us, and stimulate us to struggle for national independence and respectable equality, and then, when we had made ourselves ready for the effort, in confident belief in the integrity of your promise, that its realization will be withheld." When several Black colonizationists (perhaps including Menard) called at the White House "to express their disappointment in the delay of their being sent, as promised, to Central America," Lincoln replied through a secretary that he "was as anxious as he ever was for their departure" but "that he had placed everything in the hands of Senator Pomeroy of Kansas, and that he could not now see the deputation of colored men, but that he would do so in the course of a few days." But he did not do so, to his discredit.[152] This uncharacteristic behavior further suggests that Lincoln did not take the Chiriquí project seriously.

ACTUAL COLONIZATION ON HAITI'S ÎLE-À-VACHE

The collapse of the Chiriquí project created a vacuum quickly filled by another colonization scheme, the brainchild of a disreputable adventurer named Bernard Kock, who proposed to resettle 5,000 African Americans on a small island off the coast of Haiti (Île-à-Vache, or Cow Island) for $50 a head. The administration began considering Kock's plan in the early fall of 1862, and Lincoln signed a contract with Kock on December 31, a few hours before issuing the Emancipation Proclamation.

It is not clear why the president trusted Kock, thus authorizing the only colonization project that actually resettled some African Americans abroad (for a brief time). By year's end, there was no longer a need to prepare the public mind for emancipation, for he had done that dramatically in August at the widely publicized meeting with five Black Washingtonians, as well as with his public letter to Horace Greeley and his annual message to Congress on December 1. He probably wanted to continue his quest to establish an asylum for those African Americans who despaired of achieving equality in the US and also for those suffering in "contraband camps," where conditions were truly deplorable. In September 1862, the celebrated former slave Harriet Jacobs reported that at a refugee camp on Capitol Hill she found "men, women and children all huddled together, without any distinction or regard to age or sex. Some of them were in the most pitiable condition. Many were sick with measles, diphtheria, scarlet and typhoid fever. Some had a few filthy rags to lie on; others had nothing but the bare floor for a couch."[153]

Bernard Kock's "home agent," Jacob R. S. Van Vleet, appealed to Lincoln's sensitive conscience by stressing how the Île-à-Vache plan would benefit the people in such an unfortunate situation. "The present condition of the 'Contrabands' has excited my warmest sympathies," Van Vleet wrote in October. If Lincoln were to sign Kock's contract, he would "instantly take thousands of these poor, houseless, homeless, friendless beings, from the depths of poverty, and place them in a land where there is no prejudice against them—where they will have good homes, constant employment—and the care of attentive and sympathizing friends, who will surround them by all the institutions of New England civilization."[154] Since Van Vleet was known as a reliable friend of African Americans, and because he served as an editor at the pro-administration *National Republican,* Lincoln may well have been disposed to take him seriously.[155] His argument was echoed by the *Philadelphia Press,* edited by Lincoln's friend and ally, John W. Forney; he wrote that Kock's proposal "will give a home to thousands of our unfortunate people who have escaped from slavery."[156] Forney may well have been expressing Lincoln's views.

In November 1862, a month before Lincoln signed the fateful contract, New York Quakers Benjamin Tatham and William Cromwell inspected refugee camps in Washington and Alexandria and called in person on the president, on Secretary of War Stanton, and on Attorney General Bates. In their report about camp conditions, they described their meeting with those officials on November 28 and 29: "We explained to them the object of our visit, and also reported what we had seen in Washington and Alexandria, believing that, in the multiplicity of their engagements, they were uninformed of the facts, and urging the importance of prompt measures to remedy existing evils. We were received with great kindness, and full approbation was expressed of the motives and action of Friends in this matter. The President was glad that Friends were ready to aid in the relief of these people. We assured him he had our sympathy, and that of our Friends, in the cares and responsibilities which devolved upon him, that our object was not to add to those cares, but to do what little we could toward relieving them. We had an interesting interview, and took a leave of him with renewed interest in his behalf."[157]

Immediately afterward, Cromwell and Tatham visited Norfolk to inspect refugee camps in and about Fort Monroe, where conditions were as appalling as those they had seen in Alexandria and Washington. At the "Grand Contraband Camp" located on the site of Hampton, a town that Confederates had burned to the ground, thousands of refugees were "quartered in small rooms, sometimes containing ten to twelve persons each, with insufficient fuel and clothing to keep warm throughout the winter months." Those Black refugees "said they had come for freedom, but would gladly return to their former plantations if they could be unmolested. Not one wanted to go north."[158] A similar report, prepared by Sergeant Albert Howe of the Quartermaster's Department at Old Point Comfort, indicated that some "blacks were housed in an old tobacco barn with chalk lines drawn on the dirt floor to delineate assigned living spaces for each family. Other freedmen were housed in dilapidated sheds and barns in an area west of Hampton known as Slabtown because the houses were constructed from old packing crates. They lacked clothing and firewood; few could find work of any sort; and there were frequent deaths from disease, exposure, and hunger."[159]

Lincoln was also receiving information about conditions at the Alexandria and Washington camps from other sources, including the Quaker abolitionist Julia Wilbur, who deplored the camps' "squalid poverty, suffering & filth."[160] On November 7, she wrote Lincoln describing the plight of the refugees and appealing for help to create better housing for them.[161] Five days earlier, Mary Lincoln had written her husband from New York saying that her African American dressmaker and confidante Elizabeth Keckly "has been very unsuccessful" in raising money for the benefit of refugee slaves: "She says the immense number of contrabands in W[ashington] are suffering intensely, many without bed covering & having to use any bits of carpeting to cover themselves—Many dying of want—Out of the $1000 fund deposited with you by Gen Corcoran, I have given her the privilege of investing $200 here [in New York] in bed covering. She is the most deeply grateful being, I ever saw, & this sum, I am sure, you will not object to being used in this way—The cause of humanity requires it."[162] As noted previously, Lincoln was fond of Elizabeth Keckly, who in 1862 established the Relief Association for the Contrabands in the District of Columbia.

In mid-December, Van Vleet met with Lincoln and presented letters of support from some New York merchants praising Kock.[163] Two weeks later, Lincoln signed the contract, which Secretary Seward then refused to certify and seal. Soon thereafter, Kock fired Van Vleet, who disclosed embarrassing information about Kock to Danforth B. Nichols, a Methodist minister serving as Superintendent of Contrabands in Washington.[164] That led to the cancelation of Kock's contract, soon to be replaced by another, more modest contract concluded with some of his New York financial backers, calling for 500 refugees to be resettled on Île-à-Vache. Lincoln signed it in mid-April.

The modified Île-à-Vache plan went into effect almost immediately. William Watkins, who had co-edited *Frederick Douglass' Paper* and served as an agent for James Redpath's Haitian Emigration Bureau, had been busy recruiting emigrants from among the many refugees living in the Fort Monroe area of Virginia.[165] Watkins's Haitian-born wife was enthusiastic about the project. Many volunteers had become convinced "that there [Haiti] & there alone they will be free from annoyance," as a Congregationalist missionary noted. Such "annoyances" included not only Confederate raiders but also Union soldiers, some of whom committed rape and stole the property of refugees. Watkins told the volunteers that he had visited Haiti, a country he said he knew well, and that "ample preparations had been made" for them, including "houses well furnished," and that therefore they need take little with them other than the clothes on their backs. They would, he assured them, first sail to Washington to meet the president before proceeding to Haiti, where they were to receive $50, housing, work paying $10 monthly, and schooling. He persuaded 453 refugees to become pioneers in the resettlement effort. They sailed a few days after Lincoln signed the new contract with Kock's financial backers.

But when they arrived at Île-à-Vache, they received none of the benefits Watkins had promised. Instead, the project's agent (amazingly, Kock himself) stole their money while en route to Haiti, and once there compelled them under duress to sign unfavorable labor contracts. The immigrants suffered so badly from cramped quarters, poor medical care, unpalatable food, lack of pay, inclement weather, poisonous insects, hostility of the Haitians, and tropical diseases that, after a few months, they begged to be returned.[166]

Distraught by the plight of those African Americans, Lincoln told army chaplain John Eaton that they "were suffering intensely from a pest of 'jiggers' [sand fleas] from which there seemed to be no escape or protection." An infestation of jiggers (usually on the toes, heels, or hands) can be extremely painful, as a survivor of the Île-à-Vache project, William Henry Nelson, testified. Upon returning to the US in 1864, he reported that the insects on the island were "very troublesome, particularly the jiggers, a small insect like a flea, which works into the flesh, and multiply there." He added that "I was down with the Haitian fever a long time, and as soon as I got over that the jiggers commenced at me and lamed me up so that sometimes I could not walk at all." When asked if he could get rid of the jiggers, Nelson replied, "No, Sir, there was no such thing as getting rid of them. They work into your foot at night when you are asleep. They are the same all year round. . . . There is no way to keep clear of them—not on that island there ain[']t. Boots don't keep them out of your feet—they will get in in spite of them, and there is no living for them."[167]

Chaplain Eaton recalled that the president's "distress was as keen as it was sincere, and I have often thought of it as an illustration of his kindness of heart, which found no detail too insignificant upon which to expend itself. The spectacle of the President of the United States, conducting the affairs of the Nation in the midst of a civil war, and genuinely affected by the discomfort occasioned a little group of Negroes by an insect no bigger than a pinhead, was a spectacle that has stayed by me all my life."[168] That distress may well have been compounded by a sense of guilt that Lincoln probably felt for having authorized the venture in the first place, despite Attorney General Bates's accurate warning that Kock was a "charlatan adventurer" and an "errant humbug."[169] Both Lincoln's conscience and his sense of compassion were unusually sensitive.

In late January 1864, when Interior Secretary John Palmer Usher received a report from Île-à-Vache recommending that the colonists be retrieved, he promptly informed Lincoln, who ordered it done forthwith. In March, 368 of the original 453 colonists arrived back in Virginia. In dispatching a vessel to repatriate them, Lincoln acted on the basis of a statute authorizing the government to rescue slaves who had been sent by their masters to Cuba or Brazil in order to evade the government's emancipation measures. Congress sought to thwart that strategy by outlawing it, mandating the repatriation of slaves thus deported, and declaring them free. That statute, in effect an anti-colonization measure, was signed by Lincoln in 1862 and implemented by him in 1864.[170]

Lincoln never mentioned colonization publicly after December 1862. In March 1863, he told an African American clergyman, the Rev. Dr. H. Parker Gloucester, that he "was opposed to colonization" and "in favor of colored soldiers, colored chaplains, and colored physicians."[171] Yet in 1863 and 1864, his administration did explore small-scale resettlement schemes with the British and Dutch governments.[172] Nothing came of those efforts, which officially ended in June 1864, when Congress rescinded the legislation providing Lincoln with $600,000 for colonization purposes. By that time, he had spent only six percent of those funds ($38,000). On July 1, John Hay noted in his diary, "I am glad the president has sloughed off that idea of colonization. I have always thought it a hideous & barbarous humbug."[173]

Of the 4,500,000 African Americans in the US in 1860, a total of 453 (one one-hundredth of one percent) had been colonized, 368 of whom returned after less than a year abroad. No participants in the ill-fated Île-à-Vache project had been colonized against their will by the government, though some had been deported by their owners.

REFLECTIONS ON THE CONTROVERSIAL MEETING AND ITS AFTERMATH

In words that could just as easily be applied to Lincoln, historian David G. Smith remarked that Radical Republican Thaddeus Stevens's "support of colonization does not necessarily mean that he was racist or favored the elimination of African-Americans from America."[174] Far from it; Stevens and Lincoln, though temperamentally and stylistically quite different, were both racial egalitarians. According to Phillip Magness, Stevens endorsed a "federal colonization enterprise" as "something of a safety valve for African-Americans to escape racial oppression."[175] Lincoln did the same, though as president, he had to be more mindful than Stevens of constitutional and political constraints and thus was not as outspoken as the Pennsylvania congressman, but "inwardly he was just as progressive."[176] His actions, however, demonstrate that neither he nor Stevens shared the widespread belief that African Americans were biologically inferior and therefore should be treated as second-class citizens. As historian Paul Scheips observed in 1952, "although Lincoln's plans for colonization failed, it is to be remembered that as far as he was concerned, they were the product of a genuine regard for humanity, however ethically undesirable the Radical Abolitionists believed and we may now believe them to have been."[177]

LEFT: Frederick Douglass around the time that he delivered his famous 1852 Independence Day oration, in which he said, "This Fourth of July is yours, not mine. You may rejoice, I must mourn." *Samuel J. Miller, ca. 1847–1852, Art Institute of Chicago, colorized by Jordan J. Lloyd of Sussex, England, Dynachrome.com.* BELOW: Frederick Douglass in 1879, three years after he delivered his widely known speech at the unveiling of the Freedmen's Monument in Lincoln Park, Washington. *George K. Warren, National Archives, colorized by Jordan J. Lloyd of Sussex, England, Dynachrome.com.*

ABOVE: In 1876, Frederick Douglass delivered the keynote speech at the dedication of this work, depicting a rising slave, broken shackles, and Lincoln holding the Emancipation Proclamation. Located in Washington's Lincoln Park, it is known as the Freedman's Memorial (alternatively, the Emancipation Memorial) and contains the following inscription: "In Grateful Memory of ABRAHAM LINCOLN this monument was erected by the western sanitary commission of Saint Louis, MO: with funds contributed solely by emancipated citizens of the United States declared free by his proclamation January 1st A.D. 1863. The first contribution of five dollars was made by Charlotte Scott a freed woman of Virginia, being her first earnings in freedom and consecrated by her suggestion and request on the day she heard of President Lincoln's death to build a monument to his memory." *National Park Service.* BELOW: On March 4, 1865, Frederick Douglass was initially refused admittance to the White House reception following Lincoln's second inauguration. When the president immediately overruled the constables, Douglass was ushered into the huge East Room, where he found himself "in a bewildering sea of beauty and elegance, such as my poor eyes had never before seen in any one room at home or abroad." Douglass thought the scene "so splendid, so glorious" that he almost regretted his decision to attend the event. That reception resembled the gala depicted here, held in February 1862. *Frank Leslie's Illustrated Newspaper, February 22, 1862.*

ABOVE: In 1862, Lincoln placed Kansas Senator Samuel Pomeroy in charge of the planned-but-eventually-scuttled colonization effort in Panama. The following year, he escorted Frederick Douglass to the White House to meet the president for the first time. Colorized version of an undated photo (ca. 1860–1870), *Mathew Brady Studio.* BELOW LEFT: In 1863, George Luther Stearns, a wealthy Massachusetts industrialist/abolitionist who had helped fund John Brown, successfully urged Frederick Douglass to call on Lincoln and protest against the discrimination suffered by Black troops in the Union Army. *Image based on a photograph taken during the Civil War, in Sidney H. Morse, "An Anti-Slavery Hero," New England Magazine, June 1891.* BELOW RIGHT: Chaplain John Eaton, Superintendent of Negro Affairs for the Department of the Tennessee, was a colonel in the United States Colored Troops. He facilitated Frederick Douglass's meeting with Lincoln in 1864. *CDV by John Cadwallader, William L. Clements Library, University of Michigan.*

RIGHT: Martin Delany, widely regarded as the father of Black nationalism, was one of the few African American callers on Lincoln who was not of mixed race. The president described him as a "most extraordinary and intelligent black man." *Alamy stock.* BELOW: This hand-colored lithograph print is based on a carte de visite of Martin Delany by photographer Abraham Bogardus, ca. 1865. Wearing his full dress major's uniform, Delany is situated in an imaginary army camp. He was the first Black line officer in the Union Army. *National Portrait Gallery, Washington.*

In April 1862, Bishop Daniel Payne of the African Methodist Episcopal Church met with Lincoln and urged him to sign the law abolishing slavery in Washington. James Redpath described him at the time as "probably the most influential and respected colored American in this country." Educated at the Lutheran Seminary in Gettysburg, Pennsylvania, Payne helped found Wilberforce University in 1856 and eventually served as its president. *Photo by C. M. Bell, early 1890s, colorized by Jordan J. Lloyd of Sussex, England, Dynachrome.com.*

In 1862, Alexander Crummell, a philosophy professor and Episcopal priest who had emigrated from New York to Liberia, lobbied the president on behalf of the government of his adoptive country. *Image from* Crummell, The Greatness of Christ: And Other Sermons *(New York: Thomas Whittaker, 1882), colorized by Jordan J. Lloyd of Sussex, England, Dynachrome.com.*

On New Year's Day 1864, abolitionist Charles Lenox Remond of Massachusetts was one of the four African Americans who first breached the color line at White House receptions. *Photo by Samuel Broadbent, Philadelphia, ca. 1851–1856, Boston Public Library, Wikimedia Commons.*

Dr. Alexander T. Augusta, born free in Virginia, studied medicine in Canada after being denied admission to American medical schools. When Lincoln issued the Emancipation Proclamation, authorizing the enlistment of Black men in the army, he immediately volunteered, was appointed a major, and served throughout the war, experiencing much discrimination before being mustered out after Appomattox as a lieutenant-colonel. He was the highest ranking Black officer in the Union Army. *Oblate Sisters of Providence Archives, Baltimore, Maryland.*

In 1861, after four years studying medicine under the supervision of Alexander Augusta, Anderson R. Abbott became the first Canadian-born Black physician in that country. During the American Civil War, he served the Union Army as a contract surgeon, working with his mentor, Dr. Augusta. In February 1862, those two physicians breached the color line at a White House reception. *CDV by Mathew Brady, Toronto Public Library.*

John T. Costin was one of the five leaders of Washington's Black community who met with Lincoln on August 14, 1862. His family was one of the pillars of Washington society. *Image dated Washington, 1849, in* Official History of Freemasonry among the Colored People of North America *(New York: Broadway Publishing Company, 1903), digital collection, New York Public Library.*

ABOVE LEFT: John F. Cook Jr. was one of the five Black Washingtonians who called on the president in August 1862. He was described in the press as a prominent member of the capital's African American "aristocracy." *http://johnfcook10.org/History.html*. ABOVE RIGHT: In 1862, Lincoln named James Mitchell of Indiana, former agent of the American Colonization Society and a Methodist minister, as Commissioner for Emigration in the Interior Department. He facilitated Lincoln's August 1862 White House meeting with John F. Cook, John T. Costin, and three other Black leaders. That occasion was the first time that African Americans were invited to the Executive Mansion to consult with a president on matters of state. *University of Michigan Library.*

John Palmer Usher of Indiana, Lincoln's secretary of the interior, supported colonization efforts, which were supervised by his department, ca. 1860–1870. *Library of Congress.*

Henry Highland Garnet, a leading Presbyterian minister in New York, acquired a radical reputation in 1843 when he publicly called for a slave revolt. He championed the Black emigrationist movement and defended Lincoln's 1862 proposal to have the government establish a sanctuary for African Americans in Central America. Garnet called the president's plan "the most humane, and merciful movement which this or any other administration has proposed for the benefit of the enslaved." *James U. Stead, ca. 1881, National Portrait Gallery, Washington, colorized by Jordan J. Lloyd, Sussex, England, Dynachrome.com.*

Henry McNeal Turner, the charismatic, young abolitionist/emigrationist minister of Washington's Israel African Methodist Episcopal Church, defended Lincoln's 1862 colonization proposal, assuring Black Washingtonians that the president had no desire to compel them to leave the country. Rather, Turner wrote, it was made to calm the fears of White Northerners who dreaded the prospect of newly liberated slaves flooding their region if emancipation were not coupled with colonization. Harper's Weekly, *12 December 1863, Alamy stock.*

E. Arnold Bertonneau, secretary of the Union Radical Association in New Orleans, was a well-to-do wine merchant and coffee shop proprietor who in 1861–1862 had served as a captain in the Louisiana Native Guards. In 1864, along with a fellow African American from Louisiana (Jean Baptiste Roudanez), he submitted to Lincoln a petition calling for the enfranchisement of Black men in the Crescent City. *Image from the collection of Herbert G. Ruffin II.*

In 1864, Abraham Galloway led a deputation of Black men from New Bern, North Carolina, who called on Lincoln and urged him to enfranchise African Americans. *Image from William Still,* The Underground Railroad *(1872).*

In 1863, Congregationalist minister George LeVere of Brooklyn headed a five-man delegation from the African Civilization Society of New York that called on the president. The following year, Lincoln appointed him to be an army chaplain. *Image from fold3.com.*

In 1863, Richard H. Cain, a pastor in the African Methodist Episcopal Church in Brooklyn, called on Lincoln along with other directors of the African Civilization Society. During Reconstruction, he was elected to the U.S. House of Representatives from South Carolina. Taken at the C. M. Bell Studio, Washington, ca. 1873-1890, when Cain was a bishop of the A.M.E. Church. *Library of Congress.*

The former slave Sojourner Truth (née Isabella Van Wagener), a celebrated champion of women's rights and abolitionism, met with Lincoln in 1864 but the following year was denied admittance when she sought to attend one of Mrs. Lincoln's receptions. She said of the president, "I never was treated by any one with more kindness and cordiality than were shown to me by that great and good man." *Colorized version of a CDV, Library of Congress, Alamy stock.*

Born a slave, Elizabeth Keckly became a successful dressmaker in Washington, where she befriended Mary Lincoln and published a memoir revealing much about the First Couple. She recalled that the president "was as kind and considerate in his treatment of me as he was of any of the white people about the White House," and that "I loved him for his kind manner towards me." *From her book,* Behind the Scenes *(New York: Carleton, 1868).*

At the Lincoln White House, William Slade was a messenger-valet-steward-majordomo as well as a gifted storyteller, a confidant of the president, and a leader of Washington's Black community. *Abraham Lincoln Presidential Library, Springfield.*

ABOVE: Lincoln surrounded by a jubilant crowd of recently freed slaves and White Unionists while touring Richmond in a carriage with Admiral David Dixon Porter on April 4, 1865. *Oil painting by Dennis Malone Carter, 1866, Chicago History Museum.* RIGHT: Thomas Nast, the eminent artist and political cartoonist, drew this image of Lincoln entering Richmond (April 4, 1865) based on an eyewitness account provided to him by the journalist Charles Carleton Coffin. It was published in *Harper's Weekly*, February 24, 1866.

ABOVE: This imaginary scene, drawn in 1883, depicts Lincoln reviewing Black troops in Richmond with his son Tad and Senator Charles Sumner in April 1865. Months earlier, near Petersburg, the president had reviewed African American units who greeted him joyously. An observer noted that he was "so broken by emotion that he could scarcely articulate the words of thanks and congratulation which he tried to speak to the humble and devoted men through whose ranks he rode. The scene was affecting in the extreme, and no one could have witnessed it unmoved." BELOW: On January 1, 1863, Lincoln issued the Emancipation Proclamation, officially liberating all slaves held in areas still in rebellion. The famed cartoonist/artist imagines its likely effect. In the center, a Black family enjoys freedom beside a "Union" stove. Below, a child represents the New Year unshackling slaves. On the left are scenes illustrating the horrors of slavery; on the right contrasting scenes depict the future. This 1865 woodcut is a colorized version of an image that appeared in *Harper's Weekly*, 24 January 1863. *Library of Congress.*

James Redpath, a Radical abolitionist who ran the Haitian Emigration Bureau, urged Lincoln to extend diplomatic recognition to Haiti, which Congress did in 1862 at the president's suggestion. Cosmopolitan, *April 1896, Alamy stock.*

The Contraband Hospital in Alexandria, a town where conditions for refugee slaves were truly deplorable. Even this hospital was "a loathsome place," according to relief agent Julia Wilbur, a Quaker abolitionist who recorded in her 1863 diary that "those poor women are dying from neglect." When she and others informed Lincoln of the misery suffered by so many African Americans in contraband camps, he was moved to support a misguided colonization effort in Haiti which seemed on paper like a better alternative than life in those camps. *Mathew Brady, ca. 1862–1865, National Archives.*

Journalist David Ross Locke, whose "Nasby Papers" satirized Negrophobes mercilessly, was Lincoln's favorite humorist. Based in Ohio, he has been aptly described as "a one-person battering ram against racial prejudice." *Library of Congress.*

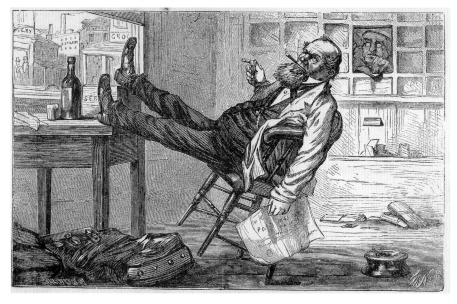

The heavy-drinking minister Petroleum Vesuvius Nasby, a fictional Ohio Democrat created by humorist David Ross Locke, was a deep-dyed Negrophobe whose over-the-top anti-Black fulminations reportedly caused Lincoln to say, "For the genius to write such things I would gladly give up my office." In this Thomas Nast drawing, the lazy, ignorant, vulgar Nasby realizes his dream of being appointed a postmaster. *Locke,* The Struggles of Petroleum V. Nasby *(Boston: Lee Shepard, 1893), 194. It originally appeared in Locke,* Swingin' 'Round the Cirkle *(Boston: Lee Shepard, 1867).*

5

"Abraham Lincoln Takes No Backward Step"

Frederick Douglass and Other African American Callers in 1863

M ost of Lincoln's African American callers were estimable, but not all of them.

On January 30, 1863, the president met with another Black Washingtonian promoting emigration to Liberia, Baptist minister Chauncey Leonard, accompanied by fellow Baptist minister Thomas S. Malcom, assistant treasurer of the Pennsylvania Colonization Society.[1] Leonard turned out to be a rather disreputable character, though that was doubtless unknown to Lincoln. Born in 1821 in Connecticut, Leonard attended Wilbraham Wesleyan Academy and the New Hampshire Academical and Theological Institution, a Baptist school. There he received a scholarship contingent on his serving as a missionary in Liberia after graduation. Rather than fulfilling that obligation, he accepted a pastorate in Providence, Rhode Island. After he spent two years in that post, his alma mater tracked him down and insisted that he either pay his educational bills or go to Liberia for a year. By that time he had a family and, evidently reluctant to leave the country, took a remunerative job running a school in Baltimore and serving as pastor of that city's Union Baptist Church.[2] But even there he could not earn enough to settle his student debts, so in 1859 he took a post as a teacher and minister at Washington's First Colored Baptist Church.[3] By 1862, he was apparently desperate. On November 1 of that year and again three months later Leonard, along with Malcom, met with Lincoln and appealed for money to underwrite an inspection tour of Liberia.[4] Lincoln agreed to fund such a venture, advancing the Colonization Society $200 to pass along to Leonard for "visiting Liberia, with reference to the establishment of a colony on the St. John's river."[5] A few days thereafter, Leonard sailed for Monrovia "as a pioneer of about fifty Baptists, who are to follow on the 1st of May with two or three preachers."[6] If the Baptist Church was paying his way, Leonard may have been double-dipping by getting the federal government via the Colonization Society to give him $200 while also receiving funds from the Baptists or the Colonization Society, or both. That is not certain but seems plausible in light of his subsequent conduct.

Years later, Leonard said that the president commissioned him to inspect "the acclimating houses" in Liberia and "obtain a percentage of the sickness and death of the colored colonists who had emigrated from the United States." ("Acclimating fever" was often fatal.) Leonard submitted a report that "was not favorable to sending the colored people in a mass to Africa, mostly on account of the inconveniences while acclimating and lack of provisions."[7] Early in 1864, Leonard grew sick and returned to the US, where Lincoln appointed him an army chaplain.[8] Stationed at the L'Ouverture Hospital for Freedmen in Alexandria, he acted as a teacher as well as a minister before being mustered out in 1865.

Leonard's reminiscences about his fact-finding mission may not be entirely reliable, for his postwar career was so checkered that it makes him seem like an untrustworthy informant. In 1866, he became minister of the Shiloh Baptist Church in Philadelphia, but his tenure was brief. That year he was arrested for defrauding a Philadelphian of $200 and soon thereafter dismissed from his pulpit. A Baptist newspaper in the City of Brotherly Love described him as "an utterly vile reprobate" who "at different times collected money for various objects." Police court records in Washington indicated that Leonard "has been repeatedly before the court for indecent exposure and kindred infamous offenses, and has been found guilty and sentenced to the workhouse. He has been a minister, and a member of the Shiloh (Colored) Church" in Philadelphia but was "unanimously excluded" from its ranks.[9] According to a history of that church, for a few months after his appointment in 1866, "everything seemed to progress nicely, but the brother was beginning to show evidence of certain proclivities that still clung to him that he was unable longer to conceal. These facts became known, not only to the Deacons, but to the church and community. Under these trying circumstances there was no other alternative but dismiss him from the pastorate of the church. After serving in a weak manner one year and about four months his administration came to an end."[10]

AFRICAN AMERICANS' REACTION TO BLACK DIPLOMATS

In March 1863, Washington's African Americans were excited by the arrival of the first Haitian diplomats to represent their country in the US. Previous administrations had refused to extend recognition to Haiti for fear that its government might send a Black emissary to Washington.[11] In 1825, Jean-Pierre Boyer, president of Haiti, offered to appoint a diplomat "such in color as not to offend the prejudices of the country."[12] But that gesture was not enough. As Senator Thomas Hart Benton of Missouri explained in 1836, "We receive no mulatto consuls, or black ambassadors, from her [Haiti]. And why? Because the peace of eleven states will not permit the fruits of a successful negro insurrection to be exhibited among them. It will not permit black ambassadors and consuls to . . . give their fellow blacks in the United

States proof in hand of the honors that await them for a like successful effort on their part. It will not permit the fact to be seen, and told, that for the murder of their masters and mistresses, they are to find friends among the white people of these United States."[13] (See the Appendix for a discussion of Lincoln's views on the acceptability of Black diplomats.)

In December 1861, Lincoln told Congress that he could see no good reason "why we should persevere longer in withholding our recognition of the independence and sovereignty of Hayti and Liberia." Unwilling to inaugurate such a "novel policy" unilaterally, he suggested that Congress pass legislation authorizing such recognition.

In 1862, soon after Congress did so, Democrats ridiculed the idea. Ohio Representative Samuel S. "Sunset" Cox exclaimed mockingly, "How fine it will look . . . to welcome here at the White House an African, full-blooded, all gilded and belaced, dressed in court style, with wig and sword and tights and shoe-buckles and ribbons and spangles and many other adornments which African vanity will suggest! How suggestive of fun to our good-humored, joke-cracking [Chief] Executive! With what admiring awe will the contrabands approach this ebony demi-god! while all decent and sensible white people will laugh the silly and ridiculous ceremony to scorn!"[14]

As its first diplomatic representative to the US, the Haitian government in 1863 appointed a young army colonel, Ernest Roumain, variously described as "bright copper colored," "mahogany-colored," and "black and shiny." He was accompanied by a Black secretary.[15] In the colonel's honor, Secretary of State Seward hosted a formal diplomatic dinner where the two Haitians were described as "elegant colored gentlemen, white kid gloves, Parisian toilet, conversing in Spanish, French and English, yet unmistakably darkey."[16]

When some of Washington's African Americans extended greetings to those gentlemen and asked permission to pay a courtesy call, the diplomats replied that they "were not receiving calls from negroes just yet." The rebuff incensed the capital's Black community, which held a meeting to consider the snub. One attendee allegedly expressed his indignation heatedly, saying, "those damned niggers think themselves better than the president. Old Abe lets colored folks come into the White House and talks to them like a father, and those cusses won't even let us look at 'em."[17]

THE FREMONT LEGION

In March 1863, the Rev. Dr. H. Parker Gloucester of Poughkeepsie, New York, who "believed that colored people could fight as well as white men if they had sufficient cause to impel them to do it," called on the president.[18] A few weeks earlier, Lincoln's announcement that Black men would be eligible for military service inspired African Americans in Poughkeepsie to try raising a 10,000-man all-Black army to be known as the "Fremont Legion." It would be commanded by General John C. Frémont, a hero to many African Americans because of his August 1861 unilateral order freeing slaves in Missouri. Reporting from Washington, the radical abolitionist journalist Jane Grey Swisshelm described Gloucester as "a polished gentleman, the son of a Kentucky slave," with "a small mixture of Caucasian blood." He "has entered into the business of raising the Fremont Legion with great spirit and has had several interviews with the President, by whom, he says, he has been most cordially received and assured that the legion shall be heartily welcomed to the service, and their wishes respected in the choice of their commander."[19] Another journalist similarly noted that Gloucester "has been holding interviews with President Lincoln nearly every day for over a week" and has also been the "guest of Mrs. Lincoln on one or two occasions."[20] A Washington newspaper stated that he had arrived around March 16, and that two days later "gave an interesting account of the interview of the delegation with the President and Gen. Frémont, by both of whom they were cordially received."[21] A month thereafter, Gloucester delivered a lecture in which he "stated many facts in connexion [sic] with conversations he had had with the President and his wife, which showed old Abe's firmness and determination to put down the rebellion, and his wife's loyalty and patriotism. Mr. Lincoln was opposed to colonization. He was in favor of colored soldiers, colored chaplains, and colored physicians."[22]

It is not clear if Gloucester was alone or accompanied by others, nor is it certain that the president met with him/them more than once in March.[23] In any event, Gloucester presented Lincoln with an appeal that African Americans in Poughkeepsie had adopted thanking the president "for proclaiming liberty to the suffering millions of our oppressed fellow countrymen. . . . We prayed for a deliverer likened unto Moses." They believed "that our prayer has been answered, and that God has raised up your Excellency as a deliverer, and a lamp by which our feet are guided into the paths of liberty." Observing that Black men had fought in earlier wars as loyal Americans, they declared their willingness "to follow the example of our fathers, and rally to our country's call. We have been called cowards. We deny the charge. It is false." They "humbly" asked Lincoln "to accept the service of the Fremont Legion."[24]

A leading African American abolitionist, James W. C. Pennington, worried that Gloucester "has undertaken a big thing," perhaps too big, but Pennington was nonetheless confident that "he is the right man" for the job.[25] On April 6, when Gloucester returned to Poughkeepsie, "the Sons and Daughters of Freedom" there adopted resolutions hailing him as "our American Kossuth" and stating "that we highly appreciate the kind reception given Dr. Gloucester by President Lincoln and his excellent lady, Mrs. Lincoln."[26]

In early May, some White New York abolitionists established the Fremont Legion Committee to help forward the project. On the morning of May 30, a subcommittee of the organization, including Gloucester and his brother James, called at the White House, where Senator Charles Sumner introduced them to the president.

(The Rev. Dr. James N. Gloucester founded Brooklyn's Siloam Presbyterian Church, served as president of the American Freedman's Friend

Society, and supported the American and Foreign Anti-Slavery Society. An ardent foe of slavery, he was a friend of Frederick Douglass and John Brown, both of whom he entertained at his home. After Brown was captured, a letter from Gloucester's wife, Elizabeth, enclosing a modest contribution, was found among his papers. Another donation from the Gloucesters was handed to Brown by Douglass.[27])

According to a press report, Lincoln, on the morning of May 30, "was in council with Secretary Chase, but received the committee in his own business-like, bland, and genial manner. To the appeals of the committee he listened with attention and respect, granted them a further hearing [for June 1], assuring them of his profound interest in their mission, his willingness to serve his country to the entire extent of his ability, his unshaken adherence to the claims of humanity, and his implicit confidence in God, affirming that it was the settled purpose of the government to bring into its active service, in the most effective form, this class of persons, for whom the petitioners pray."[28] Another paper stated that Lincoln "declared that he would gladly receive into the service not 10,000 but ten times 10,000 colored troops; expressed his determination to protect all who enlisted, and said that he looked to them for essential service in finishing the war. He believed the command of them afforded scope for the highest ambition, and he would with all his heart offer it to Gen. Fremont." The delegation was "profoundly impressed by the earnestness of the president, and his determination to employ all within his reach to the suppression of the Rebellion."[29]

Two days later, the committee met again with the president, who spoke at greater length. According to some committee members, Lincoln said "that the policy of the Government, so far as he represented it, and his will controlled it, was fixed, and that the Government would avail itself of any plausible instrumentalities to obtain the cooperation of the emancipated slaves of the South as a military organization; that we had been drifting to this result, and had partly been compelled to it by the exigencies of the war; that he was thoroughly in earnest in this purpose, and he only labored under embarrassment in regard to how to carry it out. He confessed the partial failure in recruiting colored troops both North and South, but admitted their patriotism, their enthusiasm, and their devotion to the cause of liberty. Indeed, he could not very well account for the seeming possibility we had arrived at in this enterprise, which he deemed an essential one to an early and complete success of the Union arms."

The president further told the Gloucester brothers and their colleagues, "You ask a suitable command for Gen. Fremont? There I see difficulty. Gen. Fremont is the second officer in rank in the active service of the United States; a suitable command would certainly mean a department. I have not a department vacancy to give him; I do not think I would be justified in dismissing any commander of a department for the purpose of placing him upon duty as contemplated by your memorial.'" Citing an anecdote allegedly involving the British playwright Richard Brinsley Sheridan, he remarked, "You place me in the position of the English lord who, when told by his paternal relative to take a wife, replied, 'whose wife shall I take, father?'" His administration "could not always carry out promises about special men, special numbers and special commands." Lincoln then showed the committee a map with shaded areas indicating where slaves were most numerous. Pointing to the territory around Vicksburg, Mississippi, he said, "My opinion is that the colored population will have to take these places and will have to hold them." He "hoped for cooperation from the negroes in that section to take Vicksburg and to hold it." He had "explained that matter to various officers of high rank," but had "always found on these occasions that I ran afoul of somebody's dignity." He "could not prevail on them, because they had stars on their shoulders." He continued: "I would like anybody who can to undertake the matter. I believe Gen. Fremont peculiarly adapted to this special work. I would like to have him do it." He "assured them that he would do all in his power to forward the movement" and "that if they had the entire ten thousand troops they promised raised, he would give

Gen. Fremont a department that very morning. He was disposed, in that case, to waive obstacles."[30]

Later that day (June 1), Lincoln wrote to Charles Sumner explaining that if there was "a fair prospect that a large force of this sort could thereby be the more rapidly raised," he would waive the rule against having "troops raised on any special terms, such as to serve only under a particular commander, or only at a particular place or places" and "cheerfully" place Frémont in command of the 10,000 Black soldiers and whatever White troops could be added. But he could not create a new department for Frémont (known as the Pathfinder) because there were not enough spare troops, nor could the Pathfinder be appointed to head an existing department because there were insufficient grounds "to relieve the present commander of any old one." Moreover, in "the raising of the colored troops, the same consent of Governors would have to be obtained as in case of white troops, and the government would make the same provision for them during organization, as for white troops."[31]

In July, a convention of African Americans met in Poughkeepsie to promote the enlistment effort.[32] Attendees listened to speeches, approved a manifesto, and heard remarks written by William Whiting, the solicitor of the War Department, who had been invited to speak. His long letter concluded, "Abraham Lincoln takes no backward step. . . . The President wishes the aid of all Americans, of whatever descent or color, to defend the country. He wishes every citizen to share the perils of the contest, and to reap the fruits of victory."[33] (This reference to "every citizen" plainly suggested that Black men who served would be granted citizenship rights.)

Ultimately, nothing came of the Fremont Legion proposal. The recruiters failed to meet their goal, partly because other states were offering generous bounties to New York's Black men as an inducement to join their regiments. In addition, Frémont himself was unenthusiastic, and the Democratic governor of New York, Horatio Seymour, refused to cooperate, declaring that he opposed "the whole system of using Negro regiments, from principal."[34]

In the late spring, H. Parker Gloucester and a friend called on the governor, who told them that he "had too much sympathy for colored men to encourage the sending of colored troops" into battle, where they were likely to be slaughtered.[35] When Lincoln was urged to grant "authentications" allowing the recruitment of Black troops in New York without gubernatorial approval, he refused on procedural grounds to override Seymour; governors were instrumental in raising troops, and he had already clashed unhappily with Seymour's predecessor over that very matter.[36]

BLACK PREACHERS CALL ON THE PRESIDENT

In August 1863, a dozen African American Baptist ministers visited the White House and asked Lincoln "to ascertain what protections they might have from the government in 'sending missionaries on Southern soil to promulgate the gospel of Christ within the lines of the military forces of the United States.'"[37] The president "favored them with a very flattering audience" and gave their chairman a letter: "To whom it may concern: To-day I am called upon by a committee of colored ministers of the Gospel, who express a wish to go within our military lines and minister to their brethren there. The object is a worthy one, and I shall be glad for all facilities to be afforded them which may not be inconsistent with or a hindrance to our military operations."[38]

Massachusetts Governor John A. Andrew appointed the first Black chaplains in the Union Army, William Jackson and William Grimes. Two of only fourteen African American chaplains to serve in the Union Army, they joined the 55th Massachusetts regiment. Though they were officers, Black chaplains did not command troops, nor did White soldiers have to salute them. The other ninety-plus chaplains in Black regiments were White.[39]

THE AFRICAN CIVILIZATION SOCIETY SEEKS MONEY

In November 1863, Lincoln met with five leaders of the African Civilization Society based in New York. Two months earlier, they had written
Commissioner of Emigration James Mitchell, enclosing a copy of the
organization's new constitution and asking him to call Lincoln's attention
to the society, founded in 1858 by Henry Highland Garnet. That year
Garnet told a Black audience, "Let those who wished to stay, stay here, and
let those who had enterprise and wished to go, go and found a nation, of
which the colored American could be proud." The society originally aimed
to settle African Americans in Nigeria (then known as Yoruba), where they
might prosper by growing cotton. They could thus reduce American and
European reliance on Southern states' cotton, weakening both slavery
and the slave trade. They would also help modernize the region and convert
its residents to Christianity. Moreover, as Garnet put it, the society would
help establish "a grand centre of Negro nationality, from which shall flow
commercial, intellectual, and political power which shall make colored
people respected everywhere."[40]

In their letter to Mitchell, the society's leaders requested a $5,000 credit
to enable their organization "to carry out the general objects of its forma-
tion." Enclosed with the letter was an endorsement from prominent White
New Yorkers, including Henry W. Bellows, president of the United States
Sanitary Commission; Henry J. Raymond, editor of the *New York Times*;
Peter Cooper, a generous industrialist-philanthropist; and David Hoadley,
president of the Panama Railroad. Mitchell replied that the funds they
sought were earmarked for the resettlement of emancipated slaves only, but
the president might be able to accede to their wishes.[41]

Mitchell arranged for a delegation from the society to call at the White
House on November 5, 1863. It was headed by the organization's president,
George W. LeVere, who was accompanied by its secretary, Henry M. Wilson,
and three of its directors: Richard H. Cain, Peter S. Porter, and William

Anderson. Like the five-man Black deputation that had met with Lincoln the previous year to consider colonization in Central America, these men were prominent members of the African American community.

George LeVere was a Congregationalist minister in Brooklyn whom Lincoln appointed in 1864 as one of the few Black men to serve as an army chaplain. Fellow ministers described him as "respected in the community for his intelligence, devotedness and fidelity." After the war he moved to Knoxville, where he founded an influential church and became the leader of the Grand Lodge of Colored Masons in Tennessee.[42] He enjoyed a reputation as "one of the brightest colored men who ever lived in the South."[43]

Richard Cain, a pastor in the African Methodist Episcopal Church, had studied at Wilberforce University before being assigned in 1861 to a parish in Brooklyn. There he became active in politics, serving as a delegate to the 1864 Syracuse National Convention of Colored Men. After the war he was reassigned to Charleston, South Carolina, where he founded a newspaper and pursued political office while expanding the size of his congregation dramatically. In 1868, he won election to both the state constitutional convention and to the state senate. Two years later, voters sent him to the US House of Representatives, where his oratorical gifts and keen sense of humor helped him champion the cause of equal rights, an effort culminating in the passage of the landmark 1875 Civil Rights Act. In 1880, the AME Church named him a bishop.[44]

Henry M. Wilson, an 1848 graduate of the Princeton Theological Seminary, was the minister at New York's Seventh Avenue Presbyterian Church. In 1858, he worked closely with fellow Presbyterian Henry Highland Garnet, speaking at various sites around Manhattan. He had helped establish the American League of Colored Laborers, which provided job training and business loans for African Americans. Immediately after the war, he co-founded and administered the Brooklyn Colored Orphan Asylum (also known as the Home for Freed Children and Others and later as the Howard Colored Orphan Asylum), which cared for many children, including some of those who had been in the Manhattan orphanage that mobs burned to the ground during the city's 1863 draft riots. Wilson advocated an all-Black approach to organizing and administering the orphanage.[45] During Garnet's 1861 visit to England, Wilson assumed control of the African Civilization Society and allied it with the Freedmen's Aid Society; together they maintained schools in Maryland and Washington.

A successful businessman and treasurer of the New York Legal Rights Association, Peter S. Porter helped found the New York State Suffrage Association in 1855 and had been instrumental in the semi-successful antebellum struggle to desegregate the city's streetcars.[46] During the "horsecar wars," he was savagely beaten for refusing to leave the interior of a car.[47] "He who would be free must strike the first blow," was his motto.[48] He was esteemed as a "manly, plucky, and wise" leader of New York's Black community. His palatial mansion in Manhattan served as a luxury hotel for African Americans.[49] An obituarist described him as a humble man who "enjoyed the intimate friendship of such men as Garnet, Fred Douglass, Lloyd Garrison, Gerrit Smith, and other leaders in the anti-slavery movement. Porter was himself an important factor in abolition, and his advice and his race were prized by the philanthropic coterie who devoted their lives to the cause of freedom."[50]

Commissioner Mitchell drafted a document appropriating $5,000 for Lincoln's signature, but the president did not sign it. The only account of the meeting simply states that Lincoln "gave them a patient hearing, and said he would bestow upon their written communication due consideration." The ostensible reason for the request was to fund the organization's unspecified "general objects," but it seems likely that the society wanted to facilitate the immigration of African Americans to British Honduras, a project then being considered by the administration. Nothing, however, came of plans to resettle African Americans there.[51]

LINCOLN MEETS FREDERICK DOUGLASS FOR THE FIRST TIME

Other African Americans called at the White House to make political appeals. Frederick Douglass had been actively recruiting Black men for the Union Army. If captured, they faced the alarming prospect of being killed or enslaved. When Confederates threatened to do just that, the *New-York Tribune* complained that Lincoln took no steps to stop them. The president called the subject of retaliation "one of the most vexing which has arisen during the war."[52] An abolitionist officer, angry that "the President was very weak on the subject of protecting black troops and their officers," expressed the wish that Lincoln "had said a rebel solider shall die for every negro soldier sold into slavery."[53] Responding to that criticism, he protested to a group of clergy: "*I am very ungenerously attacked*" and asked plaintively, "What *could* I do?"[54]

One thing Lincoln did do was to issue an order of retaliation, which "enforced the idea that the life of a black person was just as valuable as that of a white one," as David S. Reynolds put it.[55] On July 30, 1863, the president wrote Stanton: "It is the duty of every government to give protection to its citizens, of whatever class, color, or condition, and especially to those who are duly organized as soldiers in the public service. The law of nations and the usages and customs of war as carried on by civilized powers, permit no distinction as to color in the treatment of prisoners of war as public enemies. To sell or enslave any captured person, on account of his color, and for no offence against the laws of war, is a relapse into barbarism and a crime against the civilization of the age. The government of the United States will give the same protection to all its soldiers, and if the enemy shall sell or enslave anyone because of his color, the offense shall be punished by retaliation upon the enemy's prisoners in our possession. It is therefore ordered that for every soldier of the United States killed in violation of the laws of war, a rebel soldier shall be executed; and for every one enslaved by the enemy or sold into slavery, a rebel soldier shall be placed at hard labor on the public works and continued at such labor until the other shall be released and receive the treatment due to a prisoner of war."[56]

Despite the prospect of being either murdered in cold blood or enslaved if captured, Black men joined the army in large numbers. Many, however, were angry because they were paid less than White troops and because they could serve only as enlisted men, not officers. "We have an imbecile administration, and the most imbecile management that is possible to conceive of," wrote the Black novelist William Wells Brown.[57] Douglass was so dismayed that he quit his recruitment efforts, explaining to abolitionist and army recruiter George Luther Stearns, "I owe it to my long-abused people, and especially to those already in the army, to expose their wrongs and plead their cause. I cannot do that in connection with recruiting. When I plead for recruits I want to do it with all my heart, without qualification. I cannot do that now. The impression settles upon me that colored men have much over-rated the enlightenment, justice, and generosity of our rulers at Washington. In my humble way I have contributed somewhat to that false estimate."[58]

In reply, Stearns recommended that Douglass urge the administration to provide more protection for Black POWs. Taking that advice, on August 10, 1863, Douglass visited the White House, escorted by Kansas Senator Samuel C. Pomeroy.[59] Looking back later, Douglass wrote that he required much nerve to undertake this mission, for the "distance then between the black man and the white American citizen was immeasurable. I was an ex-slave, identified with a despised race, and yet I was to meet the most exalted person in this great republic. It was altogether an unwelcome duty, and one from which I would gladly have been excused. I could not know what kind of a reception would be accorded me. I might be told to go home and mind my business, and leave such questions as I had come to discuss to be managed by the men wisely chosen by the American people to deal with them. Or I might be refused an interview altogether."[60]

Upon arrival at the Executive Mansion, Douglass found the stairway jammed with office seekers, and since he "was the only dark spot among them," he expected he would have "to wait at least half a day." But, as he recalled, "in two minutes after I sent in my card, the messenger came out, and respectfully invited 'Mr. Douglass' in. I could hear, in the eager multitude outside, as they saw me pressing and elbowing my way through, the remark, 'Yes, damn it, I knew they would let the nigger through.'"[61]

Upon entering the room, Douglass observed the president sitting "in a low armchair with his feet extended on the floor, surrounded by a large number of documents and several busy secretaries." Lincoln appeared "much over-worked and tired. Long lines of care were already deeply written on Mr. Lincoln's brow, and his strong face, full of earnestness, lighted up as soon as my name was mentioned. As I approached and was introduced to him he arose and extended his hand, and bade me welcome. I at once felt myself in the presence of an honest man—one whom I could love, honor, and trust without reserve or doubt."[62]

Lincoln greeted him "cordially," as Douglass put it, "just as you have seen one gentleman receive another, with a hand and voice well-balanced between a kind cordiality and a respectful reserve." Douglass was immediately taken with the president: "I have never seen a more transparent countenance," Douglass wrote two days later. "There was not the slightest shadow of embarrassment."[63]

When he began to explain who he was, Lincoln put him at ease, saying, "I know you; I have read about you, and Mr. Seward has told me about you."[64] Douglass later said that he felt "quite at home in his presence" and characterized the interview as "a man in a low condition, meeting a high one. Not Greek meeting Greek, exactly, but railsplitter meeting nigger." He was impressed by Lincoln's habit of calling him "Mr. Douglass."[65]

Douglass explained that for months he had been helping to recruit Black troops for the Union Army, an effort that at first went well, but in time faltered, for it seemed that the administration was not treating African Americans fairly. When Lincoln asked him to elaborate, Douglass said Black soldiers should receive the same pay as White troops; and like White soldiers, they should be promoted from the ranks to officerships if their conduct warranted it. Lincoln "listened with patience and silence." Troubled by what he heard, he replied earnestly, impressing Douglass "with the solid gravity of his character."[66]

When Douglass thanked him for the July 30 order of retaliation, Lincoln immediately "proceeded with . . . an earnestness and fluency of which I had not suspected him, to vindicate his policy respecting the whole slavery ques-tion and especially that in reference to employing colored troops." Noting that Douglass had recently criticized him for his "tardy, hesitating, vacil-lating policy," Lincoln told his guest, "Mr. Douglass, I have been charged with being tardy, and the like" to which he replied that while he might be slow at times, he was not vacillating. "Mr. Douglass, I do not think that charge can be sustained; I think it cannot be shown that when I have once taken a position, I have ever retreated from it." This comment Douglass interpreted as "an assurance that whoever else might abandon his antislavery policy President Lincoln would stand firm."[67]

In justifying his initial reluctance to issue an order of retaliation, Lin-coln "said that the country needed talking up to that point. He hesitated in regard to it when he felt that the country was not ready for it. He knew that the colored man throughout this country was a despised man, a hated man, and he knew that if he at first came out with such a proclamation, all the hatred which is poured on the head of the negro race would be visited on his Administration. He said that there was preparatory work needed." He added that "he had difficulty in getting colored men into the United States uniform; that when the purpose was fixed to employ them as soldiers, several different uniforms were proposed for them, and that it was something gained when it was finally determined to clothe them like other soldiers."[68]

In time, the necessary "preparatory work" was done, he said, by brave African American troops: "Remember this, Mr. Douglass; remember that [the battles of] Milliken's Bend, Port Hudson, and Fort Wagner are recent events; and that these were necessary to prepare the way for this very proclamation of mine." If he had issued the order earlier, he said, "such was the state of public popular prejudice that an outcry would have been raised against the measure. It would be said 'Ah! We thought it would come to this. White men are to be killed for negroes.'" Douglass found the argument "reasonable."

Lincoln called retaliation for Confederate mistreatment of Black captives "a terrible remedy, and one which it was very difficult to apply." Once commenced, "there was no telling where it would end." If "he could get hold of the Confederate soldiers who had been guilty of treating colored soldiers as felons he could easily retaliate, but the thought of hanging men for a crime perpetrated by others was revolting to his feelings." He believed "that the rebels themselves would stop such barbarous warfare" and "that less evil would be done if retaliation were not resorted to." This line of reasoning revealed to Douglass "the tender heart of the man rather than the stern warrior and commander-in-chief of the American army and navy, and, while I could not agree with him, I could but respect his humane spirit."[69]

As for equal pay, the president explained that "we had to make some concession to prejudice. There were threats that if we made soldiers of them that all white men would not enlist, would not fight beside them. Besides it was not believed that a negro would make as good a soldier as a white man, and hence it was thought he should not have the same pay as a white man." He added: "I assure you, Mr. Douglass, that in the end they shall have the same pay as white soldiers." Lincoln pledged to insist that captured Black troops be treated as honorable prisoners of war, just like White captives.[70]

Though Douglass "was not entirely satisfied" with Lincoln's replies, he was "so well satisfied with the man and with the educating tendency of the conflict" that he resumed his recruiting efforts.[71] In a letter describing this conversation, Douglass said it "was gratifying and did much to assure me that slavery would not survive the War and that the country would survive both slavery and the War."[72] In December, Douglass told a Philadelphia audience that while in the White House, he "felt big."[73]

The day Douglass had his interview with Lincoln, he also spoke with Secretary of War Stanton, who proposed to commission him as an army officer and assign him to join the staff of General Lorenzo Thomas, who was leading efforts to recruit Black men in the Mississippi Valley. Both leaders assured him "that justice would ultimately be done," and so he "gave full faith and credit to their promise."[74] But they did not follow through on all their commitments. Douglass never received a commission and declined to aid General Thomas's recruiting efforts without one. Similarly, though 179,000 Black men served in the ranks, only about 100 became officers, most of them chaplains and doctors without authority to issue orders to White troops, nor would White soldiers have to salute them. In 1864, Congress belatedly equalized pay for Black and White troops, retroactively applied to most (but not all) African American recruits.[75]

Lincoln's order of retaliation was never implemented, even though Confederates did kill some Black prisoners in cold blood, most notoriously at Fort Pillow, Tennessee, in April 1864.[76] After accounts of that massacre sparked public outrage, Lincoln declared that no retaliation would be undertaken while the matter was under investigation, but that if the reports proved accurate, "the retribution shall . . . surely come. It will be a matter of grave consideration in what exact course to apply the retribution; but . . . it must come."[77]

But it did not come. After the Congressional Committee on the Conduct of the War reported that the allegations were true, the cabinet discussed possible responses. According to Interior Secretary John Palmer Usher, Lincoln was "very much in earnest about the matter" but argued that the "difficulty is not in stating the principle, but in practically applying it." Blood, he said, "can not restore blood, and government should not act for revenge."[78] On May 17, 1864, after mulling over the matter, Lincoln ordered Stanton to notify Confederate authorities that if they did not abandon their policy, the Union would set aside a number of Rebel prisoners and "take such action as may then appear expedient and just."[79] That threat proved idle, however, for Grant's spring offensive distracted the administration's attention.

(On the related issue of prisoner-of-war exchanges, Lincoln took a principled but politically unpopular stand. Because Confederates refused to swap Black captives, the president suspended the exchange cartel, leaving many Union POWs to suffer the horrors of Andersonville and other Southern camps. As David S. Reynolds observed, this was "another example of Lincoln's commitment to blacks, even at great political cost to himself as well as injury to whites. It further belies the charges of those critics that Lincoln was really a racist or indifferent to the plight of blacks."[80])

Reflecting on his White House meeting, Douglass called Lincoln "not only a great President, but a GREAT MAN—too great to be small in anything." While with the president, "I was never in any way reminded of my humble origin, or of my unpopular color" and felt as though he "was in the presence of a big brother" and "that there was safety in his atmosphere."[81]

The following year, Douglass would return to the White House, this time unescorted and at the president's request.

6

"To Keep the Jewel of Liberty Within the Family of Freedom"

African American Callers in 1864, Including Frederick Douglass Again

n 1864, Lincoln met with several African Americans; of all those interviews, arguably the most significant took place in early March, when two educated Black men from New Orleans—Jean Baptiste Roudanez, an engineer, and E. Arnold Bertonneau, a former officer in the Union Army—presented him a petition signed by several hundred free Black residents of the Crescent City, an unusually literate, sophisticated African American community.

BLACK COMMUNITY LEADERS IN NEW ORLEANS

After Union forces gained control of New Orleans in the spring of 1862, Lincoln appointed George Shepley to act as military governor of Louisiana and Benjamin Butler to command the Department of the Gulf.[1] In 1863, the president urged both generals to help establish a new civilian government in the Bayou State by holding elections for state officers and delegates to a constitutional convention. The question immediately arose: should Louisiana's Black men be enfranchised? If so, would voting rights be granted just to the freeborn or also to those who were liberated during the war? The 11,000 freeborn Black Louisianans had arguably been recognized as citizens in November 1862, when Attorney General Edward Bates ruled that citizenship was determined by birthplace and not by race or color (the *Dred Scott* case to the contrary notwithstanding). "Is a man legally incapacitated to be a citizen of the United States by the sole fact that he is a *colored* and not a white man?" he asked. Replying to this rhetorical query, Bates wrote, "The Constitution says not one word, and furnishes not one hint, in relation to the color or to the ancestral race of the 'natural-born citizen.'" Therefore, he concluded, "I give it is my opinion that the *free man of color*, if born in the United States, is a citizen of the United States."[2] Bates's opinion was "constructively the opinion of the President," according to the editor of *The Congregationalist*.[3] Though it broadly implied that skin color had nothing to do with citizenship, it ignored the matter of voting rights for Black men. Evidently acting on Bates's opinion, the State Department began issuing passports to Black applicants.[4] Freeborn African Americans in New Orleans—eighty percent of whom were Creoles (descendants of French and Spanish colonials)—had traditionally enjoyed far more rights than did free African Americans in other slave states.

Many of those New Orleans Black Creoles were educated, tax-paying property owners who regarded themselves as far superior to Louisiana's slaves. (Only ten percent of those Creoles were unskilled laborers.) They disliked being held responsible "for the ignorance that the laws of the Black Code have inflicted on the unhappy slaves."[5] In August 1864, the *New Orleans Tribune*, which reflected the views of the city's Black Creoles, said, "while we are of the same race as the unfortunate sons of Africa who have trembled until now under the bondage of a cruel and brutalizing slavery, one cannot, without being unfair, confuse the newly freed people with our intelligent population which, by its industry and education, has become as useful to society and the country as any other class of citizens."[6] Those Creoles felt entitled to voting rights, for they constituted, in their own eyes, a class able "to exercise the right of suffrage in an intelligent manner."[7]

Black Creoles began discussing the suffrage question in late 1862. In November of the following year, at a meeting of several hundred African Americans, speakers both Black and White resolved to demand the immediate enfranchisement of freeborn Black men. Captain P. B. S. Pinchback, who would become the first African American to act as a state governor, spoke for many Black Louisianans who served in the Union Army: they "only demanded, as a right, that they should be allowed the suffrage." They "did not ask for *social equality*, and did not expect it, but they demanded *political rights*. They wanted to be MEN." He "believed that if colored people were citizens they had a right to vote; if they were not citizens, they were exempt from the draft."[8] The meeting's participants approved a long petition embodying their demand to be submitted to Governor Shepley.[9] (That same petition, evidently written by the secretary of the Union Radical Association, E. Arnold Bertonneau, would be presented to Lincoln four months later, with only minor changes.[10]) Rather than replying, Shepley passed the document on to General Butler's successor, Nathaniel P. Banks, who also failed to respond.

Frustrated by the generals' silence, the Union Radical Association convened another meeting on January 5, 1864, where the petition addressed to Governor Shepley that had been adopted two months earlier was modified slightly and addressed to Lincoln and the US Congress. Two weeks later, at yet another mass meeting, it was resolved to have the petition delivered to the authorities in Washington. But before their designated messenger, Pascal M. Tourne, left for the nation's capital, Colonel James M. McKaye of the American Freedmen's Inquiry Commission addressed another mass meeting on February 8, announcing that the president had sent him to New Orleans "as a special commissioner to inquire into their condition and ascertain their wishes."[11] Resolutions were drawn up offering thanks for the "realization of their new position in social life" and expressing the hope that "wise and judicious legislation for the just equalization of human rights" would be passed.[12] No direct allusion was made to suffrage, although the popular Jordan P. Noble, known as "the drummer boy" in Andrew Jackson's army that had defeated the British in 1815, "went into a history of the colored people of Louisiana, stating that there were two classes introduced here, one of slaves from the wilds of Africa, an ignorant, degraded people, and the other an intelligent, educated and enlightened and wealthy class from Jamaica, Haiti and Cuba." Those free Black Creoles "wanted the right to be protected in their rights. They wanted to be assured that this protection was to be given them by having a voice in the legislation of the country, the voice and the selection of the president of the legislative officers at the ballot box."[13]

An 1859 editorial in the New Orleans *Picayune* offered a more elaborate description of the social structure of New Orleans' Black community: "Our free colored population form a distinct class from those elsewhere in the United States. Far from being antipathetic to the whites, they have followed in their footsteps, and progressed with them, with a commendable spirit of emulation, in the various branches of industry most adapted to their sphere. Some of our best mechanics and artisans are to be found among the free colored men. They form the great majority of our regular, settled masons, bricklayers, builders, carpenters, tailors, shoemakers, &c. . . . whilst we count among them in no small numbers, excellent musicians, jewelers, goldsmiths, tradesmen and merchants. As a general rule, the free colored people of Louisiana, and especially of New Orleans—the 'creole colored people,' as they style themselves—are a sober, industrious and moral class, far advanced in education and civilization."[14] Similarly, the Northern abolitionist B. Rush Plumley, who in 1863 had come to organize

Black troops in Louisiana, noted that the "free colored Creoles are divided into castes, very sharply defined." The divisions included "the free against the bound, the light against the dark, the loyal against the disloyal." Some of them had contributed "to the rebel fund for the defence [sic] of the city against the Federal forces." There were "not more decided confederates to be found in the South than may be found among the free colored Creoles of Louisiana." That segment of the Creole population "is not large, but it is rich, aristocratic, exclusive, and bitterly hostile to the black, except as a slave." In fact, some Black Creoles "do not believe in freedom for the black," and "others who would limit colored suffrage to their own class."[15]

AFRICAN AMERICANS URGE LINCOLN TO SUPPORT BLACK SUFFRAGE

Instead of Pascal M. Tourne, Jean Baptiste Roudanez and E. Arnold Bertonneau were chosen to carry the petition to Washington.[16] A reporter described those two as "gentlemen well known in business circles in New Orleans, and in every respect accomplished and able men."[17] Another journalist depicted them as "fine specimens of that mixed blood which characterizes a large portion of the population of the Crescent City"; they both had a "European cast of features" and "present the appearance of quite scholarly personages and polished gentlemen."[18]

According to that reporter, the forty-six-year-old Roudanez "was educated in Paris, having access to the best society of that metropolis."[19] Colonel McKaye called Roudanez, who had testified before his commission about the mistreatment of slaves, "a man of great intelligence and probity" and added that no one in New Orleans "bears a higher reputation for truth and sobriety."[20] Born into a prominent Creole family (his father Louis was a French merchant and his mother, Aimes Potens, was a free Black woman), he prospered as a mechanical engineer and building contractor working on sugar plantations. Before the war, in advertisements targeting sugar planters, he described himself as a "kettle-setter."[21] In 1863, Roudanez, along with his more prominent brother Charles, founded and helped run the *New Orleans Tribune*, the first Black daily newspaper in the country. It championed the radical faction of the Republican party in Louisiana. Initially, the paper supported enfranchising only freeborn Black men, but by mid-1864 it added newly freed slaves to its reform agenda.[22] Roudanez was to serve as vice president of the New Orleans Freedmen's Aid Association, established in February 1865 to help liberated slaves by acquiring land for them, teaching them how best to manage it, lending them money, providing them necessary supplies, and encouraging the establishment of schools.[23]

During their 1864 sojourn in the North, the twenty-seven-year-old Bertonneau was more outspoken than Roudanez. A short, light-skinned, blue-eyed, well-to-do wine merchant and coffee shop proprietor, he had in 1861–1862 been a captain in the Louisiana Native Guards, a unit that was in effect a branch of the state militia and hence formed part of the Confederate Army.[24]

When war broke out in April 1861, several free Black men in New Orleans, including Bertonneau, said they were resolved "to take arms and form themselves into companies for the defense of their homes, together with the other inhabitants of the city, against any enemy who may come and disturb its tranquility." Over 1,500 free African Americans rallied to express support for the authors of that resolution. In keeping with their pledge, free Black men formed a regiment consisting of thirty-three officers and 731 enlisted men. (The lieutenants and captains were Black, while the higher-ranking field officers were White.) Their action was not unprecedented; both slaves and free Black men had served in the Louisiana militia during the eighteenth and early nineteenth centuries. Captain Bertonneau later explained why he and other Black Creoles joined the Confederate Army: "Without arms and ammunition, or any means of self-defense, the condition and position of our people were extremely paralyzed; could we have adopted a better policy?" Many free Black Creoles owned property they wished to protect; some had plantations worked by scores of slaves. A captain in the Louisiana Native Guard, Charles Sauvinet, said, "If we had not volunteered, they would have forced us into the ranks, and we should have been suspected. We have property and rights here, and there is every reason why we should take care of ourselves."[25]

Confederate authorities did not supply the Native Guards with arms or uniforms, nor were they assigned duties other than company drilling. When Union forces captured New Orleans, General Butler urged the Native Guards to join the Union Army. They responded positively, and in late September 1862 the first regiment of the Native Guards was mustered into service as the Sixth Louisiana Infantry. Not all the recruits were freeborn; as many as half were fugitive slaves. A second regiment of Native Guards, consisting largely of former slaves, joined up in October, and a third regiment followed suit six weeks later. Bertonneau served in the second regiment as a captain, the rank he had held in the Native Guards.

In 1863, General Banks decided to purge the Black officers, whom White troops resented. To weed them out, Banks created examining boards that inspected only African American officers, and did so in a blatantly prejudicial manner. To protest, Bertonneau resigned his commission in March 1863, stating, "When I joined the Army I thought that I was fighting for the same cause, wishing only [that] the success of my country would suffice to alter a prejudice which had existed. But I regret to say that five months experience has proved the contrary."[26] In July 1863, when Banks feared that Confederates might attack New Orleans while most of his men were a hundred miles away besieging Port Hudson, he called for short-term, emergency volunteers. Disillusioned though Bertonneau was by the prejudice he had experienced, he reenlisted for a sixty-day tour, during which the threatened Confederate attack failed to materialize.[27]

Accompanied by Pennsylvania Congressman William D. Kelley, a leading Radical Republican, Bertonneau and Roudanez met with Lincoln on the evening of either March 3 or 4.[28] Their petition asserted that, of the

30,000 free African Americans in Louisiana, all but 1,000 were literate; they paid taxes on property worth over $15,000,000; many were descended from French and Spanish settlers and from men who in 1815 had fought alongside Andrew Jackson against the British at the Battle of New Orleans; many had lighter complexions than some White people; and they had rallied to protect the city from a feared attack by Confederates. "We are men; treat us as such," they insisted in their appeal for the right to vote.[29]

(After meeting with Senator Charles Sumner, Congressman Kelley, and other Radical Republicans, Roudanez and Bertonneau on March 10 tacked on an addendum arguing that both morality and political exigency dictated that freed slaves should also be enfranchised.[30] They later reported that the first draft of their petition had called for that, but White allies in Louisiana had urged them to limit the appeal to benefit the freeborn.)

After reading their petition (minus the addendum), Lincoln remarked, "I regret, gentlemen, that you are not able to secure all your rights, and that circumstances will not permit the government to confer them upon you. I wish you would amend your petition so as to include several suggestions, which I think will give more effect to your prayer, and after having done so please hand it to me." When Bertonneau volunteered to rewrite the document on the spot, Lincoln asked, "Are you, then, the author of this eloquent production?"

"Whether eloquent or not, it is my own work," he replied, and thereupon swiftly incorporated the president's suggestions into the petition.[31] (It is unknown just what changes were made at that point.)

Lincoln was courteous and respectful to his Black guests. Though Bertonneau and Roudanez agreed to make his suggested changes to the petition, the president denied their request, explaining "that the restoration of the Union in all its parts being his primary aim, all other questions, in his mind, were subordinate to this. Hence, whatever he did to attain this end arose from his estimate of the political necessity demanding the action, and not from any moral aspects of the case. Inasmuch as the reasons given for admitting the free people of color to the voting privilege in Louisiana were purely of a moral nature, in no wise affecting the relation of that State to the Union, he would not depart from his established views, and would decline to take any steps in the matter until a political urgency rendered such a course proper."[32] According to another account of this interview, Lincoln said that he "saw no reason why intelligent black men should not vote; but this was not a military question, and he would refer it to the Constitutional Convention in Louisiana."[33] In yet another version, Lincoln is quoted as saying "it was his business to finish the job he had on hand, and if he was convinced that it was necessary, in order to secure the restoration of Louisiana, that they should be allowed to vote, he would do it. But this petition rests its claim on moral grounds, and with those he had, and would have nothing to do. He must, therefore, refer them to the constitutional convention soon to be held in Louisiana."[34]

In fact, by the time Roudanez and Bertonneau met with him, Lincoln had twice approved the enfranchisement of at least some freeborn Black men. In August 1863, Secretary of War Stanton had directed Governor Shepley to register "all the loyal citizens of the United States" as eligible voters; the qualifier *white* was conspicuously absent. Four months later, Chase reported that Lincoln "said he could see no objection to the registering of such citizens, or to their exercise of the right of suffrage."[35]

In December 1863, when Lincoln had received an appeal from a White Louisiana Unionist urging him to deny Black men the right to vote for constitutional convention delegates, he endorsed the document: "On very full consideration I do not wish to say more than I have publicly said."[36] Just as he would not yet openly support Black voting, he would not oppose it either.

A few days after meeting with Roudanez and Bertonneau, Lincoln took a further step. In a March 13 letter congratulating Michael Hahn on his recent election as governor of Louisiana, the president alluded to the state's imminent constitutional convention: "Now you are about to have a Convention which, among other things, will probably define the elective franchise. I barely suggest for your private consideration, whether some of the colored people may not be let in—as, for instance, the very intelligent, and especially those who have fought gallantly in our ranks. They would probably help, in some trying time to come, to keep the jewel of liberty within the family of freedom. But this is only a suggestion, not to the public, but to you alone."[37] Though phrased tentatively, the president's letter was really an order. As James G. Blaine later wrote, "The form of the closing expression, quite unusual in Mr. Lincoln's compact style, may have been pleonastic, but his meaning was one of deep and almost prophetic significance. It was perhaps the earliest proposition from any authentic source to endow the negro with the right of suffrage."[38] When the letter to Governor Hahn was first published in the summer of 1865, the knowledgeable journalist Whitelaw Reid observed that it was written at a time "when negro suffrage was a thing to speak of in bated breath, and with many a shudder. Even then, in advance of almost every leading man of the party which supported him, Mr. Lincoln was found inquiring—in a quarter where he knew inquiry to be almost equal to command," he endorsed Black voting rights.[39] To be sure, Lincoln supported only limited Black suffrage—for the "very intelligent" and military veterans. Some radicals went further, demanding equal suffrage, that is, stipulating that any qualifications restricting suffrage to some categories of Black men should also be applied to White men. A few Radicals went even further, insisting on universal suffrage (at the time understood as unrestricted voting rights for all adult males).[40]

Governor Hahn showed Lincoln's letter to many constitutional convention delegates while urging them to enfranchise at least some Black men. General Banks also worked behind the scenes to the same end. Despite those efforts, an overwhelming majority of delegates rejected what they called the "nigger resolution" and instead approved a measure to prohibit the legislature from ever enfranchising Louisiana's Black men. Banks and Hahn managed to persuade the majority to backtrack somewhat by empowering the legislature to grant the vote to Black men based on military service, intellectual merit, or payment of taxes. This hardly satisfied Lincoln's desire for immediate enfranchisement of some Black men, but it did pave the way for the eventual adoption of Black voting rights in 1868.[41]

That was as far as White Louisianans were willing to go in 1864. Chase's principal informant about affairs in the Bayou State, George S. Denison, told the treasury secretary that "constitutions & laws are without good effect, unless sustained by an enlightened public opinion—and any law giving suffrage to negroes, could not be so sustained at present, in any State county or town throughout the whole South. I do not think you appreciate or understand the intense antipathy with which Southerners regard negroes. It is the natural antipathy of races, developed & intensified by the servile, brutal condition of one—[and] the insolent, despotic position of the other." Given those conditions, the constitution's provision allowing the legislature to enfranchise Black men seemed like "a great step in the right direction."[42] Similarly, the abolitionist Major B. Rush Plumly maintained that "although the movement for a free State may not have promised immediately all that the free colored creoles desired, it was a complete change of front for Louisiana—a facing toward justice, on the straight line to the goal of freedom and of all rights."[43]

Lincoln's March 13, 1864, letter to Hahn had made it possible for a clause in the new constitution authorizing the legislature to enfranchise Black men to be adopted. In 1865, Hahn revealed that the president's missive, "though marked 'private,' was no doubt intended to be seen by other Union men in Louisiana beside myself, and was consequently shown to many members of our Constitutional Convention and leading free-State men." He added that the "letter, written in the mild and graceful tone which imparted so much weight to Mr. Lincoln's simple suggestions, no doubt had great effect on the action of the Louisiana Convention in all matters appertaining to the colored man."[44]

After sending his letter to Hahn, Lincoln worked to promote the interests of Louisiana's African Americans, recalling General Banks from New

Orleans to lobby Congress on behalf of the Hahn government. Frustrated by the lack of cooperation between the military forces in Louisiana and the civilian government there, he sent Banks back to New Orleans. The president did not write instructions for him, but his intent can be inferred from Banks's remarks upon arriving in New Orleans soon after Lincoln's assassination. There he addressed a mass meeting: "To the colored people of this State, I will say that the work is still going on; and, by being patient, they will see that the day is not far distant when they will be in the enjoyment of all rights. . . . Abraham Lincoln gave his word that you will be free, and enjoy all the rights guaranteed to all citizens."[45]

While lobbying Congress on behalf of the Hahn government, "Lincoln had been earnestly anxious to permit the extension of the right of suffrage to American citizens of African descent in Louisiana," according to Pennsylvania Congressman William D. Kelley. As that Radical Republican wrote, it "was not a mere sentiment with Mr. Lincoln. He regarded it as an act of justice to the citizens, and a measure of sound policy for the States, and doubtless believed that those whom he invested with power were using their influence to promote so desirable an object. Of this he assured me more than once, and in the presence of others to whose memories I may safely appeal."[46]

To demonstrate his sincerity, Lincoln showed members of Congress his letter to Hahn. Among them was Missouri Senator B. Gratz Brown, a leading supporter of Black voting rights. Writing an open letter to his constituents in late 1864, Brown quoted the president's missive to Hahn and said that the provision of the Louisiana constitution authorizing the legislature to enfranchise Black men "was prompted by the executive head of our nation himself."[47] Congressman Thomas D. Eliot of Massachusetts was also assured by "the highest sources" that the Hahn government would enfranchise Black men.[48]

Lincoln also showed the Hahn letter to abolitionists, including J. Miller McKim, who told William Lloyd Garrison in May 1864: "I . . . have seen some of the correspondence between Mr. Lincoln and New Orleans. It is greatly to Mr. Lincoln's credit as a friend to the black man. Mr. Lincoln is in advance of his party on the question of negro suffrage. Not in advance of all, but of the majority."[49] While the president and Banks lobbied Congress, their allies on the ground in Louisiana championed the cause of Black suffrage.[50]

(Lincoln also worked unostentatiously to persuade White Arkansans to enfranchise Black men. In the summer of 1864, he appointed one of his White House secretaries, William O. Stoddard, as US marshal for the eastern district of that state with instructions to "do all you can, in any and every way you can, to get the ballot into the hands of the freedmen! We must make voters of them before we take away the troops. The ballot will be their only protection after the bayonet is gone, and they will be sure to need all they can get." Stoddard wrote that Lincoln "believed that it might be obtained as a part of the processes of reconstruction."[51])

⁂

Bertonneau and Roudanez, by prompting Lincoln to write a letter to Hahn, had not labored in vain. After their White House meeting, they traveled to Boston, where they were feted at a gala banquet hosted by Massachusetts Governor John A. Andrew and attended by prominent abolitionists like William Lloyd Garrison and Frederick Douglass. There Bertonneau delivered an impassioned plea for equal rights: "In order to make our State blossom and bloom as the rose, the character of the whole people must be changed. As slavery is abolished, with it must vanish every vestige of oppression. The right to vote must be secured; the doors of our public schools must be opened, [so] that our children, side by side, may study from the same books, and imbibe the same principles and precepts from the Book of Books—learn the great truth that God 'created of one blood all nations of men to dwell on all the face of the earth'—so will caste, founded on prejudice against color, disappear."[52] Frederick Douglass hailed Bertonneau and Roudanez as representatives of "the future South" and urged his fellow diners to use their influence for "the complete, absolute, unqualified enfranchisement of the colored people of the South, so that they shall not only be permitted to vote, but to be voted for, eligible to any office."[53]

In January and September 1865, Bertonneau and Roudanez played leading roles at important New Orleans conventions of Louisiana's Black community.[54] The following year, Bertonneau joined other New Orleans African Americans in protesting against President Andrew Johnson's Reconstruction policies, which allowed former Confederate states to gain political rehabilitation without enfranchising Black men. When the 1864 constitutional convention reconvened in Mechanics Hall on July 30, 1866, African Americans including Bertonneau urged it to support Black suffrage. While doing so, they were savagely attacked by a mob, including firemen and police, who regarded the convention as extralegal. Over three dozen African Americans were killed and more than a hundred wounded. That massacre proved a turning point in Reconstruction, persuading Northerners that Black Southerners needed far more protection than the Johnson administration was providing. Bertonneau barely escaped with his life, largely because the murderous rioters thought he was White.[55] (When he died in 1912, the death certificate identified his race as White.)

In 1867–1868, Bertonneau served as a delegate to the Louisiana state constitutional convention which enfranchised Black men. He was instrumental in persuading the delegates to approve an article stating that "there shall be no separate school or institution of learning established exclusively for any race by the State of Louisiana."[56] On January 2, 1868, in response to a White delegate who "warned the colored members of the Convention that any attempt to regulate social equality was simply suicidal," he insisted that "he didn't want to force white persons to drink with him, but simply to have the privilege of drinking in the same saloons."[57]

Bertonneau also fought against segregation in other forms. In 1867, he helped establish racially-integrated Masonic lodges in Louisiana.[58] Eleven years later, he unsuccessfully sued the city of New Orleans for re-segregating its schools, some of which had been integrated between 1870 and 1877.[59] Two decades later, the decision in *Bertonneau v. School Directors* was cited by the US Supreme Court to justify its ruling in the infamous case of *Plessy v. Ferguson*, which established the "separate but equal" doctrine legalizing racial segregation.

As Michael Vorenberg observed, Lincoln's meeting with Roudanez and Bertonneau "probably did more than anything to convince him that at least some Southern blacks should be granted the ballot."[60] He was willing to do so not only because of the persuasive example of those two men but also because of the impressive presentations of earlier Black callers, including Frederick Douglass, Bishop Daniel Payne, Alexander Crummell, Edward M. Thomas, John F. Cook, Cornelius C. Clark, John T. Costin, Benjamin McCoy, Henry Highland Garnet, and Henry McNeal Turner, among others. Equally important, Lincoln was influenced by the heroic service of Black troops.

MORE AFRICAN AMERICANS APPEAL FOR VOTING RIGHTS

On April 29, 1864, a deputation of Black North Carolinians presented Lincoln with a petition asking him to support Black enfranchisement. Those six men from New Bern did not resemble the urbane, freeborn New Orleans visitors of the previous month. The delegation consisted of a brick mason, two barbers, a farmer, a baker, and a preacher, four of whom were ex-slaves, including their leader, Abraham H. Galloway, a tall, handsome, proud, fiery, illiterate abolitionist and Union scout/spy in his mid-twenties.[61] The charismatic Galloway was a "very shrewd, smart, accomplished man," according to a New England abolitionist.[62] A journalist who observed Galloway dominate a meeting of New Bern's Black community in 1865 described him as "a light yellow man whose features seem to indicate that there was a cross of Indian blood in his veins." He was a "well shaped man" who when speaking "stood erect, using forcible and graceful gestures. His voice was powerful, and, though an illiterate man, his speaking was effective," marred only by his tendency to laugh inappropriately. His "power of sarcasm and brutal invective, and the personal influence given to him by his fearlessness and audacity, always secured him hearing."[63] Politically ambitious, Galloway was chosen as a delegate to the National Convention of Colored Men, held at Syracuse in October 1864, and four years later won election to both the North Carolina constitutional convention and the state senate. He died in 1870 at the age of thirty-three, mourned by several thousand Tarheels.

According to the group's preacher, Lincoln "didn't tell us to go round to the back door, but, like a true gentleman and noble-hearted chief, with as much courtesy and respect as though we had been the Japanese Embassy, he invited us into the White House," where they presented their petition. Pointing out that North Carolina's Black men had enjoyed voting rights until 1835, and that some Northern states still allowed Black men to vote, they asked the president "to finish the noble work you have begun, and grant unto your petitioners that greatest of privileges when the State is reconstructed, to exercise the right of suffrage, which will greatly redound to your honor, and to cause posterity, to the latest generation, to acknowledge their deepest sense of gratitude. We feel proud in saying that we have contributed moral and physical aid to our country in her hour of need, and expect so to continue to do until every cloud of war shall disappear."[64] After reading their appeal, Lincoln spoke with them "freely and kindly," saying among other things "that he had labored hard and through many difficulties for the good of the colored race, and that he should continue to do so, and in this matter would do what he could for us, but as it was a matter belonging to the State it would have to be attended to in the reconstruction of the state. He was glad to see colored men seeking for their rights, and said that this was an important right which we, as a people, ought to have." After their long interview, during which the president's interlocutors requested and received "his sympathies and promises to do for us all he could," they "took a hearty shake" of Lincoln's hand and bade farewell.[65] According to a press account, their "interview was a pleasant one, and they received from Mr. Lincoln assurances of his sympathy and earnest co-operation."[66]

In addition to appealing for suffrage rights, the visitors may well have followed Frederick Douglass's lead and urged Lincoln to do more to ensure that captured Black troops would not be slaughtered, as they had been a few days earlier when Confederates overran Plymouth, seventy miles from New Bern.[67]

A BLACK WOMAN CALLS AT THE WHITE HOUSE

In April 1864, Caroline Johnson, an illiterate former slave who served as president of the Colored Women's Sanitary Commission of Philadelphia and was an active member of the Colored Persons Union League of Philadelphia, presented the First Couple with wax fruits she had made, along with a stem-table, to express her gratitude for the president's emancipation policies.[68] She was accompanied by James Hamilton, minister of the Union Baptist Church, which she attended. She recalled that Secretary of Agriculture Isaac Newton, who had arranged the interview, "received us kindly," and had the box of wax fruit "sent to the White House, with directions that it should not be opened until I came. The next day was reception day, but the President sent me word that he would receive me at one o'clock. I went and arranged the table, placing it in the centre of the room. Then I was introduced to the President and his wife. He stood next to me; then Mrs. Lincoln, Mr. Newton, and the minister."

James Hamilton delivered a brief address in which he "touchingly alluded to the past sufferings of his people, to the rapid progress of their deliverance under the present administration, and their hopes of the future, and asked the president to accept the gift as a specimen of the handiwork of a lady of color, and as an evidence of their confidence and esteem for their chief who had brought them this far out of the land of bondage." At the conclusion of his remarks, he suggested that Mrs. Johnson might "like to say a few words."

As she recalled, "I looked down to the floor, and felt that I had not a word to say, but after a moment or two, the fire began to burn, and it burned and burned till it went all over me. I think it was the Spirit, and I looked up to him and said: 'Mr. President, I believe God has hewn you out of a rock, for this great and mighty purpose. Many have been led away by bribes of gold, of silver, of presents; but you have stood firm, because God was with you, and if you are faithful to the end, he will be with you.' With his eyes full of tears, he walked round and examined the present, pronounced it beautiful, thanked me kindly, but said: 'You must not give me the praise— it belongs to God.'" According to another account, Lincoln "briefly responded, returning thanks for the beautiful present, referring to the difficulties with which he had been surrounded, and ascribing the wondrous changes of the past three years to the rulings of an all-wise Providence."[69] Mrs. Lincoln was "exceedingly pleased" with the gift.[70]

A BLACK COLONIZATIONIST DISCUSSES TROOPS

Also that April, Lewis H. Putnam, a Black New Yorker who (like many other African Americans) had long been active in the colonization movement, called on Lincoln to discuss the United States Colored Troops. The president referred him to Secretary of War Stanton with a note: "please see L. H. Putnam, whom you will find a very intelligent colored man; and who wishes to talk about our colored forces their organization, &c."[71]

Putnam may also have discussed colonization with Lincoln himself, who at the time was desultorily supporting efforts to enable some African

Americans to resettle in the Caribbean Basin if they wished to emigrate. Born in North Carolina, Putnam spent time in Canada before moving to New York. There, in the 1840s, he helped fugitive slaves and in the following decade promoted Liberian colonization. Described in the press as "a plausible colored gentleman, having more of the *suaviter in modo* [pleasant in manner] than of the *fortiter in re* [powerful in deed]," he found it "truly humiliating to think that every organization in existence which aims at the elevation of our race was under the management of those who cannot comprehend the difficulties under which we are laboring." So he established the United African Republic Emigration Society (later called the Liberian Agricultural and Emigration Association), an all-Black alternative to the White-dominated American Colonization Society.[72] He drew up elaborate plans to resettle 46,000 African Americans on 9,300 farms in Liberia. Although Governor Washington Hunt of New York endorsed the scheme in his 1852 annual message, it went nowhere, partly because leading abolitionists denounced colonization in general and partly because Putnam allegedly misused funds. Deposed from the leadership of the organization, he still soldiered on throughout the decade, promoting his vision. The same concern that led him to try making African Americans independent farmers in Liberia before the war prompted him after it to champion the cause of Black land ownership in the South.[73]

BLACK WASHINGTONIANS SEEK PERMISSION TO USE THE WHITE HOUSE GROUNDS

In June 1864, some of Washington's Black Catholics sought presidential assistance in raising money to fund a chapel and school for African Americans. They had been denied access to the sanctuary of the principal Catholic church in town, and their children were barred from public schools. Since Sunday schools of various denominations traditionally held picnics on

July Fourth in Washington's parks, they thought that perhaps they could hold one on the White House grounds, which were open to the public on weekdays but not Sunday. With permission, special events could be held there. A parish priest suggested that Edward McManus, a doorkeeper at the Executive Mansion who served as superintendent of Sunday schools for the priest's church, should consult Commissioner of Public Buildings Benjamin Brown French about obtaining the necessary permission. He did so and learned that the president must approve any such request. A delegation of three African Americans, led by successful businessman/ cabinetmaker Gabriel Coakley, visited the White House and asked Lincoln's approval of their plan. The president replied to Coakley, "Certainly you have my permission. Go over to General French and tell him so." French provided the necessary document, which Coakley presented to Lincoln on June 30. The president endorsed it then and there: "I assent." As he handed it back to Coakley, he wished him and his friends success.[74]

Four days later, hundreds of Black Catholics entered the White House grounds, where a festive atmosphere prevailed and a substantial sum was raised. According to Francis B. Carpenter, Washington's African Americans never presented "a busier or more jubilant scene." On the grounds "a platform was erected, upon which accommodations were placed for speakers. Around this were rows of benches, which, during the greater part of the day, were not only well filled but crowded. Meanwhile groups reposed under every tree or walked to and fro along the shaded paths. From the thick-leaved branches of the trees were suspended swings, of which all, both old and young, made abundant use. Every contrivance which could add to the pleasure of the time was brought into energetic requisition, and altogether no celebration of the day presented a greater appearance of enjoyment and success."[75] Washington attorney William E. Doster noted that a "stranger would imagine himself in the palace gardens of [Emperor Faustin] Soulouque of Hayti. Negroes [were] in hacks, with standards on gayly-caparisoned horses, and generally in the costume of the Southern aristocracy."[76] John Hay recorded that there "was a pic-nic yesterday, in the President[']s grounds of the negroes of Washington. They were very neatly & carefully dressed very quietly & decently behaved: the young fellows buckishly & the young girls like ill bred boarding school maids."[77]

Indignant Democrats declared that up until then, "no body of citizens had been allowed to assemble there for purposes of diversion—not even white Sabbath school children!"[78] White Washingtonians were reportedly "much exercised" by the president's decision to authorize the picnic.[79] A Pennsylvania newspaper protested that within and around the nation's capital "thousands of wounded and languishing white men" with "parched lips and fevered brows" could not enjoy "the rich cold lemonade" and "balmy cool shade" that were provided to the "motl[e]y crowd of reveling niggers."[80] An Ohio soldier wrote home, "On the Fourth of July there was a *nigger* picnic on the White House grounds, while *white* soldiers stood guard around. Don't that beat h[el]l!"[81] The president "looked on and enjoyed it hugely," according to an Indiana paper, which averred that the "same spot would have been refused the white children of Washington for a similar purpose." The editor exclaimed, "God save the Republic!"[82]

Later that month, Protestants followed the Catholics' lead. The superintendent of Washington's Third Colored Baptist Sabbath School sought permission for another fundraising event to be held on the Executive Mansion grounds. It was described as a "demonstration of the appreciation of the colored people of the much-desired and highly appreciated privileges they are permitted to enjoy since the freeing of the slaves and abolishing of the black laws of the District of Columbia."[83] The money raised would be used to purchase a banner for the school "to be called 'The Banner of Freedom,' and which was to contain a life-size picture of President Lincoln, together with a design representing the freeing of slaves from bondage to freedom." Lincoln approved the request, and on August 4 more than 400 African Americans attended the celebration, during which the organizer of the affair "thanked the President for granting the use of the grounds and doing so much for the colored people."

The event began with religious exercises, after which "the assembly gave themselves up to social enjoyment. Watermelons, cantaloupes, smaller fruits, cakes, lemonades and other refreshments were spread out in abundance. Swings were suspended from the branches of the trees, and promenading parties continually moved about. All seem to enjoy themselves hugely. Outside the grounds the scene was equally animated. Numerous tables, for the sale of refreshments occupied every available space and trade was brisk."[84]

Local Democratic papers denounced both Lincoln and the event: "The grounds, held by all patriots as something set apart and sacred, because invested with a national character, were prostituted and disgraced by the erection of stands for negro merchants to vend fruits and cakes and drinks to negro customers," fulminated the Washington *Constitutional Union*. "Negro speeches were made." The incredulous editor emphasized that "these were *negroes* who did these things," and did so "with the high approval and warm commendation of our president," who refused to allow "the use of the public grounds around the White House for picnic purposes by Sabbath Schools of white men and ladies!" The "*negro* is wooed to accept the gracious permission—nay, it may be, the urgent request—and the aghast country beholds the terrible spectacle of white men rudely spurned in requesting a privilege most eagerly anxiously thrust forward to the blacks."[85]

A paper in nearby Georgetown similarly bemoaned the fact that "the grounds of the house furnished by the people, by the white people of the country, were again polluted by the escapades of a negro pic-nic." It roundly criticized Lincoln: "his demagoguism may lead him to affect, and to induce others to believe, in social equality; but his partisans are few in number; and no sensible man credits his sincerity or the sanity of his followers."[86]

BLACK MINISTERS PRESENT A BIBLE TO LINCOLN

In September 1864, five African American clergymen from Baltimore presented Lincoln with an ornate Bible as "a token of respect and gratitude to him for his active part in the cause of emancipation."[87] This delegation was led by the Rev. Dr. Samuel W. Chase, a widely admired Presbyterian minister whose funeral in 1867 was reportedly "one of the largest of the kind ever witnessed" in Baltimore.[88] A local paper noted that "he had a high reputation among his colored brethren and enjoyed the confidence of many white persons."[89]

When the group of five clergymen entered the White House, Lincoln shook hands with each member, whereupon Dr. Chase said, "The loyal colored people of Baltimore have entrusted us with authority to present this Bible as a testimonial of their appreciation of your humane conduct towards the people of our race." Since the day of "our incorporation into the American family, we have been true and loyal," and now were "ready to aid in defending the country, to be armed and trained in military matters, in order to assist in protecting and defending the star-spangled banner." With hearts "warm with gratitude," they were presenting a special Bible "as a token of respect for your active participation in furtherance of the cause of the emancipation of our race." Whenever "our children shall ask what mean these tokens, they will be told of your worthy deeds, and will rise up and call you blessed."

In accepting the gift, Lincoln apologized for not having prepared an appropriately "lengthy response to the address which you have just made." Instead he could "only now say, as I have often before said, it has always been a sentiment with me that all mankind should be free. . . . I have always acted as I believed to be right and just; and I have done all I could for the good of mankind generally. In letters and documents sent from this office I have expressed myself better than I now can."

Lincoln went on to describe the Bible as "the best gift God has given to man. All the good the Saviour gave to the world was communicated through this book. But for it we could not know right from wrong. All things most desirable for man's welfare, here and hereafter, are to be found portrayed in it. To you I return my most sincere thanks for the very elegant copy of the great Book of God which you present."

The president "spent some time in examining the present, and expressed himself highly pleased." After a "pleasant conversation," the ministers shook the president's hand "and bade him adieu, wishing him great success in his office, and re-election for another four years."[90]

LINCOLN'S SECOND MEETING WITH FREDERICK DOUGLASS

By August 1864, Lincoln understandably feared he might lose that reelection bid, a defeat which would lead to the preservation of slavery, for it seemed highly unlikely that a Democratic president would make emancipation a sine qua non for peace. To meet that contingency, he wanted to gather as many slaves as possible under the tent of freedom. The Emancipation Proclamation would liberate all who had escaped to Union lines by March 4, 1865, but none who remained in Confederate territory. (When the war ended, approximately 3,000,000 slaves still lived in areas controlled by Confederates; as many as 500,000 had been liberated before hostilities ceased.[91]) In August, Lincoln told Colonel John Eaton, Superintendent of Freedmen in the Department of the Tennessee, "that he wished the 'grapevine telegraph'" that kept slaves informed about the progress of the war "could be utilized to call upon the Negroes of the interior peacefully to leave the plantations and seek the protection of our armies." When Eaton mentioned Frederick Douglass's recent criticism of the administration (the president had, Douglass charged, "robbed our statesmanship of all soul-moving utterances"), Lincoln modestly asked if the famed orator might be persuaded to come to the White House for a discussion. Eaton, who knew Douglass well, facilitated an interview.[92]

On August 19, Lincoln and Douglass met again, this time at the president's invitation. Among other things, they discussed a recent letter he had drafted but not yet sent to Charles D. Robinson, editor of a Democratic newspaper which had criticized Lincoln's so-called "Niagara Manifesto," a document stating that emancipation was a precondition for any peace settlement. Discussing the "manifesto," Lincoln in his letter appeared to renege on that statement. In a lawyerly quibble, he maintained "that saying re-union and abandonment of slavery would be considered, if offered, is not saying that nothing *else* or *less* would be considered, if offered." He reminded Robinson that "no one, having control of the rebel armies, or, in fact, having any influence whatever in the rebellion, has offered, or intimated a willingness to, a restoration of the Union, in any event, or on any condition whatever." If Jefferson Davis wanted "to know what I would do if he were to offer peace and re-union, saying nothing about slavery, let him try me."

Lincoln went on to write, "I am sure you would not desire me to say, or to leave an inference, that I am ready, whenever convenient, to join in re-enslaving those who shall have served us in consideration of our promise. As a matter of morals, could such treachery by any possibility, escape the curses of Heaven, or of any good man? As a matter of policy, to *announce* such a purpose, would ruin the Union cause itself. All recruiting of colored men would instantly cease, and all colored men now in our service, would instantly desert us. And rightfully too. Why should they give their lives for us, with full notice of our purpose to betray them?" The employment of Black troops "is not a question of sentiment or taste, but one of physical force, which may be measured, and estimated as horsepower, and steam power, are measured and estimated. And by measurement, it is more than we can lose, and live. Nor can we, by discarding it, get a white force in place of it. There is a witness in every white man[']s bosom that he would rather go to the war having the negro to help him, than to help the enemy against him."[93]

While Douglass heartily agreed with Lincoln's arguments regarding the importance of Black soldiers, he emphatically objected to the implied backsliding on emancipation as a precondition for peace. He urged the president not to send the letter to Robinson, for it "would be given a broader meaning than you intend to convey; it would be taken as a complete surrender of your anti-slavery policy, and do you serious damage. In answer to your Copperhead accusers, your friends can make the argument of your want of power, but you cannot wisely say a word on that point."[94] Lincoln decided to leave the missive to Robinson in his desk, unsigned and unsent.

Seeming troubled, Lincoln expressed to Douglass with "great earnestness and much solicitude" his regret that "he was being accused of protracting the war beyond its legitimate object and of failing to make peace when he might have done so to advantage." Though the president was fearful "of what might come of all these complaints," he nonetheless felt sure "that no solid and lasting peace could come short of absolute submission on the part of the rebels." As Douglass recalled, Lincoln understood "the danger of premature peace," and like the "thoughtful and sagacious man he was, wished to provide means of rendering such consummation as harmless as possible." To Douglass, this "showed a deeper moral conviction against slavery than I had ever seen before in anything spoken or written by him. I listened with the deepest interest and profoundest satisfaction."[95]

As they conversed, a White House aide twice announced that the governor of Connecticut was sitting in an adjacent room, eager for an interview. Douglass offered to retire, but Lincoln instructed the aide to "tell Governor Buckingham to wait. I want to have a long talk with my friend Douglass."[96]

Their conversation continued for another hour. Douglass later speculated that this "was probably the first time in the history of the country when the Governor of a State was required to wait for an interview, because the President of the United States was engaged in conversation with a negro." This, Douglass said, vividly illustrated Lincoln's "kindly disposition towards colored people."[97] Several months later, Douglass said of the president's decision to keep the governor waiting, "It was a telling rebuke to popular prejudice, and showed the moral courage of the man."[98]

Getting to the main point, Lincoln told Douglass that the "slaves are not coming so rapidly and so numerously to us as I had hoped." His guest "replied that the slaveholders knew how to keep such things from their slaves, and probably very few knew of his Proclamation." Lincoln tasked Douglass with ensuring that slaves in the Confederacy knew about the Proclamation: "I want you to set about devising some means of making them acquainted with it, and for bringing them into our lines."

In a letter to the president written ten days after their conversation, Douglass referred to Lincoln's "suggestion that something should be speedily done to inform the slaves in the Rebel states of the true state of affairs in relation to them" and "to warn them as to what will be their probable condition should peace be concluded while they remain within the Rebel lines: and more especially to urge upon them the necessity of making their escape."[99]

As he told an abolitionist friend a few weeks later, Douglass agreed "to undertake the organizing of a band of scouts, composed of colored men, whose business should be somewhat after the original plan of John Brown, to go into the rebel States, beyond the lines of our armies, and carry the news of emancipation, and urge the slaves to come within our boundaries."[100]

Lincoln's appeal to Douglass casts doubt on the notion that the slaves freed themselves by absconding to Union lines in such overwhelming numbers that the government was forced to adopt an emancipation policy.[101] As historian Mark E. Neely stated flatly, "The theory is not true."[102] Similarly, historian James McPherson observed, "Slaves did not emancipate themselves; they were liberated by Union armies. Freedom quite literally came from the barrel of a gun." Rhetorically, McPherson asked, "And who was the commander in chief that called these armies into being, commanded their generals, and gave them direction and purpose?" Answering his own question, he added, "Ending the institution of bondage required Union victory; it required Lincoln's reelection in 1864; it required the

Thirteenth Amendment. Lincoln played a vital role, indeed the central role, in all of these achievements. It was also his policies and his skillful political leadership that set in motion the processes by which the reconstructed or Unionist states of Louisiana, Arkansas, Tennessee, Maryland, and Missouri abolished the institution during the war itself."[103] In 1865, when a young Union officer thanked him for emancipating the slaves, Lincoln modestly disclaimed credit, which he said belonged to abolitionists like William Lloyd Garrison and to the army. "I have only been an instrument," he told Lieutenant Daniel H. Chamberlain. "The logic and moral power of Garrison, and the anti-slavery people of the country and the army have done all."[104]

Douglass also asked the president to discharge his ailing son Charles from the army. "Now, Mr. President—I hope I shall not presume to[o] much upon your kindness—but I have a very great favor to ask. It is not that you will appoint me General Agent to carry out the Plan now proposed—though I would not shrink from that duty—but it is, that you will cause my son Charles R Douglass . . . now stationed at 'Point Lookout' to be discharged—He is now sick—He was the first colored volunteer from the State of New York—having enlisted with his Older Brother in the Mass—54th partly to encourage enlistments—he was but 18. When he enlisted—and has been in the service 18 months. If your Excellency can confer this favor—you will lay me under many obligations[.]"[105]

Lincoln granted that request, but nothing came of the proposal to create a kind of militarized Underground Railroad encouraging slaves to flee to Union lines. Douglass industriously drew up such a plan, but by the time he finished doing so, the political tide had turned as Union forces won major victories, most notably General Sherman's capture of Atlanta in early September, thus ensuring Lincoln's reelection and eliminating the need to implement a John Brown-like scheme.

Several months later, Douglass said that Lincoln repeatedly declared that "he was in favor of the enfranchisement of two classes of the Southern people. First, all those who had taken any part in suppressing the rebellion;

and secondly, all those who could read and write."[106] Presumably he meant both Black and White men, for as noted above, in March 1864, he had written to the governor of Louisiana recommending that African American men who were "very intelligent" or who had served in the armed forces should be enfranchised.

After his White House meeting, Douglass excitedly told Chaplain Eaton that Lincoln "treated me as a man; he did not let me feel for a moment that there was any difference in the color of our skins! The President is a most remarkable man. I am satisfied now that he is doing all that circumstances will permit him to do." The feeling was mutual, for Lincoln said to Eaton "that considering the conditions from which Douglass rose, and the position to which he had attained he was, in his judgment, one of the most meritorious men in America."[107]

Douglass found the president's willingness to summon him remarkable; several months after their second meeting, he wrote that Lincoln "knew that he could do nothing which would call down upon him more fiercely the ribaldry of the vulgar than by showing any respect to a colored man." He added, "Some men there are who can face death and dangers, but have not the moral courage to contradict a prejudice or face ridicule. In daring to admit, nay in daring to invite a Negro to an audience at the White House, Mr. Lincoln did that which he knew would be offensive to the crowd and excite their ribaldry. It was saying to the country, I am President of the black people as well as the white, and I mean to respect their rights and feelings as men and as citizens."[108] (A few months later, Douglass recalled those words somewhat differently: "I am president of all the people of the United States—not merely of white people, but of black people, and of all the people. And I regard the rights of all people, and respect the feelings of all the people."[109])

In the fall of 1865, Douglass said that a "noticeable feature" of Lincoln's "personal demeanor" was his ability "to talk easily and freely to a negro without reminding him that he was a negro."[110] Recalling his two White

House interviews, Douglass wrote that Lincoln "set me at perfect liberty to state where I differed from him as freely as where I agreed with him. From the first five minutes I seemed to myself to have been acquainted with [him] during all my life." Lincoln "was one of the very few white Americans who could converse with a negro without anything like condescension, and without in anywise reminding him of the unpopularity of his color."[111]

Much later, Douglass wrote, "In all my interviews with Mr. Lincoln I was impressed with his entire freedom from popular prejudice against the colored race. He was the first great man that I talked with in the United States freely, who in no single instance reminded me of the difference between himself and myself, of the difference of color, and I thought that all the more remarkable because he came from a State where there were black laws."[112]

Reflecting on Lincoln's ability to relate to him so easily, Douglass speculated, "I account partially for his kindness to me because of the similarity with which I had fought my way up, we both starting at the lowest round of the ladder."[113] Lincoln doubtless did identify with Douglass as an ambitious, talented, articulate man who overcame his lowly background and made the most of himself. Sometime in the 1850s, Lincoln told an audience, "I used to be a slave."[114] Years earlier, describing his relief at escaping from an engagement to be married, he wrote, "Through life I have been in no bondage, real or immaginary [sic] from the thraldom of which I so much desired to be free."[115]

The "imaginary form of bondage" he referred to was his treatment at the hands of his father. As an adolescent, Lincoln had worked not only on his family's farm but also for neighbors to whom his father Thomas rented him. Whenever Thomas found himself in financial trouble, which was often, he removed his boy from school and hired him out. During his teenage years, Abraham evidently felt himself to be a quasi-slave to his father, toiling as a farmhand, butcher, ferry operator, riverman, wood chopper, and sawyer, earning anywhere from 10¢ to 31¢ a day. These meager wages he handed over to Thomas, in compliance with the rule stipulating that children's labor was owed to their father and that any money they earned belonged to him. As a champion of the antislavery cause, he stressed one argument repeatedly (and to the virtual exclusion of other arguments); namely, that slavery was wrong because it represented a form of systematized robbery, an outrageous rewording of God's injunction: "In the sweat of thy brow shalt thou eat thy bread." Lincoln's difficult childhood helped him to empathize with Black Americans better than many of his White peers. By dint of talent, self-education, and hard work, he liberated himself from his father's "parental tyranny" (Lincoln's term); as president, he helped liberate 4,000,000 others from a more cruel and systematic tyranny.[116]

"A Practical Assertion of Negro Citizenship for which Few Were Prepared"

White House Receptions, 1864–1865,
Including Frederick Douglass (Again)

n 1901, Theodore Roosevelt famously sparked an outcry when he invited a Black man, Booker T. Washington, to dine at the White House.[1] A generation earlier, Lincoln less famously created a similar outcry when he greeted African Americans at Executive Mansion receptions.[2]

FREDERICK DOUGLASS AT THE INAUGURAL RECEPTION, MARCH 1865

The best known such reception is the one following Lincoln's second inauguration on March 4, 1865, when Frederick Douglass was temporarily barred. In his autobiography, Douglass described how guards denied him admittance to the White House on that memorable day and how the president at once overruled them and heartily welcomed the famous Black orator.[3]

That account, from the *Life and Times of Frederick Douglass*, is familiar but not as richly detailed as the one Douglass gave in an 1894 speech: "Having witnessed the inauguration of Mr. Lincoln in the morning, my colored friends urged me to attend the inauguration reception at the executive mansion in the evening." Mistakenly believing that no African American had ever attended such a reception other than as a servant or waiter, he decided to set a precedent. To him it seemed "a serious thing to break in upon the established usage of the country, and run the risk of being repulsed; but I went to the reception, determined to break the ice, which I [did] in an unexpectedly rough way."

Accompanied by Louise Dorsey, wife of Douglass's friend Thomas J. Dorsey (a leading Philadelphia caterer), Douglass presented himself at the White House, where they "were met by two sturdy policemen" who forbade them entrance. Ignoring their warning, Douglass tried to pass beyond the gendarmes, only to be resisted "with some violence." Determined "not to be repulsed," he forced himself and his companion inside, where a "red-faced, burly, blue-coated" policeman greeted them "with a show of friendliness," saying, "Oh, yes; come this way! come this way!" Thinking they were being led to the reception area, Douglass and Mrs. Dorsey suddenly realized that in fact they were being diverted to an exit. "This will not do," Douglass told himself, and called out to a passing gentleman, "Tell Mr. Lincoln that Frederick Douglass is at the door and is refused admission." Less than a minute later the constable was informed that the president "wishes Mr. D. to come in," whereupon Douglass and Mrs. Dorsey were admitted to the immense East Room. There they found themselves "in a bewildering sea of beauty and elegance," such as Douglass had never before witnessed. Towering above the crowd and surveying the scene was the president, "completely hemmed in by the concourse of visitors passing and taking his hand as they passed."

He recalled that "as soon as President Lincoln saw me I was relieved of all embarrassment. In a loud voice, so that all could hear, and looking toward me, he said, 'And here comes my friend, Frederick Douglass!' I had some trouble in getting through the crowd of elegantly dressed people to Mr. Lincoln. When I did succeed, and shook hands with him, he detained me and said, 'Douglass, I saw you in the crowd to-day, listening to my inaugural address. How did you like it?'

"I replied, 'Mr. Lincoln, I must not stop to talk now. Thousands are here, wishing to shake your hand.'"

But the president insisted, "You must stop. There is no man in the United States whose opinion I value more than yours. How did you like it?"

Douglass replied, "Mr. Lincoln, it was a sacred effort," and continued on "amid some smiles, much astonishment and some frowns."[4]

The abolitionist Julia Wilbur recorded in her diary that when "it was seen & known how cordially the Pres. received him," Douglass "was the observed of all observers, & many were ready to shake hands with him."[5]

Elizabeth Keckly recollected that Douglass "was very proud of the manner in which Mr. Lincoln received him. On leaving the White House he came to a friend's house where a reception was being held, and he related the incident with great pleasure to myself and others."[6]

Other Black callers were admitted to the White House that day, though Douglass did not mention them. The *New York Herald* reported that "Douglass, another negro [man], and two negro women were in the East room and marched about with the rest of the company."[7] The pro-administration *Washington Chronicle* ran a similar account: "Many colored persons appeared to pay their respects to the President and his lady, among whom were Frederick Douglass and his wife [actually Mrs. Dorsey]."[8] A Washington correspondent of the Democratic *New York News* observed that "[s]everal other negroes called during the evening and paid their respects to the President. It was a strange spectacle to see black and white elbowing each other for an opportunity to crook . . . the knee before the throne of the new-fashioned royalty."[9]

More African Americans might have been received had it not been for the First Lady, who, according to the *New York Evening Express*, "was very indignant at the intrusion of a number of negroes" and "gave directions to admit no more, and eject those who were admitted."[10] That news prompted the Columbus *Ohio Statesman* to remark, "Mr. and Mrs. Lincoln are tenants at the White House upon the strength of the negro's popularity, and now they turn around and exclude him from its precincts."[11]

Though Douglass believed that he was the first Black caller to attend a White House reception, in fact the color line had been crossed on at least four other such occasions in the preceding fourteen months.[12] It may have been crossed several times earlier by light-skinned Black guests, including a Haitian diplomat. An African American physician wrote that he had once asked "an attaché of the Haitian Embassy whom I met in Washington if he had visited any of those [White House] levees and he replied that he had done so frequently, without any embarrassment. But I can understand that in his case, as he was so light complexioned, that he would pass unnoticed in a throng like that."[13] But there is no evidence of a recognizably Black visitor attending a White House reception before 1864.

POLICY REGARDING AFRICAN AMERICANS AT WHITE HOUSE RECEPTIONS

During the 1860s it was not entirely clear what rules were in force regarding the admittance of African Americans to White House receptions. After his Inauguration Day confrontation in 1865, Douglass learned that "the officers at the White House had received no orders from Mr. Lincoln, or from any one else. They were simply complying with an old custom, the outgrowth of slavery, as dogs will sometimes rub their necks, long after their collars are removed, thinking they are still there."[14]

Between 1864 and 1866, there seems to have been at least an informal understanding that African Americans might be admitted after White callers had left. On January 1, 1866, Commissioner of Public Buildings Benjamin Brown French recorded in his journal that at the annual New

Year's Day reception at the White House "a constant crowd of humanity poured along for two hours, closed up by 15 minutes devoted to '*our colored brethren*,' who seemed delighted at having a chance to take their places among men."[15] The Washington *Evening Star* reported that when the general reception ended at 2 p.m., "such of the colored people who were in waiting outside, were admitted."[16]

It is not certain that President Andrew Johnson (1865–1869) greeted those African Americans. According to the Boston *Commonwealth*, some journalists "say that the colored people were not 'received' by the President on New Years' Day—when they were admitted, half an hour after the other guests had retired, the President was in his private apartments, and the blacks had the public rooms alone to look at."[17] One such account appeared in the *Baltimore Sun*: "The colored visitors yesterday [January 1] at the White House were disappointed at not seeing the President, who had retired previous to their admission. Many mistook [Supreme Court] Marshal [David S.] Gooding for him, and put him through a course of handshaking. The police, in excluding the colored people pending the reception of the whites, stated that they were carrying out their orders." Evidently those police were replying to some Black visitors "who expressed displeasure at the discrimination."[18] Those African Americans apparently thought they should have been allowed to enter with the White callers, as had happened at the 1865 New Year's Day reception.[19]

After hosting a contentious meeting with African American leaders in February 1866, President Johnson reimposed the color line.[20] In March, a newspaper announced that "the most profound excitement exists in Washington with reference to the course which President Johnson has determined to pursue. He has excluded negroes from the receptions at the White House, at which they have been admitted for three years hitherto."[21]

Just as Andrew Johnson abandoned Lincoln's small-scale policy of racial inclusion, so too did he abandon Lincoln's large-scale project to make African Americans full-fledged citizens. Johnson undermined Congress's attempt to build a superstructure of racial equality on the foundation that Lincoln had laid, an attempt that would not be revived until the civil rights movement of the 1960s.[22]

BREAKING PRECEDENT: NEW YEAR'S DAY, 1864

During Lincoln's presidency, it is uncertain just when the color line at receptions was initially crossed (and reported in the press). As noted above, in 1866 one paper indicated that the racial bar had been taken down starting in 1863; others suggested it was first lowered three years later. Echoing several other papers, the *New York Observer* asserted that on January 1, 1866, "colored citizens were admitted, for the first time in our history."[23]

In reality, the first recorded breach of the color line took place in 1864. According to a widely copied account in the *Washington Chronicle,* on New Year's Day that year "a few of the freed Africans" were among those outside the White House watching diplomats and other invited eminent guests pass by on their way to the traditional reception.[24] Of that handful of African American onlookers, four men "of genteel exterior and with the manners of gentlemen" entered the Executive Mansion and were presented to Lincoln. Two of them were Massachusetts abolitionists, Charles Lenox Remond and Joshua Bean Smith. Remond, the "spare, thin-faced, and dark-skinned" scion of an elite Black family in Salem, was a professional antislavery lecturer who helped recruit Black troops.[25] He was arguably the best known African American abolitionist other than Frederick Douglass.[26] Smith, who also recruited Black volunteers for the army, enjoyed a reputation as "the Prince of Caterers" in Boston, where he befriended Senator Charles Sumner. Smith allegedly refused to cater an event for Daniel Webster because that senator supported passage of the infamous Fugitive Slave Act of 1850.[27] Smith had at one time worked for the family of Robert Gould Shaw, the colonel who led the storied 54th Massachusetts Infantry of the United States Colored Troops in its heroic attack on Fort Wagner, South Carolina.

A diarist noted that Redmond and Smith "with 2 other colored gentlemen called on the President New Years & were received just like the others."[28] Reportedly, one of those two was the Haitian consul general and chargé d'affaires, Ernest Roumain, who later "spoke with veneration of Mr. Lincoln, and the hearty reception he had given him."[29]

The other member of that precedent-setting quartet was Henry J. Johnson, minister of the African Methodist Episcopal Zion Church in Ithaca, New York. He described Lincoln as "a gentleman, straight and tall, modest, with pleasing features" who looked "firm and determined." Johnson told some Black Washingtonians that "the President received him as one gentleman ought to receive another." Johnson was also introduced to Secretary of State Seward, who in turn presented him to his daughter and other women. "As great as the crowd was of gentle and noble men, these privileges were granted me without molestation or insult," Johnson wrote. A journalist described him as a former slave who, "after being dogged by bloodhounds, shot at and wounded by his master, and enduring great hardships," had managed to escape, "bringing away four buckshot [pellets] in his leg, as mementos of the tender mercies of the 'patriarchal institution.'"

Apropos of the four Black men calling at the White House, the same journalist speculated that "had such a thing been attempted three years ago, they [the Black guests] would have got their heads broke for their presumption, and I suppose the bare statement of the fact now may throw some negrophobes into convulsions, nevertheless, the White House stood firmly on its foundations through it all as far as is known."[30] Similarly, the *Washington Chronicle* observed that in previous years "had a colored man presented himself at the White House, at the President's levee, seeking an introduction to the Chief Magistrate of the Nation, he would have been in all probability roughly handled for his impudence." That paper heartily approved of the proceedings: "We are neither amalgamationists [i.e., supporters of interracial marriage] nor advocates of the leveling of all social distinctions, but we rejoice that we have a [Republican] President who is a democrat [i.e., egalitarian] by fact as well as by nature."[31]

Democratic newspapers, however, did "go into convulsions," including one in Maine: "What a hideous travestie [sic] this is—what an abject and shameful truckling to the shocking and unnatural doctrine of negro equality—what a terrible humiliation at any time—and what a shameless boast at a period when the nation is undergoing the horrors of civil war, engendered by this same insane craving for negro equality, forbidden by the decrees of the Almighty."[32] In Indiana, a Democratic editor tut-tutted, "There could be no possible objection to Mr. Lincoln's course as a private individual in associating with negroes," but "when as the representative of a great nation, he chooses to inaugurate a reign of social equality between the white and black races, democrats, and old time gentlemen generally, we think, have the right to enter their emphatic protest."[33] Another Indiana paper sneered, "Four niggers were among the throng that visited the White House on New Year's Day, and presented to the President, who was, no doubt, highly pleased to make their acquaintance."[34] Yet another Indiana journal ran an article headlined, "Nigger at the White House! Ah! Never Before Has Cuffee's Long Heel Trod the White House Floor."[35]

TWO BLACK DOCTORS ATTEND A RECEPTION IN FEBRUARY 1864

It is unclear whether any of the four Black men who in 1864 attended the New Year's reception at the White House thought of themselves as civil rights pioneers crossing a traditional color line, but there is little doubt about the two African American military physicians who the following month also breached that color line: Dr. Alexander T. Augusta and his protégé, Dr. Anderson Abbott, were self-consciously flouting the rules of a segregated social order.

The elder of the two—thirty-nine-year-old Major Augusta—was at that time regularly taking a seat in the senate gallery, much to the dismay of some other spectators. In late February 1864, a newspaper reported that he "daily ingratiates himself into a seat in the Senate gallery among the large number of battle stained and war-worn private soldiers. Many of them change their seats or go out of the gallery altogether."[36] In the Capitol, he was also trying to attend deliberations of the Supreme Court but was blocked by the marshal's staff.[37]

More dramatically, a few weeks earlier Major Augusta had launched a campaign to integrate Washington's streetcars. On a rainy February 1, clad in his officer's uniform, the doctor had been en route to testify at the trial of a White soldier accused of murdering a Black patient of his.[38] When Major Augusta hailed a streetcar, it stopped, and he violated the rule dictating that African American passengers were restricted to the exposed front portion of the vehicle where the driver stood. Major Augusta instead tried to enter the car, to the alarm of the conductor, who told him it was illegal for Black passengers to do so. In a letter to the judge advocate presiding over the trial at which he was scheduled to testify, Dr. Augusta explained why he had been delayed: "I told him [the conductor] that I would not ride on the front, and he said I should not ride at all. He then ejected me from the platform, and at the same time gave orders to the driver to go on. I have therefore been compelled to walk the distance in the mud and rain." In closing, he added an appeal: "I therefore most respectfully request that the offender may be arrested and brought to punishment."[39] Newspapers published the letter, which Massachusetts Senator Charles Sumner read aloud to his legislative colleagues; they authorized an investigation into what Sumner deemed an "outrage." Congress debated the matter off and on for weeks, finally passing legislation outlawing discrimination on Washington streetcars.[40]

Dr. Augusta was no stranger to such discrimination. Born free in 1825 in Virginia, he moved to Baltimore, where he practiced the barber's trade and, with the help of some clients, learned to read. Ambitious, bright, determined, and assertive, he sought admission to medical schools in Philadelphia and Chicago, but in vain; eventually the persistent young man moved to Toronto, entered Trinity Medical College, and became the one of the first African Americans in North America to graduate from a medical school. He then established a private practice and headed the Toronto City Hospital.

A week after the promulgation of Lincoln's Emancipation Proclamation, authorizing the enlistment of Black men into the military, Dr. Alexander wrote to the president volunteering his services: "Having seen that it is intended to garrison the U.S. forts with coloured troops, I beg leave to apply to you for an appointment as surgeon to some of the coloured regiments, or as a physician to some of the depots of 'freedmen.' I was compelled to leave my native country, and come to this [one] on account of prejudice against color, for the purpose of obtaining a knowledge of my profession, and having accomplished that object, at one of the principle educational institutions of this Province, I am now prepared to practice it, and would like to be in a position where I can be of use to my race."[41] He also wrote a similar letter to Secretary of War Edwin Stanton expressing a desire "to be of use to my race, at this important epoch."[42]

When the Army Medical Board ruled Dr. Augusta ineligible to serve, both because of his race and because of his Canadian residency, he explained that he had been born and raised in the US and was not a Canadian citizen; he added that he had "come near a thousand miles at a great expence [sic] and sacrifice hoping to be of some use to the country and my race at this eventful period."[43] When Secretary Stanton ordered the board to reverse its earlier decision, it resolved to give Dr. Augusta an unusually rigorous examination.[44] According to a journalist, he was "put through a squeezing process which few surgeons, in or out of the service, could have sustained unscathed. The fun of the thing is, that it is highly probable that Augusta knew more than all his questioners. And any rate, against their prejudices they were obliged to give him a certificate that he was competent for the duties and responsibilities of a brigade surgeon."[45] An army medical officer reported that when the surgeon general asked the chairman of the examining board, "How did you come to let that nigger pass?" he was told, "The fact is, General, that nigger knew more than I did and I could not help myself."[46]

Because the War Department at first decided to commission Black physicians as officers, Dr. Augusta was appointed a major. But the authorities quickly abandoned the policy when White officers below that rank protested against taking orders from an African American. Only a few other Black doctors received commissions; most were taken on as civilian "contract surgeons."

Dr. Augusta's appointment as a major offended not only White subordinate officers (captains and lieutenants) but also many civilians. Under the headline, "Uncle Abe Appoints a Negro Surgeon for the Army," the *Chicago Post* ran a story observing that the "amalgamation bedlamites who run the governmental machine at Washington have commissioned a negro doctor . . . with the rank of major. Whether it was intended by this appointment to insult the sense of the army or the country, does not yet fully appear."[47]

To some ruffians in Baltimore, Major Augusta's appointment was so offensive that they physically attacked him as he sat on a train awaiting its departure. A mob, numbering about 200 souls, took special umbrage at his effrontery in wearing an officer's uniform. Some toughs assaulted him in his seat; they began by tearing off his shoulder straps. Before they could proceed much further, troops stationed at the depot hastened to his rescue and escorted him to safety at their headquarters, pursued by an angry horde. After a while, armed detectives conveyed Major Augusta back to the depot. As they proceeded, one young man struck the doctor in the face, drawing much blood. At that point the mob cried out "kill him," prompting the detectives to draw their revolvers and force the crowd back. Dr. Augusta then boarded a train and went on his way.[48]

Northern outrage at this violence was reflected in a dispatch by a Washington journalist: "Better burn Baltimore even with the ground than permit any agent of the government to be deliberately mobbed in the streets." The "brutal attack upon Dr. Augusta is the first outbreak in the border country against the policy of employing colored men to fight in this war." Therefore, the "government must show that it is determined to defend its deliberately-chosen position with all the military power at its command."[49]

In May 1863, after a brief period spent examining Black recruits, Major Augusta was put in charge of Washington's Contraband Hospital, which served both African American troops and fugitive slaves who had begun pouring into the city after slavery ended there the previous year. Five months later he was removed, causing an abolitionist admirer to complain, "I hear that Dr. Augusta has been relieved from his duties as chief surgeon in the Con[traband] Camp at W[ashington]. His white enemies & despisers have succeeded it seems in having him removed. I am disgusted with mankind. Especially those who are living on the government."[50]

Dr. Augusta was transferred to the Seventh Colored Troops Infantry, where he served as the principal regimental surgeon, with two White assistant surgeons under his command. Those subordinates, along with some of their counterparts in other regiments, protested: "When we made application for position on the Colored Service, the understanding was universal that all commissioned officers were to be white men. Judge of our surprise when, upon joining our respective regiments, we found that the Senior Surgeon of the Command was a Negro. We claim to be behind no one, in a desire for the elevation and improvement of the colored race in this Country, and we are willing to sacrifice much in so grand a cause, as our present positions may testify. But we cannot in any cause, willingly compromise what we consider a proper self-respect; nor do we deem that the interests of either the country or of the colored race, can demand this of us. Such degradation, we believe to be involved in our voluntarily continuing in the service, as subordinate to a colored officer. We therefore most respectfully, yet earnestly, request that this unexpected, unusual, and most unpleasant relationship in which we have been placed, may in some way be terminated."[51] And so the major was reassigned to "detached duty," with no responsibility more serious than recruiting.

Dr. Augusta was subjected to yet another indignity: he was paid far less than other majors. When he called this to the attention of Henry Wilson, chairman of the senate military committee, that Massachusetts legislator intervened, and in April 1864 Secretary Stanton ordered that Major Augusta receive the same pay as White officers of that rank.

⤛⤜

Alluding to the Black guests at the 1864 New Year's reception, the *Dayton Daily Empire* snidely noted that on February 1, a "negro Major, in full uniform, was put off the street-cars, in Washington . . . and made to walk. Let him go to the White House for consolation. There he will be received as 'one gentleman receives another.'"[52] On February 23, 1864, that major— Dr. Augusta—took up the *Empire*'s sarcastic challenge. Along with his assistant surgeon and protégé, Dr. Anderson R. Abbott (also Black), he attended a White House reception, where, according to a Connecticut newspaper, they were "received by Mr. Lincoln with marked attention."[53] (The *Baltimore Sun* reported that they "were kindly received."[54]) Dr. Abbott recalled that Commissioner of Public Buildings Benjamin Brown French greeted them with "with all the urbanity imaginable" and conducted them to the president. Upon catching sight of Major Augusta, Lincoln "advanced eagerly a few paces" and "grasped his hand." As they exchanged greetings, Lincoln's son Robert, who had been standing nearby next to his mother, approached and, as Dr. Abbott remembered, "asked a question very hastily, the purport of which I took to be, 'Are you going to allow this invasion?' refer- ring, doubtless, to our presence there!" (Robert was almost certainly acting at the behest of his mother.) Lincoln responded, "Why not?" Without a further word, Robert retreated to the First Lady's side. The president then continued to heartily greet both Dr. Augusta and Dr. Abbott.[55]

The author of an 1864 biography of Lincoln described that scene: "When two or three colored gentlemen availed themselves of the privilege to call upon him," the president gave no sign that he regarded them as different from other guests at the reception. "They were greeted with the same cordiality and freedom that he had bestowed upon white men." It was highly unusual for Black callers to appear at such events, "yet Mr. Lincoln treated the affair as of ordinary occurrence, much to his credit and renown."[56]

A presidential secretary recalled that same occasion: "I shall never forget the sensation produced at a levee by the appearance of two tall and very well dressed Africans among the crowd of those who came to pay their respects. It was a practical assertion of negro citizenship, for which few were prepared. The President received them with marked kindness, and they behaved with strict propriety, not seeming to court attention, but went on their way with great self-possession."[57]

The two Black physicians may not have courted attention, but they received a great deal of it when they proceeded to the huge East Room. There, Dr. Abbott remembered, the "moment we entered the room, which was crowded and brilliantly lit up, we became the cynosure of all eyes. I had never experienced such a sensation as I did when I entered the room. We could not have been more surprised ourselves nor could we have created more surprise if we had been dropped down upon them through the skylight. . . . I felt as though I should have liked to crawl into a hole. But as we had decided to break the record, we held our ground." (Dr. Abbott did not realize that the "record" of Black exclusion had been broken the previous month.) "I bit my lips, took [Major] Augusta's arm and sauntered around the room endeavoring to, or pretending to, view the very fine pictures which adorned the wall. I tried also to become interested in the beautiful music discoursed by the Marine band, but it was the first time that music had failed to absorb my attention. Wherever we went, a space was cleared for us and we became the centre of a new circle of interest. Some stared at us merely from curiosity, others with an expression of friendly interest, while others again scowled at us in such a significant way, that left no doubt as to what views they held [on] the Negro question. We remained in the room and faced monocles and lorgnettes. Stares and fascinating eyes levelled at us for half an hour or so and then we passed out of the room and secured our wraps."[58] Thus was the color line at White House receptions breached a second time.

Lincoln's willingness to receive Black callers was politically risky, not least because many newspapers across the country attacked him for doing so. Soon after the New Year's reception, a correspondent of the *Chicago Times*, the Midwest's leading Democratic newspaper, complained that "[f]ilthy buck niggers, greasy, sweating, and disgusting, now jostle white people and even ladies everywhere, even at the President's levees." (The writer was evidently referring to Drs. Augusta and Abbott as well as the four African American men "of genteel exterior and with the manners of gentlemen"—including Charles Lenox Remond and Joshua Bean Smith—who had attended the White House levee on New Year's Day.) Worse still, the *Times* correspondent observed, "the beastly doctrine of the intermarriage of black men with white women [is] openly avowed and indorsed and encouraged by the President of the United States."[59] Yet, rather than succumbing to this and other attacks in widely read editorials, Lincoln endured such criticism in order to establish a policy of racial equality at White House receptions.

MANY BLACK CALLERS TRY TO ATTEND THE 1865 NEW YEAR'S RECEPTION

A third breach of the color line took place at the New Year's Day reception on January 2, 1865 (January 1 fell on a Sunday). That morning, the *Washington Chronicle*, widely viewed as an organ of the Lincoln administration, announced that "all the people present [in the District of Columbia], of every creed, clime, color and sex, are invited by the President to call upon him" at the New Year's reception that day.[60] As a result, many more Black guests attended that reception than had shown up for the same event a year earlier.

African Americans were admitted that day only briefly, however. According to a Democratic newspaper, a large crowd gathered near the portico of the White House, including several hundred well-dressed African Americans. Among them were some clergy and a few soldiers, as well as "the *bon ton* of negro society in Washington." When the front door opened, members of both races surged forward, much to the astonishment of the White attendees, who expected the Black callers to wait until the Caucasian guests had left. Alerted by jeers and curses, police quickly moved to stop the African Americans, who nonetheless persisted in their attempts to enter. Despite the constabulary's best efforts, at least twenty managed to gain admittance.[61]

The Lincolns greeted some of them, but not many. The Quaker abolitionist Julia Wilbur "saw a few colored persons" who "had a hard time to get in, but when once in[,] all were treated alike."[62] A second-hand account of the affair described how the Black guests were received: when "a colored woman presented herself, Mr. Lincoln shook hands with her, and Mrs. Lincoln gave the invariable bow; on the passage of the second one Mrs. Lincoln looked aghast; and when the third colored woman appeared, Mrs. Lincoln sent word to the door that no more colored persons would be admitted to mingle with the whites. But if they would come at the conclusion of the levee, they should receive the same admittance." The author of this article added that "I was told that quite a number availed themselves of the privilege to constitute a colored levee at the close of the white one."[63]

This account is corroborated in part by coverage appearing in the Washington *National Intelligencer*: "For a brief time some excitement was created by the refusal to admit such of the colored population as were eagerly pressing forward to pay their respects to the President. Many of them gained admission, but finally the doors were closed upon them, and they were compelled to wait patiently until after the whites had gotten through, when they were admitted and received by the President. During the excitement caused by the incident Mrs. Lincoln retired."[64]

A reporter for the New York *Independent*, edited by antislavery stalwarts Henry Ward Beecher and Theodore Tilton, noted that after the White crowd departed, the Black visitors who had been waiting outside "summoned up courage, and began timidly to approach the door." Some "were richly and gaily dressed, some were in tattered garments, and some of them in the most fanciful and grotesque costumes. All pressed eagerly forward." The president "welcomed this motley crowd with a heartiness that made them wild with exceeding joy. They laughed and wept, and wept and laughed, exclaiming, through their blinding tears, 'God bless you!' 'God bless Abraham Lincoln!' 'God bress Massa Linkum!'" The reporter observing this event wrote that "those who witnessed this scene will not soon forget it. For a long distance down the walk, on my way home, I heard fast young men cursing the President for this act; but all the way I kept saying to myself, 'God bless Abraham Lincoln!' He has within him a great heart, that feels for his brother man of whatever hue or condition."[65]

In Lincoln's hometown of Springfield, a scandalized Democratic editor had a different reaction, asking rhetorically, "Are not such scenes at the White House disgusting? When will the white people of this country awake to the sense of shame that the dominant party is bringing upon us by the practical establishment of the social equality of the negro?"[66] The *Milwaukee Daily News* deplored "the fact that negroes flock to the outer rooms of the White House!"[67]

On February 6, a fourth breach of the color line occurred at a reception attended by hundreds of guests, including a Black journalist who wrote, "In the good old days of the slaveholding Democracy . . . the habituants of the White House never in their wildest fantasies, dreamed of the possibility, even, of a colored face entering within its sacred portals except as a servant or a slave; but behold! now, at a public Reception a few days since, it was the privilege and pleasure of the writer hereof, in his place as a citizen of the Republic, to grasp by the hand the Chief Magistrate of the nation in the great hall of this self-same White House, amid assembled hundreds of other citizens present for the same purpose of doing him honor."[68]

SOJOURNER TRUTH DENIED ADMITTANCE TO THE FIRST LADY'S RECEPTION

Later that February, the color line was reinstituted, at least for Mrs. Lincoln's levees. Sojourner Truth was turned away from the First Lady's gala reception on February 25.[69] Julia Wilbur described in her diary how Truth, the well-known feminist and abolitionist, "went with Capt. [George] Carse, but they, that is the policemen[,] wd. not allow her to go in to see the President. When I went in she was sitting in the Anteroom waiting for the Capt. to come out. When I said it was too bad, she said 'never mind honey. I don't mind it.' It did not occur to me until too late that I should have gone directly in & told the President. I would like to know what he wd. have said. I cannot think it was done by his orders."[70]

If she had informed Lincoln, he may well have done then what he did a week later, when he insisted that Frederick Douglass be admitted to the post-inauguration reception. On February 27, a British journalist told Lincoln that Sojourner Truth had been denied admittance to the reception at the Executive Mansion two days earlier. The president "expressed his sorrow, and said he had often seen her, that it should not occur again, and that she should see him the first opportunity: a promise which he kept by sending for her a few days afterward."[71]

On October 29, 1864, Sojourner Truth made her only documented White House visit, which she described to a friend: "It was about 8 o'clock in the morning when I called on the President, in company with Mrs. [Lucy] C[olman]. On entering his reception room, we found about a dozen persons waiting to see him; amongst them two colored women, some white women also." Lincoln "showed as much respect and kindness to the colored persons present as to the whites." One of the Black women "was sick and likely to be turned out of her house on account of her inability to pay her rent." Lincoln "listened to her with much attention, and spoke to her with kindness and tenderness. He said he had given so much he could give no more, but told her where to go and get the money, and asked Mrs. C[olma]n to assist her, which she did."

Lucy Colman introduced her friend to the president: "This is Sojourner Truth, who has come all the way from Michigan to see you." He offered his hand, bowed, and said: "I am pleased to see you."

She replied: "Mr. President, when you first took your seat I feared you would be torn to pieces, for I likened you unto Daniel, who was thrown into the lions' den; and if the lions did not tear you into pieces, I knew that it would be God that had saved you; and I said if He spared me I would see you before the four years expired, and he has done so, and now I am here to see you for myself."

When she praised him as "the best President who has ever taken the seat," he replied, "I expect you have reference to my having emancipated the slaves in my proclamation." He demurred, "mentioning the names of several of his predecessors (and among them emphatically that of Washington) who, he modestly insisted, 'were all just as good, and would have done just as he had done if the time had come. If the people over the river (pointing across the Potomac) had behaved themselves, I could not have done what I have; but they did not, and I was compelled to do these things.'"

Said she: "I thank God that you were the instrument selected by him and the people to do it."

He then showed her the Bible that the Baltimore clergymen had presented to him earlier that year. After looking it over, she observed, "This is beautiful indeed; the colored people have given this to the Head of the government, and that government once sanctioned laws that would not permit its people to learn enough to enable them to read this Book. And for what? Let them answer who can."

Reflecting on that interview several days later, Truth wrote, "I never was treated by any one with more kindness and cordiality than were shown to me by that great and good man, Abraham Lincoln, by the grace of God President of the United States for four years more. He took my little [autograph] book, and with the same hand that signed the death-warrant of slavery he wrote as follows:

> For Aunty Sojourner Truth,
> Oct 29, 1864.
> A. LINCOLN."

As she prepared to leave, Lincoln arose, took her hand, and said "he would be pleased" if she would call again. "I felt that I was in the presence of a friend," she reported.[72]

(Lucy Colman, the abolitionist who accompanied Sojourner Truth, wrote that the president received the two women "with real politeness and a pleasing cordiality."[73])

Critics of Lincoln's racial views, among them Henry Louis Gates, regard Lincoln's use of "Aunty" as proof of his purported racism, but in fact, as historian Margaret Washington pointed out, at that time "not everyone used the term as Southern whites did after emancipation—to belittle older black women. Abolitionists used 'Aunt' and 'Aunty' as an endearment. Levi Coffin's wife Catherine was 'Aunt Kate,' Laura Haviland was 'Aunt Laura,' and freed people called Truth 'Aunt Sojourner.'"[74] Lincoln evidently followed this fashion. Rather than meaning to belittle her by signing her autograph book, Lincoln sought to express his appreciation for Truth's work, just as he had expressed it to her during their meeting.

Another White House color line Lincoln crossed was the one that barred Black guests from purely social events, such as a meal or tea. According to a historian of the White House, "no Negro received a social invitation to the White House before Booker T. Washington in 1901, nor did any thereafter for many years."[75] But in August 1864, Lincoln did invite Frederick Douglass to tea at the Soldiers' Home, where the First Family resided during the warmer months. (The only precedent for such an invitation was set in 1799 at the President's House in Philadelphia, where John Adams hosted a dinner for a White Haitian diplomat and his Black wife.[76]) In Douglass's autobiography, he described the circumstances: "At the door of my friend John A. Gray, where I was stopping in Washington, I found one afternoon the carriage of Secretary Dole [Commissioner of Indian Affairs William P. Dole], and a messenger from President Lincoln with an invitation for me to take tea with him at the Soldiers' Home. . . . Unfortunately, I had an engagement to speak that evening, and having made it one of the rules of my conduct in life never to break an engagement if [it were] possible keep it, I felt obliged to decline the honor. I have often regretted that I did not make this an exception to my general rule. Could I have known that no such opportunity could come to me again, I should have justified myself in disappointing a large audience for the sake of such a visit with Abraham Lincoln."[77]

In 1866, Douglass said that it was "a telling rebuke to popular prejudice that this man could invite the Negro not to the White House only, or to the soldiers' home, but to the table of the president of the United States."[78]

8

1865

Annus Mirabilis for African Americans

T he year 1865 began as an annus mirabilis for African Americans.

On January 2, for the first time, a significant number of Black callers attended the traditional New Year's White House reception.

On January 24, the Illinois General Assembly repealed that state's Black Laws (save the one forbidding intermarriage, which remained on the books until 1874).

On January 31, Congress passed the Thirteenth Amendment, abolishing slavery throughout the land, thus removing the possibility that courts might declare the Emancipation Proclamation unconstitutional. (By December it was ratified by the requisite number of states.) Lincoln had worked hard to persuade Democrats in the House to support the measure.

On February 1, John S. Rock became the first African American attorney admitted to practice before the US Supreme Court.

On Sunday, February 12, Henry Highland Garnet delivered a sermon in the House of Representatives, the first African American minister to be so honored. To help celebrate the passage of the Thirteenth Amendment, Lincoln had, with the approval of the cabinet and the congressional chaplain, invited the prominent Black abolitionist and emigration champion to preach there.[1]

On February 27, the first Black field officer in the Union Army, Martin R. Delany, was commissioned.

On March 3, Congress passed "An Act to Establish a Bureau for the Relief of Freedmen and Refugees," designed to provide shelter, food, clothing, medical services, and education to both newly liberated slaves and displaced White Southerners. Known as the Freedmen's Bureau, it set up schools and courts, supervised contracts that newly freed slaves made with employers, and managed land that had been abandoned or confiscated. The law was, in effect, the first piece of federal welfare legislation, establishing an agency primarily designed to protect and promote the interests of African Americans.

On March 4, members of the 45th Regiment of the United States Colored Troops became the first African Americans to participate in an inaugural parade. They were joined by Hay's African American brass band and "delegations of colored Odd Fellows" from several lodges.[2] Watching them pass by along Pennsylvania Avenue were many Black Washingtonians. According to a correspondent of the *London Times,* it "was remarked by everybody, strangers as well as natives, that there never has been such crowds of negroes in the streets of the capital. At least one-half of the multitude were coloured people, pouring in from far and near to 'assist' in the ceremonial of a day which to them . . . seemed the triumph of their race over a fast fading social prejudice and political injustice." The onlookers "held their heads high, as if they thoroughly understood that, under the beneficent sway of Abraham Lincoln, 'a man was a man for a' that.'"[3]

Later that day, Frederick Douglass and others were the first Black guests to attend an inaugural reception.

AFRICAN AMERICANS EXCLUDED FROM THE INAUGURAL BALL

On March 6, however, the series of landmark firsts came to a halt. Shortly before the inaugural ball that day, John W. Forney's *Washington Chronicle* announced, "We are authorized by the committee of management to say that there is no truth in the story which has been circulated, that tickets to the inauguration ball have been sold to colored persons. The ball is a private affair, in which the parties concerned have a perfect right to invite whom they please, irrespective of color. No modest and right thinking colored man or woman would desire to obtrude him or herself upon a company, ninety-nine in a hundred of which would repel the association; and none others are entitled to consideration. The story, therefore, if not fabricated with a view to injure the success of the ball, may at any rate be dismissed as idle and frivolous."[4]

After the ball, the *New York Herald* observed, "The absence of negroes was much remarked. They were so conspicuous during the inauguration ceremonies at the Capitol, and the reception and in the procession that every one expected to see them dance the Juba or Virginia reel before the President." Few would have objected if African Americans had been present, "for this was a thoroughly abolition ball, all of the old Washington aristocracy refusing to attend." Nonetheless, "the colored race was unrepresented."[5]

Contemptuously, the Cleveland *Plain Dealer* remarked, "Now is not this the coolest example of impudent hypocrisy that was ever perpetrated—so eminently worthy of [John W.] Forney and the men he serves? These are the people, it must be remembered, who gloat with lavish delight over the admission of a negro [John Rock]—described in their journals as of the blackest species—to the Bar of the Supreme Court; who have succeeded in commissioning negroes as officers in the army [like Major Alexander Augusta] to mess [i.e., eat] and associate with white officers and exercise the authority of their rank over white soldiers; who are patronizing orating negresses [e.g., Sojourner Truth], and the like. Oh shame, where is thy blush?"[6] Tongue in cheek, the *New*

York World protested "against this shameful attempt by Mr. Lincoln to keep negroes away from the inauguration ball." Of the Republican organizers of that event, the *World* said, "To seek any sense of shame in them were like pelting a rhinoceros with roses."[7]

Lincoln evidently had nothing to do with the decision to exclude African Americans from the ball; that had been determined by the committee in charge of the event, of which he was not a member.

APPOINTMENT OF THE ARMY'S FIRST BLACK LINE OFFICER

Like Lewis H. Putnam, another Black champion of colonization, Martin R. Delany, called in February 1865 to advise the president about African American soldiers. Delany wanted Black troops to lead efforts to improve the lot of his race. "Our elevation must be the result of *self-efforts*, and work of *our own hands*," he insisted.[8] "If I have one great political desire more than another it is that the black race manage their own affairs instead of entrusting them to others," he wrote to Frederick Douglass in 1862. In that same letter, he praised Lincoln for accepting a Black man to serve as Haiti's first diplomatic representative to the US.[9]

In 1863, when the administration first authorized the enlistment of African Americans into the army, Delany had acted as a recruiting agent for New England states. In December of that year, he wrote to Secretary of War Stanton, seeking authorization to expand his efforts into the South.[10] In response to the Confederates' decision in early 1865 to recruit slaves into their army, Delany pressed his case as a means to thwart that quixotic endeavor.

In welcoming Delany to the White House, Lincoln said he knew about his fifty-two-year-old caller, which was not surprising. Delany had attracted so much public attention that he became almost as prominent as Frederick Douglass. He took "great pride in being called a black man."[11] Notably, unlike most if not all of Lincoln's previous Black callers, Delany was not of mixed race.[12] In the late 1840s, he had worked with Douglass as co-editor and an agent of *The North Star,* the newspaper Douglass founded in 1847. (Earlier, during his residency in Pittsburgh, Delany had edited *The Mystery,* the first Black newspaper published west of the Alleghenies.) He defiantly asserted, "I care but little what white men think of what I say, write or do. My sole desire is to so benefit the colored people; this being done, I am satisfied—the opinion of every white person in the country or the world to the contrary notwithstanding."[13]

In 1850, he and two other African Americans were the first members of their race admitted to Harvard Medical School, but after a semester they left because White students objected to their presence. In a petition to the school, those White students deemed "the admission of blacks to the medical Lectures, highly detrimental to the interests, the welfare, of the Institution of which we are members, calculated alike to lower its reputation in this and other parts of the country." Oliver Wendell Holmes Sr., dean of the medical school, acceded to their demand and expelled Delany and his Black classmates. Delany nonetheless continued to practice medicine, which he had studied as an apprentice to doctors in Pittsburgh during the 1830s.[14]

With a strong ego, combative streak, and surfeit of energy and ambition, Delany was a Renaissance man: journalist, physician, novelist, explorer, Black nationalist, educator, emigrationist, and ethnographer. He was best known as a champion of Black resettlement in Africa. In the decade before the Civil War, he organized and presided over national Black emigration conventions and published two of his most important books: *The Condition, Elevation, and Destiny of the Colored People of the United States* (1852), widely regarded as the first expression of Black nationalism in print; and *Blake; or The Huts of America: A Tale of the Mississippi Valley, the Southern United States, and Cuba* (1859), a novel about a slave who organizes an uprising. Rather than mass emigration, Delany envisioned a selective, small-scale project to found a colony that would serve as a "city on a hill," demonstrating to the world in general, and to Americans in particular, that Black people were capable of attaining a high level of prosperity and civilization without White help.

While returning from an exploratory trip to Africa in 1860, Delany spent time in London, where his participation in the International Statistical Congress drew widespread attention. When other delegates welcomed him warmly, the American representative to the congress resigned in protest.

In 1862, Frederick Douglass described Delany as "[f]ine looking, broad chested, full of life and energy, shining like polished black Italian marble, and possessing a voice which when exerted to its full capacity might cause a whole troop of African Tigers to stand and tremble." To Douglass, he seemed "just the man for the great mission of African civilization to which he is devoting his life and powers."[15] Other leading Black abolitionists had mixed feelings about his racial views. In 1861, William Wells Brown sarcastically wrote that "[c]onsidered in respect to hatred to the Anglo-Saxon, a stentorian voice, a violence of gestures, and a display of physical energies when speaking, Dr. Delany may be regarded as the ablest man in Chatham [Canada], if not in America."[16] An obituarist noted that Delany's "tenacious claims for the superiority of the black race" were "untenable."[17] In his novel *Blake*, full-blooded African Americans are portrayed as superior to both White and mixed-race characters.[18] A similar theme appears in the last of his many books, *Principia of Ethnology: The Origin of Races and Color, With An Archaeological Compendium of Ethiopian and Egyptian Civilization* (1879). These two works, among his many publications, established Delany as one of the most ardent supporters of Black nationalism ever to have an audience with Lincoln.

⁂

With "a generous grasp and shake of the hand," Lincoln greeted Delany, who recalled their conversation in detail: "No one could mistake the fact that an able and master spirit was before me," he wrote. "Serious without sadness, and pleasant withal, he was soon seated, placing himself at ease, the better to give me a patient audience."

Lincoln asked, "What can I do for you, sir?"

"Nothing, Mr. President, but I've come to propose something to you, which I think will be beneficial to the nation in this critical hour of her peril."

Delany could "never forget the expression of his countenance and the inquiring look which he gave me when I answered him."

"'Go on, sir,' he said, as I paused through deference to him. I continued the conversation by reminding him of the full realization of [the Confederates' attempt at] arming the blacks of the South, and the ability of the blacks of the North to defeat it by complicity with those at the South, through the medium of the *Underground Railroad*—a measure known only to themselves.

"I next called his attention to the fact of the heartless and almost relentless prejudice exhibited towards the blacks by the Union army, and that something ought to be done to check this growing feeling against the slave, else nothing that we could do would avail. And if such were not expedited, all might be lost. That the blacks, in every capacity in which they had been called to act, had done their part faithfully and well."

After Lincoln had expressed his full agreement, Delany continued, "I would call your attention to another fact of great consideration; that is, the position of confidence in which they have been placed, when your officers have been under obligations to them, and in many instances even the army in their power. As pickets, scouts, and guides, you have trusted them, and found them faithful to the duties assigned; and it follows that if you can find them of higher qualifications, they may, with equal credit, fill higher and more important trusts."

Emphatically, Lincoln said, "*Certainly*, and what do you propose to do?"

Delany replied, "I propose this, sir; but first permit me to say that, whatever I may desire for black men in the army, I know that there exists too much prejudice among the whites for the soldiers to serve under a black commander, or the officers to be willing to associate with him. These are facts which must be admitted, and, under the circumstances, must be regarded, as they cannot be ignored. And I propose, as a most effective remedy to prevent enrolment of the blacks in the rebel service, and induce them to run to, instead of from, the Union forces—the commissioning and promotion of black men now in the army, according to merit."

The president asked, "How will you remedy the great difficulty you have just now so justly described, about the objections of white soldiers to colored commanders, and of officers to colored associates?"

"I have the remedy, Mr. President, which has not yet been stated; and it is the most important suggestion of my visit to you. And I think it is just what is required to complete the prestige of the Union army. I propose, sir, an army of blacks, commanded entirely by black officers, except such whites as may volunteer to serve; this army to penetrate through the heart of the South, and make conquests, with the banner of Emancipation unfurled, proclaiming freedom as they go, sustaining and protecting it by arming the emancipated, taking them as fresh troops, and leaving a few veterans among the new freedmen, when occasion requires, keeping this banner unfurled until every slave is free, according to the letter of your proclamation. I would also take from those already in the service all that are competent for commissioned officers, and establish at once in the South a camp of instruction. By this we could have in about three months an army of forty thousand blacks in motion, the presence of which anywhere would itself be a power irresistible. You should have an army of blacks, President Lincoln, commanded entirely by blacks, the sight of which is required to give confidence to the slaves, and retain them to the Union, stop foreign intervention, and speedily bring the war to a close."

Lincoln replied, "This is the very thing I have been looking and hoping for; but nobody offered it. I have thought it over and over again. I have talked about it; I hoped and prayed for it; but till now it never has been proposed. White men couldn't do this, because they are doing all in that direction now that they can; but we find, for various reasons, it does not meet the case under consideration. The blacks should go to the interior, and the whites be kept on the frontiers."

"Yes, sir, they would require but little, as they could subsist on the country as they went along."

"Certainly, a few light artillery, with the cavalry, would comprise your principal advance, because all the siege work would be on the frontiers and waters, done by the white divisions of the army. Won't this be a grand thing? When I issued my Emancipation Proclamation, I had this thing in contemplation. I then gave them a chance by prohibiting any interference on the part of the army; but they did not embrace it."

"But, Mr. President, these poor people could not read your proclamation, nor could they know anything about it, only, when they did hear, to know that they were free."

"But you of the North I expected to take advantage of it."

"Our policy, sir, was directly opposite, supposing that it met your approbation. To this end I published a letter against embarrassing or compromising the government in any manner whatever; for us to remain passive, except in case of foreign intervention, then immediately to raise the slaves to insurrection."

"Ah, I remember the letter, and thought at the time that you mistook my designs. But the effect will be better as it is, by giving character to the blacks, both North and South, as a peaceable, inoffensive people. Will you take command?"

"If there be none better qualified than I am, sir, by that time I will. While it is my desire to serve, as black men we shall have to prepare ourselves, as we have had no opportunities of experience and practice in the service as officers."

"That matters but little, comparatively, as some of the finest officers we have never studied the tactics till they entered the army as subordinates.

And again, the tactics are easily learned, especially among your people. It is the head that we now require most—men of plans and executive ability."

"I thank you, Mr. President, for the—"

"No—not at all. I see nothing now to be done but to give you a line of introduction to the secretary of war."

Lincoln wrote a brief note to Stanton, which he handed to Delany: "Do not fail to have an interview with this most extraordinary and intelligent black man."

That message, Delany wrote, showed that the president "perfectly understood my views and feelings; hence he was not content that my color should make its own impression, but he expressed it with emphasis, as though a point was gained. The thing desired presented itself; not simply a man that was *black*, because these had previously presented themselves, in many delegations and committees,—men of the highest intelligence,—for various objects; but that which he had wished and hoped for, their own proposed measures matured in the council-chamber had never been fully presented to them in the person of a black man."[19]

(Did Lincoln really long for an all-Black army to penetrate into the interior of the Confederacy? Perhaps. In March 1863, he wrote to Andrew Johnson: "The colored population is the great *available* and yet *unavailed* of, force for restoring the Union. The bare sight of 50,000 armed and drilled black soldiers on the banks of the Mississippi would end the rebellion at once. And who doubts that we can present that sight, if we but take hold in earnest?"[20] It is not clear that he meant an army *commanded* by Black officers. He had, however, indicated to Frederick Douglass that he wanted him to receive an officer's commission if Stanton approved.)

On February 27, 1865, Delany was appointed a major, thus becoming the highest-ranking Black line officer (i.e., officer in a combat unit) in the Union Army. He was outranked only by Dr. Augusta, who ended his military service as a lieutenant colonel. Before 1865, Black soldiers only served as enlisted men, not line officers.

Delany's appointment was hailed by the *Washington Chronicle*, which described him as "manly, intelligent, and zealous of exalting the spirit of his race. He looks to us more fit than any negro we have yet seen to be the Moses of those children of wrong."[21] A newspaper in Pittsburgh, where Delany had lived in his early adulthood, praised him as "a self-made and self-educated man" and rejoiced "that (without ever having been selected by a Congressman as a cadet at West Point), he has attained a fair position in the army."[22]

Delany was assigned to the 104th regiment of the US Colored Troops (commanded by a White lieutenant colonel) and reported for duty in South Carolina, where he recruited men for the 105th USCT regiment. He remained in the Palmetto State as an agent of the Freedmen's Bureau and later as an unsuccessful political activist. In 1888, Bishop Daniel Payne wrote of Delany: "His oratory was powerful, at times magnetic. If he had studied law, made it his profession, kept an even course, and settled down in South Carolina, he would have reached the Senate-chamber of that proud State. But he was too intensely African to be popular, and therefore multiplied enemies where he could have multiplied friends by the thousands. Had his love for humanity been as great as his love for his race, he might have rendered his personal influence co-extensive with that of Samuel R. Ward in his palmiest days, or that of Frederick Douglass at the present time."[23]

Less than a week after Lincoln's assassination, Delany proposed a tribute to "the humane, the benevolent, the philanthropic, the generous, the beloved, the able, the wise, great, and good man, . . . Abraham Lincoln the Just," a "mighty chieftain and statesman." He suggested "that, as a just and appropriate tribute of respect and lasting gratitude from the colored people of the United States to the memory of President Lincoln, the Father of American Liberty, every individual of our race contribute *one cent*."[24] Delany's proposal resembled the one that eventually produced the 1876 Freedmen's Memorial Monument to Lincoln in Washington, a statue of the standing president and a rising slave. That sculpture, sited in Washington's Lincoln Park and better known as the Emancipation Memorial, was entirely financed by former slaves, many of them veterans of the USCT.

Delany died in 1885, having lived what W. E. B. DuBois called "a magnificent life."[25] A later generation came to regard him as "the father of black nationalism."[26]

David S. Reynolds aptly noted that the "bonding between the president" and Martin Delany, as well as with Frederick Douglass, "puts to rest any doubts about Lincoln's underlying radicalism on race. His meetings with them were in the spirit of John Brown." The "combination of interracial respect and black centered militancy that Lincoln displayed in his dealings with Douglass and Delaney suggests that there was validity in proslavery comparisons between Lincoln and John Brown, one of the least racist white people in American history."[27]

But Lincoln's claim to be considered a "radical antiracist" and a "leftist abolitionist who loathed racism" rests on more than his relationship with Douglass and Delany. His unfailing cordiality to African Americans in general, his willingness to meet with them in the White House, to honor their requests, to invite them to consult on public policy, to treat them with respect and kindness whether they were kitchen servants or leaders of the Black community, to invite them to attend receptions and tea, to sing and pray with them on their turf, to authorize them to hold events on the White House grounds—all those manifestations of an egalitarian spirit fully justified the tributes paid to him by Frederick Douglass, Rosetta Wells, Sojourner Truth, Elizabeth Keckly, and other African Americans. He richly deserves the sobriquet Douglass coined: "emphatically the black man's president."

9

Emphatically the Black Man's President or Preeminently the White Man's President?

On June 1, 1865, Frederick Douglass eulogized Lincoln as "emphatically the black man's president," but in 1876, in an oration delivered at the unveiling of the Freedmen's Monument in Washington, he called him "preeminently the white man's president." What accounts for the difference?

The 1876 speech was largely based on the 1865 eulogy, despite the stark contrast between "preeminently the white man's president" and "emphatically the black man's president." In the little-known 1865 eulogy, Douglass said, "No people or class of people in the country have a better reason for lamenting the death of Abraham Lincoln, and for desiring to honor and perpetuate his memory, than have the colored people." The record of the martyred president, when compared "with the long line of his predecessors, many of whom were merely the facile and servile instruments of the slave power," was impressive. Douglass acknowledged that Lincoln was "unsurpassed in his devotion to the welfare of the white race," and that "he sometimes smote" African Americans "and wounded them severely"; nevertheless he was also "in a sense hitherto without example, emphatically the black man's President: the first to show any respect for their rights as men" or to acknowledge that African Americans "had any rights which the white man ought to respect." He "was the first American President who . . . rose above the prejudice of his times, and country." If during the early stages of the Civil War the president had favored resettling freedmen abroad, Douglass asserted, "Lincoln soon outgrew his colonization ideas and schemes and came to look upon the black man as an American citizen."

Douglass cited his personal experience with the president to show that Lincoln "desired to know the black man thoroughly." Douglass assured him "that a negro would work quite as well for himself as for his master." Lincoln "was an anti-Slavery man at heart, and his anti-Slavery was deeper than that of most men. It had its root in the very nature of the man—a conviction which was as firm in his mind as the belief in a Supreme Being."

Douglass recalled one episode in particular that demonstrated Lincoln's "kindly disposition towards colored people," the aforementioned refusal to interrupt his conversation with Douglass in order to meet with the governor of Connecticut.

Douglass did not rely solely on his own experience to explain why Lincoln should be considered "emphatically the black man's President." He told his audience about one of "the most touching scenes connected with the funeral of our lamented President," which "occurred at the gate of the Presidential Mansion: A colored woman standing at the gate weeping, was asked the cause of her tears. 'Oh! Sir,' she said, 'we have lost our Moses.' 'But,' said the gentleman, 'the Lord will send you another;' 'That may be,' said the weeping woman, 'but Ah! we had him.'"

This woman, according to Douglass, was emblematic of millions of Black Americans who "from first to last, and through all, whether through good or through evil report, fully believed in Abraham Lincoln." Despite his initial tardiness in attacking slavery, Douglass said, they "firmly trusted in him" with a faith that constituted "no blind trust unsupported by reason." African Americans had "early caught a glimpse of the man, and from the evidence of their senses, they believed in him. They viewed him not in the light of separate individual acts, but in the light of his mission, in his manifest relation to events and in the philosophy of his statesmanship. Viewing him thus they trusted him as men are seldom trusted. They did not care what forms of expression the President adopted, whether it were justice, expedience, or military necessity, so that they see slavery abolished and liberty established in the country."

Black Americans, Douglass maintained, observed with their own eyes astounding progress: "Under Abraham Lincoln's beneficent rule, they saw themselves being gradually lifted to the broad plain of equal manhood; under his rule, and by measures approved by him, they saw gradually fading the handwriting of ages which was against them. Under his rule, they saw millions of their brethren proclaimed free and invested with the right to defend their freedom. Under his rule they saw the Confederate states . . . broken to pieces, overpowered, conquered, shattered to fragments, ground to powder, and swept from the face of existence. They saw the Independence of Hayti and Liberia recognized and the whole colored race steadily rising into the friendly consideration of the American people. In this broad practical common sense, they took no captious exceptions to the unpleasant incidents of their transition from slavery to freedom. All they wanted to know was that those incidents were only transitional not permanent."[1]

Douglass's 1876 speech at the dedication of the Emancipation Memorial in Washington makes many of the same points, but he introduced a few startling changes. He declared to Black Americans in the audience, "Abraham Lincoln was not, in the fullest sense of the word, either our man or our model. In his interests, in his associations, in his habits of thought, and in his prejudices, he was a white man. He was *pre-eminently the white man's President*, entirely devoted to the welfare of white men." Elaborating, he added, "The race to which we belong were not the special objects of his consideration."

Turning to address his White auditors, Douglass said, "I concede to you, my white fellow-citizens, a pre-eminence in this worship at once full and supreme. First, midst, and last, you and yours were the objects of his deepest affection and his most earnest solicitude. You are the children of Abraham Lincoln. We are at best only his step-children; children by adoption, children by force of circumstances and necessity."

In 1876, Douglass not only inverted "emphatically the black man's president" to read "preeminently the white man's president," but also contradicted other points he had made in the 1865 eulogy.

1865: Lincoln "was the first American President who . . . rose above the prejudice of his times, and country" and was "one of the very few white Americans who could converse with a negro without anything like condescension, and without in anywise reminding him of the unpopularity of his color."

1876: "President Lincoln was a white man, and shared the prejudices common to his countrymen towards the colored race."

1865: Douglass recalled an episode that demonstrated Lincoln's "kindly disposition towards colored people."

1876: "Looking back to his times and to the condition of his country, we are compelled to admit that this *unfriendly feeling on his part* [for Black Americans] may be safely set down as one element of his wonderful success." (emphasis added)

Near the close of his 1876 oration, Douglass called Lincoln a "great and good man" and added, "Taking him for all in all, measuring the tremendous magnitude of the work before him, considering the necessary means to ends, and surveying the end from the beginning, infinite wisdom has seldom sent any man into the world better fitted for his mission than Abraham Lincoln." In his peroration, Douglass passed judgment on Lincoln's handling of slavery and racial issues: "Viewed from the genuine abolition ground, Mr. Lincoln seemed tardy, cold, dull, and indifferent; but measuring him by the senti-ment of his country, a sentiment he was bound as a statesman to consult, he was swift, zealous, radical, and determined."

Why did Douglass in 1876 portray Lincoln as "preeminently the white man's president" who "shared the prejudices common to his countrymen towards the colored race" rather than "emphatically the black man's presi-dent" who "rose above the prejudice of his times, and country"?

Douglass's motive cannot be established for certain, but he was likely tailoring his remarks to move the political elite of the day—the president, cabinet members, congressional leaders, supreme court justices—who had assembled near the Capitol to observe the dedication of the Emancipation Memorial. At the time, Douglass was in despair, for those powerful men had seemingly lost interest in protecting the rights of Black Americans guaranteed in the Fourteenth and Fifteenth Amendments and enforced rigorously for a time, but no longer. As David W. Blight, a leading biog-rapher of Douglass, noted, the famed Black orator "never spoke publicly about the sixteenth president without a political purpose that served the cause of black freedom or civil rights." That was especially true of the 1876 address, which must be understood in its historical context, as described by Professor Blight: "The experiment in racial democracy born of emancipa-tion and the remaking of the US Constitution—the dream come true in 1865 and the legacy Douglass had for more than ten years trumpeted as the long-term hope of his people—not only lay in tatters; it had been crushed by widespread, unpunished violence. . . . Each note of either cautionary woe or modest celebration in Douglass's dedication speech . . . must be considered through this story of the impending fateful defeat of Reconstruction."[2]

Douglass's oration was full of subtext, all of which seemed to be an appeal to the assembled leaders not to abandon Black Americans to the mercies and caprices of White Southerners. It is important to recall that, when Douglass delivered this speech, the violent resistance to Reconstruc-tion in the South was systematically erasing the gains that had begun with

Lincoln's Emancipation Proclamation and his public endorsement of Black voting rights. Douglass's main point was that Lincoln championed those reforms not because he was a tender-minded do-gooder whose heart bled for the downtrodden, but because he was a tough-minded realist devoted to the interests of the White race, which he thought would benefit if the Black race enjoyed citizenship rights. In 1864, Lincoln had made that point in his informal remarks to the Black Washingtonians who gathered at the White House to celebrate the abolition of slavery in Maryland: "I do believe that it will result in good in the white race as well as to those who have been made free by this act of emancipation."[3]

In his 1876 oration, Douglass began with harsh criticism that recalls his 1862 condemnation of Lincoln for his remarks about colonization, sneering at the president as "quite a genuine representative of American prejudice and negro hatred" who was in effect telling Black Americans, "I don't like you, you must clear out of the country." But after fourteen years, Douglass was acknowledging that Lincoln only *seemed* to be "a genuine representative of American prejudice and negro hatred" when in fact he really *was* a "swift, zealous, radical, and determined" opponent of slavery and racism. As James Oakes observed, in 1876 Douglass "was not merely paying his respects to Abraham Lincoln but offering his apologies" for his over-the-top rhetoric in 1862, when he heatedly condemned Lincoln for endorsing a program that two of the Black orator's three adult sons admired so much they signed up to participate in it.[4]

Douglass continued to praise Lincoln publicly for the rest of his days without such qualifiers as "seemed." In 1883, he described the sixteenth president as "a very great man, as great as the greatest," and said he felt when visiting the White House "as though I was in the presence of a big brother, and that there was safety in his atmosphere."[5] A few years later, Douglass wrote, "In all my interviews with Mr. Lincoln I was impressed with his entire freedom from popular prejudice against the colored race."[6] Five years thereafter, he described Lincoln as "a man so broad in his sympathy, so noble in his character, so just in his action, so free from narrow prejudice. . . . To have known him as I knew him, I regard as one of the grandest privileges experienced by me. . . . I would not part with that peep into that noble soul for all the wealth . . . that could be bestowed upon the most successful conqueror."[7] After another five years, Douglass declared: "I . . . [have] seen many great men . . . but I have met with no such man, at home or abroad, who made upon my mind the impression of possessing a more godlike nature than did Abraham Lincoln." Conceding that there may have been more intelligent men, Douglass added that in his mind, measuring Lincoln "in the direction of the highest quality, of human goodness and nobility of character, no better man than he has ever stood or walked upon the continent."[8]

Appendix

Evaluation of Evidence Cited to Illustrate Lincoln's Purported Racism

n 2020, David S. Reynolds observed that only by studying Lincoln's "personal interchange with black people" can "we see the complete falsity of the charges of innate racism that some have levelled at him over the years."[1] More than half a century earlier, the eminent African American historian, Benjamin Quarles, called Lincoln a "kind and considerate" man "without bigotry of any kind" who treated Black Americans "as they wanted to be treated—as human beings" and did them "favors that could bring him no political advantage or private gain."[2] Similarly, ethicist William Lee Miller observed that Lincoln was consistently "cordial and welcoming in his treatment of individual African-Americans," and Roy P. Basler, editor of Lincoln's collected works, remarked that "Lincoln's personal relations" with African Americans "were almost models of democratic correctness and friendly courtesy."[3]

But Lincoln was more than kind, cordial, courteous, and considerate, important as those qualities are. In Miller's words, his interaction with

African Americans demonstrated "a racially inclusive egalitarianism."[4] It justified the description of Lincoln by James Oakes as "at bottom a racial egalitarian" when it came to natural rights, and David S. Reynolds's similar portrayal of the sixteenth president as a "radical antiracist" and a "leftist abolitionist who loathed racism," beneath whose outer surface "of moderation and caution" there "lay a radically progressive self." Lincoln's "personal bonding with African-Americans such as Frederick Douglass, Martin Delany, Sojourner Truth, and Elizabeth Keckly," Reynolds added, "reflected the genuine humanity behind his anti-slavery activism."[5]

Not all scholars agree. Critics of Lincoln's racial views, like Henry Louis Gates, professor of English at Harvard University, point first and foremost to his opening statement in the fourth of his seven debates with Stephen A. Douglas in 1858, the one held in Charleston, Illinois, seat of one of the most Negrophobic counties (Coles) in a notoriously Negrophobic state. In 1848, over ninety-four percent of the voters in that county favored the constitutional provision forbidding African Americans to settle in the state.[6] Lincoln's friend William M. Chambers, an influential leader of the American (Know Nothing) party in Charleston, advised him to attack Senator Douglas's "political inconsistencies and tergiversations" and give his audiences "less of the favouring of negro equality" than he had provided in his Chicago speech on July 10.[7] (In that address, Lincoln had urged Chicagoans to "discard all this quibbling about this man and the other man—this race and that race and the other race being inferior, and therefore they must be placed in an inferior position." Instead of such quibbling, "Let us discard all these things, and unite as one people throughout this land, until we shall once more stand up declaring that all men are created equal."[8]) Charleston's most prominent Republican, Thomas A. Marshall, a friend with whom Lincoln stayed while in town for the debate, recommended he tell Dr. Chambers that "as for negro equality in the sense in which the expression is used you neither believe in it nor desire it. You desire to offer no temptations to negroes to come among us or remain with us, and therefore you do not propose to confer upon them any further social or political rights than they are now entitled to."[9] This counsel reinforced the advice that Lincoln's close friend and political advisor David Davis had given him about the many Kentucky-born voters in central and southern Illinois: "Among all the Kentuckians it is industriously circulated that, you favor negro equality. All the [Republican] Orators should distinctly & emphatically disavow *negro suffrage*—negro holding office, serving on juries, & the like."[10]

Responding to such advice, Lincoln opened the Charleston debate with a brief disclaimer: "When I was at the hotel to-day, an elderly gentleman called upon me to know whether I was really in favor of producing a perfect equality between the negroes and white people." Lincoln explained that he had not planned to "say much on that subject," but since he was asked, he thought he "would occupy perhaps five minutes in saying something in regard to it." Bluntly he declared, "I am not, nor ever have been, in favor of bringing about in any way the social and political equality of the white and black races; that I am not, nor ever have been, in favor of making voters or jurors of negroes, nor of qualifying them to hold office, nor to intermarry with white people; and I will say, in addition to this, that there is a physical difference between the white and black races which I believe will forever forbid the two races living together on terms of social and political equality. And inasmuch as they cannot so live, while they remain together there must be the position of superior and inferior, and I as much as any other man am in favor of having the superior position assigned to the white race."[11]

As James Oakes observed, Lincoln "didn't actually say he supported the various forms of inequality he listed," all of which were outlawed in Illinois at that time. He "simply said he had never endorsed the several forms of racial equality he specified" and that "there was a 'physical difference' between blacks and whites, but he didn't say what that difference was." Obviously he was "aware that many people believed those physical differences—whatever they were—necessitated the superiority of whites and the inferiority of blacks," but he "didn't say whether he believed that," but merely asserted that "as long as blacks and whites 'must be' assigned a position of superior and inferior he would naturally prefer to be 'assigned' to the superior category."[12]

Lincoln was careful not to say that Black Americans *were* inferior, but rather that since they could not coexist with White people on terms of political and social equality, thanks to intractable Negrophobia, he would prefer that they be *placed* in the inferior position. He did not say he liked the fact that voters had to make such a choice. As historian Don E. Fehrenbacher noted, Lincoln supported racial separation "on grounds of the incompatibility rather than the inequality of the races."[13]

Lincoln's statement was made, let it be recalled, during an election campaign pitting him against the foremost Northern champion of the doctrine that all men are *not* created equal, someone who posed the greatest threat, in Lincoln's view, to the antislavery cause, who would anesthetize the Northern conscience and have voters regard African Americans as brutes rather than humans. To defeat the senator was therefore, in Lincoln's mind, essential, and if it meant he had to pay lip service to the Negrophobia of the Illinois electorate, he was willing to do so with careful qualifiers. As historian Phillip Shaw Paludan observed, such concessions to White bigotry were "the careful efforts of a subtle politician to achieve a radical goal by wrapping it in conservative bunting."[14]

At Charleston, Lincoln promptly made such a qualifier: "I do not perceive that because the white man is to have the superior position the negro should be denied everything. I do not understand that because I do not want a negro woman for a slave I must necessarily want her for a wife. My understanding is that I can just let her alone." (This observation would be echoed by Frederick Douglass in 1862 when he wrote apropos of the question "What shall be done with the Negroes?" "What shall be done with them? Our answer is, do nothing with them; mind your business, and let them mind theirs."[15])

What are we to make of Lincoln's statement? Should we agree with historian David Herbert Donald, who alleged that those remarks "represented Lincoln's deeply held personal views"?[16] Or are we to agree with historian James McPherson, who concluded that "Lincoln the politician was a master of misdirection, of appearing to appease conservatives while manipulating them toward acceptance of radical policies," a politician who "used racism as a strategic diversion"?[17] To decide between these alternatives, we should follow the counsel of David S. Reynolds, who sensibly observed that Lincoln's "attitudes toward race must be measured against those of the surrounding culture. Only then can we responsibly come to a conclusion about this crucial topic."[18] Surely such a comparative approach is essential for a responsible historian, *pace* David Herbert Donald, who insisted that "it would be a mistake to attempt to palliate Lincoln's racial views by saying that he grew up in a racist society or that his ideas were shared by many of his contemporaries."[19] Such a comparison helps *explain* Lincoln's views rather than *palliate* them and shows that Lincoln's surrounding culture was awash in a boundless sea of Negrophobia.[20]

William Lee Miller suggested that to "appraise Lincoln fairly," one "should not compare him to unattached abolitionists in Massachusetts or to anyone a century and a half later" but rather to "the other engaged politicians in the Old Northwest in the 1850s."[21] Several of those politicians shared his views on Black citizenship rights but expressed much greater skepticism about racial equality than Lincoln ever did.[22] A good example is Lincoln's old friend Joshua R. Giddings of Ohio, Congress's leading antislavery lion after the death of John Quincy Adams in 1848. In 1859, he declared on the floor of the House, "We do not say the black man is, or shall be, the equal of the white man; or that he shall vote or hold office."[23] Though Giddings's fellow congressman Owen Lovejoy of Illinois hated slavery with a passion intensified by the murder of his abolitionist brother Elijah, he declared flatly, "We may concede it is a matter of fact that it [the Black race] is inferior."[24] He told a Chicago audience in 1860, "I know very well that the African race, as a race, is not equal to ours." He added that he also knew "that, in regard to the great overwhelming majority, the Government may be considered, in a certain sense, a Government for white men."[25] Lovejoy maintained that the White and Black races were not equal "in gracefulness of motion, or loveliness of feature; [or] in mental endowment, moral susceptibility, and emotional power; not socially equal; not of necessity politically equal."[26] And yet in some respects Lovejoy was, as James Oakes observed, a more "thoroughgoing racial egalitarian" than Lincoln, who never said anything as stark as this about Black inferiority.[27]

In 1859, another leading antislavery Illinoisan, Senator Lyman Trumbull, voiced similar opinions: "When we say that all men are created equal, we do not mean that every man in organized society has the same rights. We do not tolerate that in Illinois. I know that there is a distinction between these two races because the Almighty himself has marked it upon their very faces; and, in my judgment, man cannot, by legislation or otherwise, produce a perfect equality between these two races, so that they will live happily together."[28] When asked if he would favor admitting Arizona as a state if it were "colonized and filled up with free colored people," Trumbull replied that he "did not believe these two races could live happily and pleasantly together, each enjoying equal rights, without one domineering over the other; therefore he advocated the policy of separating these races by adopting a system to rid the country of the black race, as it becomes free. He would say that he should not be prepared under the existing state of affairs to admit as a sovereign member of the Union, a community of negroes or Indians either."[29] In recommending that Black Americans leave the country, he told Chicagoans, "I want to have nothing to do either with the free negro or the slave negro. We, the Republican party, are the white man's party. . . . I would be glad to see this country relieved of them."[30] (Yet in 1866, Trumbull would write the pathbreaking Civil Rights Act, outlawing discriminatory legislation that had been adopted by former Confederate states.)

Other leading Republicans echoed Trumbull. Salmon P. Chase told his fellow senators in 1850 that "Ohio desires a homogeneous [i.e., White] population and does not desire a population of varied character."[31] In 1865, another Buckeye, future president James A. Garfield, wrote privately while he was publicly championing Black voting rights, "It goes against the grain of my feelings to favor negro suffrage . . . for I never could get in love with [the] creatures."[32] He added that he had "a strong feeling of repugnance when I think of the negro being made our political equals and I would be glad if they could be colonized—sent to heaven or got rid of in any decent way."[33] A few years later he decided not to take a house on Capitol Hill in Washington because that neighborhood was too "infested with negroes" for his taste.[34]

Similarly candid Negrophobia was expressed by Republican Senator Timothy O. Howe of Wisconsin, who viewed Black people "in the main" as "so much animal life."[35] Minnesota Congressman Ignatius Donnelly, a thoroughgoing Radical Republican, declared that while he wished Black Americans well and wanted them to progress "to the fullest development of which they are capable," he declared that he would not "rate them above or even equal to our proud, illustrious, and dominant race—our imperial race, the colonizers of the continents, the rulers of the sea, the masters of the globe."[36]

These Midwesterners were *Republicans,* outspoken opponents of slavery. Much more flagrant racism was expressed by Democrats in the Old Northwest, most notably by Stephen A. Douglas. Those Democrats did not openly favor slavery but professed to be indifferent about it. The militantly antislavery *Chicago Tribune* explained why so many Illinoisans resisted abolition: "The greatest ally of slaveholders in this country, is the apprehension in the Northern mind that if the slaves were liberated, they would become roaming, vicious vagrants; that they would overrun the North, and subsist by mendicancy and vagrancy; and that from the day they were made free, they would cease to work."[37]

Lincoln in the 1850s was primarily concerned with ending slavery, which he considered a greater evil than the limitations placed on the civil rights of Black Northerners. There were 4,000,000 slaves in the South and 250,000 Black residents of the Free States, and deplorable as second-class citizenship for the latter might be, slavery was far worse. While it could be possible to attack both evils simultaneously in antebellum New England, it was not then politically feasible either in Illinois or in the country at large. As historian George Fredrickson observed, it "is clear that no one who did not at least pay lip service to white supremacy could get elected to a statewide office in Illinois."[38] Racial equality was an issue Lincoln was willing to soft pedal in order to win over his jury—the voters of Negrophobic Illinois—and secure the desired verdict: a death sentence for slavery and defeat at the polls for its staunch ally, Stephen A. Douglas.[39]

Of all the rights denied to African Americans, that of intermarriage seemed to be the most important one to Prairie State voters. In 1865, all of Illinois' Black Laws were repealed save the one forbidding intermarriage. When asked to explain his public support for the anti-miscegenation statute, Lincoln told David R. Locke, "The law means nothing. I shall never marry a negress, but I have no objection to any one else doing so. If a white man wants to marry a negro woman, let him do it—*if the negro woman can stand it.*"[40]

⌘

Another piece of evidence cited by critics of Lincoln's racial views is his occasional use of the N-word. In the mid-nineteenth century, this term was used freely not only by opponents of emancipation but also by supportive Republicans. As historian V. Jacque Voegeli observed, "Republican journals frequently referred to colored people as 'Sambo,' 'Cuffie,' and 'niggers,' and derisively mocked their dialect," while "[s]ome of the same newspapers that most deplored Negrophobia [also] referred to colored persons as 'niggers' or 'shades' and praised the white race for its superior intelligence and strength."[41] A Black preacher noted that some White abolitionists, no matter how much they might hate slavery, nonetheless "hate a man who wears a colored skin worse."[42] Ohio Senator Benjamin Wade, a Radical Republican critic of Lincoln, alluded derisively in private correspondence to "niggers." From Washington, which he called "a mean God forsaken Nigger rid[d]en place," the senator complained that he was "getting sick of Niggers," expressed contempt for a "D[amne]d Nigger lawyer," and deplored the necessity of hiring Black servants. "For mere Nigger power it will cost over five hundred dollars per year," he told his wife. "I wish we could get a white woman of the English or Northern Europe breed."[43]

The "overeagerness to detect insult" mentioned by Randall Kennedy in the Introduction is common among Lincoln's critics. If we examine those rare instances where Lincoln used the N-word, we do not know his intonation, facial expression, body language, or gestures, but in all likelihood he was paraphrasing the language of Stephen A. Douglas and other flagrantly racist demagogues. In responding to Douglas's unvarnished race baiting, Lincoln occasionally employed the N-word, for he "generally used" racial epithets "to satirize his opponents," according to James Oakes.[44] Elizabeth Brown Pryor agreed, noting that Lincoln uttered the N-word "when he wanted to mock those who used the term without irony—in other words, to belittle the belittlers," especially Senator Douglas. Lincoln's "references to *niggers* were in speeches lampooning" Douglas. Throughout his political career, Lincoln had "regularly called on sarcasm to make his sharpest points." He evidently thought there was no better way to illustrate "the vulgarity of the bigot than by putting his words into the mouth of a man who was known to have taken a serious stand on the side of humanity."[45]

Lincoln enjoyed reading satire that ridiculed Negrophobes, especially the humorous writings of journalist David Ross Locke, creator of the uber-racist figure Petroleum Vesuvius Nasby, a preacher in rural Ohio whose outrageous, over-the-top Negrophobia tickled Lincoln's funny bone. "For the genius to write these things I would gladly give up my office," Lincoln told Locke, who was "a one-person battering ram against racial prejudice."[46] According to Lincoln biographer Richard Carwardine, "Locke, the racial egalitarian, uses Nasby's uninhibited and exuberant recourse to the word *nigger* to ridicule its ubiquity in Democrats' political rhetoric and highlight the Copperheads' obsession—near monomania—with race." Lincoln's "delight in the egregious Nasby was more than the relish of a joke. It was the double joy of recognizing a brilliant assault on ugly racial stereotyping, too." Thus Lincoln's love of Locke had "a moral dimension."[47] Echoing this sentiment, David Reynolds wrote, "Lincoln's enjoyment of Locke's humor reveals that below his veil of moderation and caution lay a radically progressive self. Within the political centrist on his tightrope lurked a leftist abolitionist who loathed racism and wanted dramatic social change."[48]

Reynolds also noted that Lincoln's appreciation of minstrel shows, which has been cited as further evidence of his unenlightened racial views, has been misunderstood: "In Lincoln's cultural context, minstrel songs could at times have a subversive edge." For example, "Old Dan Tucker" was a Black "prankster who flouts mainstream white conventions and boasts about his toughness and sexual prowess." According to Reynolds, the "progressiveness of minstrel music is especially visible in a song that Lincoln often asked [his friend Ward Hill] Lamon to sing to him: 'De Blue Tail Fly.'" The protagonist is a slave assigned to ward off blue tail flies from his master "until one bites a horse that throws the master, who dies from the fall. As in many minstrel songs, the black speaker wears a submissive mask," but "after his master dies he says indifferently, 'Ole Massa's gone, now let 'im rest/Dey say all tings am for de best.'" The chorus "shows that the man is glad his master is gone: 'Jim crack corn an' I don't care/ Ole Massa gone away.'"[49]

Like David Ross Locke, Lincoln liked to ridicule Negrophobes. In 1864, he received a telegram from one John McMahon of Pennsylvania: "I hope you will be kind Enough to pay attention to these few lines. 'Equal Rights & Justice to all white men in the United States forever. White men is in class number one & black men is in class number two & must be governed by white men forever.'"[50] Over the signature of his principal White House secretary Lincoln replied, "The President has received yours of yesterday, and is kindly paying attention to it. As it is my business to assist him whenever I can, I will thank you to inform me, for his use, whether you are either a white man or black one, because in either case, you can not be regarded as an entirely impartial judge. It may be that you belong to a third or fourth class of *yellow* or *red* men, in which case the impartiality of your judgment would be more apparant. [sic]"[51]

When, during the 1858 senatorial campaign Lincoln used the N-word, it's easy to imagine him adopting the modern technique of enclosing the word within air quotes, just as he employed quotation marks when using the word in correspondence.[52] Audiences would have seen this as a marked difference from Stephen A. Douglas's contemptuous use of the word.

Douglas sneeringly used the N-word often. When told that the Illinois senator might become president, William Henry Seward replied, "No man can be elected President of the United States who spells negro with two g's."[53] In Springfield on July 17, 1858, Senator Douglas predicted that Lincoln would seek to eliminate the Illinois law forbidding Black Americans to settle in the state: when he "lets down the bars and the floods shall have turned in upon us and covered our prairies thick with them till they shall be as dark and black as night in mid-day," then "he will apply the doctrine of nigger equality. He will then allow them to vote and to hold office, and make them eligible to the State Legislature, so that they can vote for the right persons for Senators, you know, make them eligible for Government offices, &c. After he shall have made them eligible to the Judgeship, he will get Cuffee elevated to the bench—he certainly would not refuse the Judge the privilege of marrying any woman that would have him. . . . If he thinks the nigger is equal to the white man by Divine law, and the human law deprives him of equality and citizenship with the white man, then does it not follow that if he had the power he would make them citizens with all the rights of citizenship on an equality with the white man?"[54] The N-word appears in this account published by a pro-Douglas newspaper in Indiana but not in the senator's organ, the *Chicago Times*. This difference lends credence to the claim that Douglas regularly used the N-word instead of *Negro*, and that the *Chicago Times* as well as the *Congressional Globe* sanitized his language.[55]

In their first debate, held in Ottawa, Douglas insisted that Lincoln in 1854 had "made his speech there [in Springfield] in reply to me, preaching up the same doctrine of the Declaration of Independence that niggers were equal to white men." The *Quincy Whig* sarcastically noted that Douglas used "elegant terms," among them an accusation that Lincoln espoused "the doctrine that '*niggers* were equal to white men.'" Asked the *Whig*, "Isn't this beautiful language to come from a United States Senator?"[56] A member of the audience in Ottawa that day reported that Douglas "opened the discussion in a speech characterized by a low appeal to the vulgar prejudices of his hearers, charging the Republican Party with being 'nigger worshipers,' of favoring 'nigger equality, amalgamation' &c., which disgusted many of his warmest friends."[57]

Robert R. Hitt, a shorthand reporter who covered the campaign for the *Chicago Press and Tribune*, recalled that during the second debate (held at Freeport), Republican Congressman Owen Lovejoy became "thoroughly aroused by Douglas' reference to 'the nigger'—Douglas said 'nigger' not 'negro' as the [*Chicago*] *Times* reported him on that occasion."[58] Throughout the debate, "Douglas said 'nigger,'" though his "organ printed 'negro."[59] At Hillsboro in early August, Douglas reportedly "uttered scarcely a sentence which had not the word 'nigger' in it."[60] During the final debate (held in Alton), a reporter had difficulty hearing Douglas, but could make out some "emphatic words" like "nigger equality" and an assertion that the Declaration of Independence was not made for "niggers."[61]

In the towns of Paris, Edwardsville, and Belleville, Lincoln challenged Douglas's boast that he had invented the "popular sovereignty" doctrine, whose definition was unclear: "Was it the right of emigrants in Kansas and Nebraska to govern themselves and a gang of niggers too, if they wanted them? Clearly this was no invention of his [Douglas's], because Gen. Cass put forth the same doctrine in 1848, in his so-called Nicholson letter, six years before Douglas thought of such a thing. Gen. Cass could have taken out a patent for the idea, if he had chosen to do so, and have prevented his Illinois rival from reaping a particle of benefit from it. Then what was it, I ask again, that this 'Little Giant' invented? It never occurred to Gen. Cass to call his discovery by the odd name of 'Popular Sovereignty.' He had not the *impudence* to say that the *right of people to govern niggers* was the *right of people to govern themselves*. His notions of the fitness of things were not moulded to the brazen degree of calling the right to put a hundred niggers through under the lash in Nebraska, a *'sacred right of self-government.'* And here, I submit to this intelligent audience and the whole world, was Judge Douglas' discovery, and the whole of it. He invented a *name* for Gen. Cass' old Nicholson letter dogma. He discovered that the right of the white man to breed and flog niggers in Nebraska was POPULAR SOVEREIGNTY!"[62]

Here Lincoln was evidently alluding to Douglas's senate speech of January 30, 1854, when he sneeringly described critics' objections to his Kansas-Nebraska bill: "They say they are willing to trust the Territorial legislature, under the limitations of the Constitution, to legislate upon the rights of inheritance, to legislate in regard to religion, education, and morals, to legislate in regard to the relations of husband and wife, of parent and child, of guardian and ward, upon everything pertaining to the dearest right and interest of white men, but they are not willing to treat them to legislate in regard to a few miserable negroes." The *New York Times* reported that the senator used the N-word instead of *Negroes*: "Douglas seems to have been ashamed of the speech he delivered yesterday, if we may judge by the fact he has published quite a different one. His speech, as delivered, abounded in such delectable terms as 'nigger,' . . . 'unadulterated, Free-Soil, Abolition Niggerism.' From the speech he has published, these terms are generally excluded, and others less repulsive to decency, and better fitted to the audience the Senator addressed, and the position he fills, are substituted. But the fact that he has omitted putting upon the official record these specimens of Senatorial billingsgate, is a confession that the Senator knew they were uncalled-for, improper, and calculated to bring himself into contempt before the country."[63] So it seems clear that Douglas in 1858 was referring to a few "miserable niggers" rather than "miserable negroes," and that Lincoln's references to a "gang of niggers" and the like were designed to needle his opponent and "bring him into contempt before the country" for using terms "repulsive to decency."

Critics of Lincoln's racial views also point to his occasional use of the N-word in private conversation, but it is not known how he intoned it. Was it contemptuously, maliciously, sarcastically, mockingly? (See Randall Kennedy's observations on this matter in the Introduction.) Was he understood to imply that African Americans were inferior intellectually or morally and hence should be made second-class citizens? That is highly improbable, for, as the evidence adduced in Chapter 4 shows, Lincoln felt a degree of compassion and empathy for Black Americans unusual for his time and place. It is possible, however, that Lincoln may have had some vestigial, faint traces of anti-Black prejudice left over from his early life in Negrophobic Kentucky and Indiana, but that is a far cry from saying he was a racist by any reasonable *historical* standard of racial egalitarianism (if not the standard of twenty-first century America).

Two dramatic cases of Lincoln's use of the N-word occurred in August 1862, an exceptionally fraught time, for the Union Army had recently suffered a major defeat in its massive Peninsular Campaign against Richmond. One case involved twenty-four-year old Sergeant Lucien Waters, a member of a cavalry unit protecting Lincoln, to whom the soldier handed a petition requesting a furlough. As Waters described the scene shortly thereafter, the president "in his characteristic style but not in a very dignified manner, took the said petition & sitting down on the marble pavement of the portico of the White House with his back against one of the south pillars, & with his feet drawn close up under him thereby elevating his Knees as high as his head, turned his head up & said that it had probably something to do with 'the damned or Eternal *niggar, niggar.*'!!" (The common phrase *eternal Negro question* alluded to racial issues, especially slavery.) Waters, a serious abolitionist who nonetheless referred to Black Americans as "darkies," was so shocked that he was tempted to give Lincoln a "'right smart' talking to" and a "dressing down," but resisted the impulse to play the scold. "I pity the man from my heart," he wrote, "for he is nearly worked to death. His private hours are scarcely kept sacred to his repose & comfort, & he may have been vexed & tormented with a hundred [callers] that very day who were trying to worm something out of the government for their own personal aggrandizement. Charity, Charity should be our watch word as well as the keen acumen of criticism."[64]

Around the same time that Lincoln made his untoward remark to Sergeant Waters, he similarly lost patience with an antislavery delegation from Connecticut, headed by the state's governor, William A. Buckingham. According to the governor's biographer, Lincoln was "pressed on every side by those who were urging him onto emancipation, or who would dissuade him from it, said abruptly, and as if irritated by the subject, 'Governor, I suppose that what your people want is more nigger.'" Buckingham was surprised both by the president's unwonted impatience and his unusual language. Lincoln quickly altered his tone, earnestly remarking "that if anybody supposed he was not interested in this subject, deeply interested, intensely anxious about it, it was a great mistake. He had been doing his utmost to remove this chief cause of the war [slavery], and rid our Republic of this shame and curse. And whenever the time should come that he could proclaim emancipation, and the people would sustain him in it, it would be the satisfaction of his life."[65]

Just what prompted Lincoln's outbursts to Sergeant Waters and Governor Buckingham is unclear, though—as Buckingham's biographer indicated—he was probably not angry at Black Americans but rather at the self-righteous opponents of slavery who were hounding him mercilessly. While he shared their desire to end human bondage, he was exasperated by what he deemed "the self-righteousness of the Abolitionists" and the "petulant and vicious fretfulness of many radicals."[66] Among those abolitionists was William Lloyd Garrison, who snorted, "I am growing more and more skeptical as to the 'honesty' of Lincoln. He is nothing better than a wet rag."[67] Another Massachusetts editor sneered, "Mr. Lincoln must worship a strange God indeed, if he imagines He is not in favor of universal freedom. The Bible Society, or some other benevolent institution ought at once to present him with a copy of the New Testament, with directions to peruse several chapters daily. Unless he indulged his usual hair-splitting propensity, he might derive great benefit."[68]

Though *eternal Negro question* was a commonly used locution, it was uncommon for Lincoln to utter the N-word in situations like the ones he found himself in when Sergeant Waters presented his petition and Governor Buckingham came to call. By August 1862, Lincoln's nerves were badly strained. Office seekers were pestering him relentlessly (as Sergeant Waters noted), the military situation was discouraging in the aftermath of the Peninsula Campaign's failure, the Army of the Potomac appeared on the verge of mutiny, Republican political prospects seemed bleak (and in fact the party suffered a major setback in the fall), European nations were poised to recognize the Confederacy, he was fearful the Emancipation Proclamation which he would soon issue might generate a powerful backlash, and the country was growing restive as disenchantment with the administration's "fatal milk and water policy" grew ever more intense.[69]

Lincoln was being urged not only to fight a tougher war but also to be more aggressive in dealing with slavery. He had been subjected to that sort of pressure from the day he took office. His wife's cousin Lizzie Grimsley, who had stayed in White House for six months in 1861, recalled that "there was no one affliction (and no other word is suitable) from which Mr. Lincoln suffered more in those anxious months of the war than the importunities, meddlesomeness, impatient censure, and arrogance of preachers, politicians, newspaper writers, and cranks, who virtually dogged his footsteps, demanding that he should 'free the slaves', 'arm the slaves', 'emancipate the slaves and give them the ballot.'"[70]

Such pressure mounted during the summer of 1862. On July 4, when Massachusetts Senator Charles Sumner urged Lincoln to reconsecrate Independence Day by issuing an emancipation decree on that holiday, the president said it was "too big a lick," arguing that "half the army would lay down its arms, if emancipation were declared."[71]

When another radical senator demanded that he free the slaves, Lincoln asked: "Will Kentucky stand that?"

"Damn Kentucky!" came the reply.

"Then damn you!" exclaimed the president, who seldom used profanity.[72]

Also arousing Lincoln's ire were some Pennsylvania Quakers who in June 1862 presented him with a memorial calling for emancipation, which seemed to imply that if he did not promptly issue a proclamation abolishing slavery, he would be violating the spirit of his 1858 "house divided" speech. Lincoln bristled at the implication that he had abandoned his principles. According to Congressman William D. Kelley, who observed the exchange, the president "sought to repel this covert imputation upon his integrity and veracity" and "replied with an asperity of manner of which I had not deemed him capable."[73] Lincoln doubtless was exasperated by such critics, knowing all the while that he had already prepared an Emancipation Proclamation that he would soon issue.

Lincoln's exasperation peaked in August 1862, when he said of a "well-known abolitionist orator" (almost certainly Wendell Phillips), "He is a thistle! I don't understand why God lets him live!"[74] Lincoln usually managed to curb his temper, but the strains to which he was subject day in and day out, week in and week out, month in and month out, especially during the summer of 1862, proved too much for even his legendary patience.[75] As Mary Lincoln acknowledged, her husband, when "worn down," would speak "crabbedly to men, harshly so."[76]

While Sergeant Waters refrained from "dressing down" the president for using the N-word, another Yankee—Henry Samuel, secretary of the executive committee of the Philadelphia Supervisory Committee for Recruiting Colored Regiments—did give him a "'right smart' talking to" for referring to Black Americans collectively as *cuffie*. In 1864, according to Samuel, his Philadelphia committee called at the White House, where they found Lincoln "seated at his desk with his long legs on the top of it, his hands on his head and looking exactly like a huge katydid or grass-hopper." After hearing their appeal for equalized pay for Black and White laborers assisting the army, Lincoln "turned his head and jocularly said, with one of those peculiar smiles of his, 'Well, gentlemen, you wish the pay of 'Cuffie' raised.'" Samuels interrupted, saying, "Excuse me, Mr. Lincoln, the term 'Cuffie' is not in our vernacular. What we want is that the wages of the American Colored Laborer be equalized with those of the American White Laborer." Lincoln explained, "I stand corrected, young man, but you know I am by birth a Southerner and in our section that term is applied without any idea of an offensive nature. I will, however, at the earliest possible moment do all in my power to accede to your request." Soon thereafter, that request was honored.[77]

There is little reason to doubt Lincoln's sincerity, for *cuffie* may well have been considered an acceptable colloquialism in polite Illinois society (and hardly the equivalent of the N-word), just as "darky" may have been considered acceptable in Sergeant Waters's New York social circle but not in New England. ("Darky" was originally regarded as a proper English word but eventually came to be thought of as a slur.) Few slang dictionaries and compilations of anti-Black slurs describe *cuffie* or *cuffee* as a pejorative, so it is hard to know if it was, as one of Lincoln's critics (Henry Louis Gates) alleged, "a racist name for blacks widely in use in the nineteenth century."[78] Apparently it was understood informally to be a "a general name for a black person" and "a personal name formerly common among black Americans."[79]

On February 15, 1862, Lincoln offended another young abolitionist, Edward Lillie Pierce, who had been appointed to take charge of newly freed slaves in South Carolina. Before leaving Washington, Pierce called at the White House to discuss his mission. The president (as Pierce recollected) "listened for a few moments, and then said, somewhat impatiently, that he did not think he ought to be troubled with such details,—that there seemed to be an itching to get niggers into our lines." Pierce replied "that these negroes were within them by the invitation of no one, being domiciled there before we commenced occupation." In an attempt to understand Lincoln's unwonted testiness and use of a vulgar epithet, Pierce wrote that the president's beloved son Willie "was very ill, and quite likely that had something to do with his temper at the time."[80] (Willie died five days later after a long struggle with an unidentified fatal illness.) As in the case of Governor Buckingham and Sergeant Samuel, Lincoln evidently resented the pressure that some abolitionists were bringing to bear at that time.

⁂

Lincoln met with several White abolitionists and "no matter how hard such visitors pressed him, he was usually cordial and full of anecdotes," often telling "tales of his troubles in order to gain time and sympathy."[81] Foremost among them were Wendell Phillips and William Lloyd Garrison, two of the leading champions of Black rights.

On March 18, 1862, several days after the president delivered a message formally urging Congress to compensate any state that abolished slavery, Lincoln invited Phillips to the White House. The famed orator had likened the message to "a wedge—a very small wedge, but it is a wedge for all that." Varying the image, he declared that Lincoln "had opened the door of emancipation a foot, and he [Phillips] with a coach and six, and Wm. Lloyd Garrison for a driver, would drive right through."[82] More emphatically, Phillips told fellow abolitionist Moncure Conway, "Thank God for Old Abe! He hasn't got to Canaan yet but he has set his face Zionward."[83]

Lincoln told his guest that for three months he had labored on the message to Congress "all by himself, [with] no conference with his cabinet." Though the abolitionist spellbinder had spoken highly of that document, Lincoln evidently did not believe Phillips "valued the message quite enough" and told a story about an Irish toper in the legally dry state of Maine. Thirsty for alcohol, the son of Erin requested a glass of soda, asking his host, "Couldn't ye put a drop of the crathur in it unbeknown to meself?" Just so, said Lincoln, "I've put a good deal of Anti Slavery in it unbeknown to themselves." This was evidently a reference to the Border State congressmen and senators, for he went on to inform Phillips that he had instructed them "not to talk to him about slavery. They loved it & meant it should last—he hated it & meant *it should die*." The president added, "if only men over 50 voted we could abolish slavery. When men are soon to face their God they are Antislavery—it is the *young* who support the system—unfortunately they rule too much." Although the Bostonian was frustrated because Lincoln talked "so fast & constantly" during their one-hour interview that "it was hard to get a word in edgewise," nevertheless he "felt *rather encouraged*" and reported the president "is better than his Congress fellows." Still, though Lincoln seemed a "perfectly honest" magistrate "trying to do what he thought his duty," Phillips condescendingly deemed him "a man of very *slow mind*."[84]

In January 1863, Phillips and a few other abolitionists met with the president to recommend that General John C. Frémont be given an important command. To them Lincoln analyzed the sources of growing Northern discontent.[85] When Phillips suggested that the public disliked the way in which the administration was implementing the Emancipation Proclamation, the president replied: "the masses of the country generally are only dissatisfied at our lack of military success. Defeat and failure in the field make everything seem wrong." Bitterly, he added, "Most of us here present have been long working in minorities, and may have got into a habit of being dissatisfied." When some of his guests objected to this characterization, Lincoln said: "At any rate, it has been very rare that an opportunity of 'running' [i.e., criticizing unfairly] this administration has been lost."[86] When the delegation chided him for not issuing the Emancipation Proclamation earlier, he said the public had not been ready to support it. Moncure Conway speculated that the president "was surrounded a mile thick with Kentuckians who would not let him know the truth" and expressed doubts about the honesty of Nicolay, "who superintends his reading." Asked if Benjamin Butler would be restored to command in Louisiana, Lincoln said "he meant to return Butler to N. Orleans as soon as it could be done without hurting Gen. Banks' feelings!" Conway sarcastically exclaimed, "What a fine watchword would be 'Liberty, Union and Banks' feelings!'"[87] (Soon afterward, in a lecture titled "The Vacant Throne of Washington," Conway told a Boston audience: "we find no man, in the station of power and influence, adequate to the work."[88])

Other participants in that meeting found Lincoln more impressive than Conway did. George Luther Stearns said, "It is of no use to disparage his ability. There we were, with some able talkers among us, and we had the best position too; but the President held his ground against us." Frank Bird acknowledged that Lincoln "is the shrewdest man I ever met; but not at all of a Kentuckian. He is an old-fashioned Yankee in a Western dress."[89]

William Lloyd Garrison met with the president on June 10 and 11, 1864, and reported there "is no mistake about it in regard to Mr. Lincoln's desire to do all that he can see it right and possible to do to uproot slavery, and give fair play to the emancipated. I was much pleased with his spirit, and the familiar and candid way in which he unbosomed himself."[90] During that interview, the abolitionist editor said, "Mr. Lincoln, I want to tell you frankly that [in 1861 and 1862] for every word I have spoken in your favour,

I have spoken ten in favour of General Fremont," who was running for president as the candidate of the Radical Democracy Party. Garrison "went on to explain how difficult he had found it to commend the President when the latter was revoking the [emancipation] proclamations of Fremont [in 1861] and [General David] Hunter [in 1862], and reiterating his purpose to save the Union if he could, without destroying slavery. But, Mr. President, from the hour that you issued the Emancipation Proclamation, and showed your purpose to stand by it, I have given you my hearty support and confidence." The president "received this good-naturedly, set forth the difficulties under which he had labored, and expressed his anxiety to secure the adoption of the Constitutional Amendment [abolishing slavery, then before Congress], that the question might be forever settled and not hazarded by his possible death or failure of reelection. The resolution in favor of it adopted at Baltimore had been prepared and introduced at his own suggestion."[91]

(Curiously, according to Garrison's son William, the abolitionist editor frankly criticized Lincoln's "shortcomings,—his mistakes in not making the Proclamation universal, the wicked treatment of the colored troops. . . . Not one word of congratulation did he give the President regarding his renomination."[92])

Two years later, when Wendell Phillips refused to support Lincoln's reelection, Garrison and many other abolitionists broke with the famed Boston orator. Phillips denounced the president as "a half-converted, honest Western Whig, trying to be an abolitionist," whose "Administration has never yet acknowledged the manhood of the negro."[93] In response, Garrison insisted that the president must be judged on the basis "of his possibilities, rather than by our wishes, or by the highest abstract moral standard."[94] Garrison conceded that the president was "open to criticism and censure" but added that there "is also much to rejoice over and to be thankful for; and a thousand incidental errors and blunders are easily to be borne with on the part of one who, at one blow, severed the chains of three millions three hundred thousand slaves,—thus virtually abolishing the whole slave system . . . as an act dictated alike by patriotism, justice and humanity."[95] Garrison urged his fellow abolitionists to understand the constitutional and political constraints which Lincoln had to consider: "His freedom to follow his convictions of duty as an individual is one thing—as the President of the United States, it is limited by the functions of his office; for the people do not elect a President to play the part of reformer or philanthropist, nor to enforce upon the nation his own peculiar ethical or humanitary [sic] ideas, without regard to his oath or their will. His primary and all-comprehensive duty is to maintain the Union and execute the Constitution, in good faith . . . without reference to the views of any clique or party in the land." Garrison's "firm conviction" was that "no man has occupied the chair of the Chief Magistracy in America, who has more assiduously or more honestly endeavored to discharge all its duties with a single eye to the welfare of the country, than Mr. Lincoln."[96] Similarly, he wrote the president, "God save you, and bless you abundantly! As an instrument in his hands, you have done a mighty work for the freedom of the millions who have so long pined in bondage in our land—nay, for the freedom of all mankind. I have the utmost faith in the benevolence of your heart, the purity of your motives, and the integrity of your spirit. This I do not hesitate to avow at all times."[97]

To an Englishman who denounced Lincoln as a hopeless bigot, Garrison conceded that the president "might have done more and gone further, if he had had greater resolution and larger foresight; that is an open question, and opinions are not facts. Possibly he could not have gone one hair's breadth beyond the point he has reached by a slow and painful process, without inciting civil war at the North, and overturning the government." Such speculation, Garrison maintained, was "idle." Instead, he pointed to what could be known for certain: "that his Emancipation proclamation of January 1, 1863, liberated more than three-fourths of the entire slave population; that since that period, emancipation has followed in Maryland, Western Virginia, Missouri, and the District of Columbia, and is being rapidly consummated in Kentucky and Tennessee, thus terminating the holding of property in man everywhere under the American flag; that all the vast Territories have been consecrated to freedom and free labor; that all Fugitive Slave laws have been repealed, so that slave-hunting is at an end in all the free States; that no rebel State can be admitted to the Union, except on the basis of complete emancipation; that national justice (refused under every other Administration) has been done to the republics of Hayti and Liberia, by the full recognition of their independence; that an equitable treaty has been made with Great Britain for the effectual suppression of the foreign slave trade, through right of search; that a large portion of the army is made up of those who, until now, have been prohibited bearing arms, and refused enrolment in the militia of every State in the Union [i.e., African Americans]; . . . that free negro schools are following wherever the army penetrates, and multitudes of young and old, who, under the old slave system, were prohibited learning the alphabet, are now rapidly acquiring that knowledge which is power, and which makes slavery and serfdom alike impracticable; and that on numerous plantations free labor is 'in the full tide of successful experiment.'"[98]

Though not as laudatory of Lincoln as was Garrison, Frederick Douglass backed Lincoln for reelection. He acknowledged that after the Democrats nominated the ticket of George B. McClellan and George H. Pendleton, both hostile to the antislavery cause, "all hesitation ought to cease, and every man who wishes well to the slave and to the country should at once rally with all the warmth and earnestness of his nature to the support of Abraham Lincoln." Douglass did not actively campaign for the president because, he explained, "Republican committees do not wish to expose themselves to the charge of being the 'N[igge]r party.' The Negro is the deformed child, which is put out of the room when company comes."[99]

Several other African Americans supported Lincoln's reelection bid. The preacher-cum-abolitionist James W. C. Pennington of New York declared that Black people should regard Lincoln as "OUR president, because he is the only American President who has ever given any attention to colored men as citizens." Lincoln's "reelection will be the best security that the present well-begun work of negro freedom and African redemption will be fully completed." Pennington estimated that ninety per cent of Black Americans shared his opinion.[100] Another Black minister-cum-abolitionist, J. Sella Martin, said, "As a negro, I am for the man whose party and policy have given us a free capital, a confiscation law, and a proclamation of freedom, as against the man who, with honest enough intentions, expects to drive out the devils by Beelzebub."[101] The publisher of the New York *Anglo-African* told readers that "we may have thought that Mr. Lincoln has not done what *we think* he could have done for the overthrow of oppression in our land; *but that is not the question now. The great and overshadowing inquiry is, do you want to see the many noble acts which have been passed during Mr. Lincoln's administration repealed, and slavery fastened again upon Maryland, Louisiana, Tennessee, Virginia, and portions of [other Confederate] States now free?* This is the only question now, and if you are a friend of liberty you will give your influence and cast your vote for Abraham Lincoln, who, under God, is the only hope of the oppressed."[102] John Rock addressed a convention of the National Association of Colored Citizens and Their Friends, saying that there were only two parties: "the one headed by Lincoln is for freedom and the republic, the other one headed by McClellan is for despotism and slavery." The delegates enthusiastically applauded his statement.[103]

Even before the parties held their nominating conventions, some African Americans had called for Lincoln's reelection. On January 1, 1864, a mass meeting of Black San Franciscans adopted a resolution endorsing the president for a second term. Commenting on that resolution, a Black newspaper praised Lincoln as the only president who "has stood up in defiance of the slave-power, and dared officially to maintain the doctrine, by his official actions, that we are citizens, though of African descent—that the army and navy shall protect and defend such citizens in common with all others—that provision ought to be made for the education of freedmen."[104]

The philosopher Thomas Carson recently identified nine types of racism: belief racism, belief-discrimination racism, belief-malevolent racism, belief-exploitation racism, inadequate-respect racism, inadequate-benevolence racism, disrespect racism, malevolent racism, and cold-hearted racism. In general, he found Lincoln (at least in his final years) innocent of most varieties, though he thought him guilty of "inadequate-respect racism." That concept is hazy, and the main evidence for judging him a racist of that sort is, according to Carson, his occasional use of the N-word and his opposition to interracial marriage.[105] But, as noted above, those objections are hardly telling, for Lincoln (with rare exceptions) used the N-word when paraphrasing—indeed, mocking—Stephen A. Douglas and other flagrant racists. And what of those rare exceptions? They hardly constitute proof positive that Lincoln was a racist.[106]

Moreover, Lincoln told David Ross Locke that he was not opposed to interracial marriage, his public statements to the contrary notwithstanding.[107] Carson also faulted Lincoln for supporting Illinois' other Black Laws, but during the 1858 senatorial campaign he publicly endorsed them only because Douglas was baiting him; if he had taken the bait, it would have been political suicide. Moreover, by 1865, when he was murdered for publicly endorsing Black voting rights, he had obviously changed his mind. After concluding that Lincoln was an "inadequate-respect-racist," Carson acknowledged "there is some evidence that Lincoln was very kind and respectful to black people face to face."[108] As this book has shown, there is quite a lot of evidence to that effect.

As further evidence of Lincoln's purported racism, Henry Louis Gates cited the president-elect's statement to James Redpath that he would accept a "nigger" as a Haitian diplomat.[109] (According to Redpath, Lincoln said: "You can tell the President of Haiti that I shan't tear my shirt if he does send a nigger here.") In the letter reporting these remarks, Redpath did not indicate if Lincoln uttered the N-word sarcastically, implying contempt for Negrophobes who used such vulgar language, or contempt for African Americans.

Strong evidence provided by Richard J. Hinton, Redpath's chief assistant in the Haitian Emigration Bureau, suggests it was the former rather than the latter. A radical abolitionist, Hinton visited Lincoln in December 1860 and urged him to extend diplomatic recognition to Haiti. As Hinton recalled a few years later, having "been associated with Mr. Redpath in other anti-slavery efforts," including active support of John Brown in Kansas, "at his request, I acted as special agent of the movement" to have the US recognize Haiti diplomatically. In that role, Hinton "made a tour through many of the Northern States," interviewing Salmon P. Chase and several other prominent Republicans, among them Lincoln. During his conversation with the president-elect, Hinton was struck by "a remark of Mr. Lincoln which showed how little the prejudice against color affected his own conclusions. It is more distinct in my memory because other Republican statesmen, to whom the same view was presented, expressed a different conclusion from that given by Mr. Lincoln. In the arguments made in behalf of the [diplomatic] recognition of Hayti, I suggested, as a matter of policy, that [Haitian] President [Fabre] Geffrard would send, in the event of recognition, as a representative of the republic at Washington, some one of the educated men of mixed blood, of whom there were many who would pass muster for Creole or Spanish American whites. In short, Hayti would send a representative as near like a white man as she could find among her worthy citizens." (White people were not accorded citizenship in Haiti at the time.) "Mr. Lincoln remarked, in an animated manner, 'I don't see the necessity for that. An educated black man would be as dignified, I have no doubt, as a ginger-colored one.'" Hinton recalled that he "had presented the same suggestion to others who were, at that hour, considered as able and more radical than was Abraham Lincoln. His manner assured me that the question of receiving a black man as a diplomatist, would not at all affect his conduct, and aroused no special prejudice in his mind."[110] According to this John Brown-assisting abolitionist, Lincoln was more of a racial egalitarian than reputedly "more radical" antislavery leaders whom he had lobbied, notably including Salmon P. Chase.

∽

Further evidence of Lincoln's purported racism is a statement made in 1877 by Gideon Welles, his secretary of the navy, who claimed that the sixteenth president "doubted if the Africans as a race were themselves capable of organizing as a community and successfully maintaining a government without supervision, or individually susceptible of high intellectual cultivation. There might be and were exceptional cases, but they [i.e., most African Americans] were by nature dull, inert, dependent, and of little foresight—an ignorant and inferior race, who needed to be governed, were not as a class able or qualified to participate intelligently in self-government. If they were to exercise the high privilege of suffrage—the first and most impressive step in free government—it must be at some distant day in the future after several generations of education and nurture."[111]

Welles demonstrably misrepresented Lincoln's racial views, ascribing his own opinions to the president. On September 28, 1865, Welles wrote in his diary, "I would not enslave the negro, but his enfranchisement is another question, and until he is better informed, it is not desirable that he should vote." He added, "I am no advocate of social equality, nor do I labor for political or civil equality with the negro. I do not want him at my table, nor do I care to have him in the jury-box or in the legislative hall, or on the bench."[112]

Pace Welles, Lincoln did not believe that voting rights for African Americans should be delayed until "some distant day in the future after several generations of education and nurture." As Welles knew, on April 11, 1865, the president publicly endorsed Black voting rights and three days later was assassinated for doing so. To be sure, Lincoln recommended that only African Americans who had served in the armed forces and those who were "very intelligent" (presumably he meant literate) should be enfranchised, but in making that announcement he was laying the groundwork for unrestricted voting rights for all Black men. Frederick Douglass acknowledged in a little-noted December 1865 speech that Lincoln's support for Black suffrage was disappointing because of its limited scope. It "seemed to mean but little," but Douglass soon realized that it actually "meant a great deal. It was just like Abraham Lincoln. He never shocked prejudices unnecessarily. Having learned statesmanship while splitting rails, he always used the thin edge of the wedge first—and the fact that he used it at all meant that he would if need be, use the thick as well as the thin."[113] As noted above, Lincoln repeatedly declared to Douglass that "he was in favor of the enfranchisement of two classes of the Southern people. First, all those who had taken any part in suppressing the rebellion; and secondly, all those who could read and write."[114]

To support his point, Douglass could have cited Lincoln's steps on the road to emancipation: the president first inserted the thin edge of the wedge in late 1861, when he worked behind the scenes to persuade Delaware's General Assembly to emancipate that state's slaves; in March 1862, he drove the wedge deeper with a recommendation that Congress help compensate any state, not just Delaware, that adopted gradual emancipation; he drove the wedge deeper still in 1863 with the Emancipation Proclamation, covering most Confederate states; and finally in 1864–1865 he drove home the thick edge of the wedge by facilitating passage of the Thirteenth Amendment, abolishing slavery throughout the country.

Lincoln dealt similarly with Black suffrage. In March 1864, he inserted the thin edge of the wedge by privately urging Louisiana Governor Michael Hahn to support the enfranchisement of at least some Black men (those who served in the military as well as the intelligent/literate) in the Bayou State. During the spring and summer of 1864, he also worked behind the scenes to get the Louisiana constitutional convention to do so. It is possible that Lincoln did not mean to extend suffrage to uneducated Black men in other states, but that seems unlikely, for if he wanted to enfranchise only the educated, he would not have suggested that Black soldiers, regardless of educational background, be granted voting rights. In 1865, he drove the wedge still deeper by publicly endorsing the same policy. If he had not been murdered, he probably would have driven home the thick edge of the wedge by urging that all adult Black males be enfranchised. Historian Martha Hodes concluded that if Lincoln had lived, "African Americans would have petitioned him and visited him in the White House, advancing the same demands for equality and rights that they asked of his successor. The difference was that Lincoln would have answered without Johnson's defensiveness, ridicule, and dismissal. Lincoln's record of words and actions all during the war, even if marked by slow deliberation, indicated that he would have listened to, absorbed, and responded to the demands of African Americans."[115]

Did Lincoln really believe that most African Americans "were by nature dull, inert, dependent, and of little foresight," thus constituting "an ignorant and inferior race," as Gideon Welles claimed? Lincoln *never* said that they were inferior to White Americans in any respect except in terms of *color*, which was probably a satirical concession designed to make White supremacists look ridiculous.[116] What, after all, is an inferior color? On July 17, 1858, he told a Springfield audience, "Certainly the negro is not our equal in color—perhaps not in many other respects—still, in the right to put into his mouth the bread that his own hands have earned, he is the equal of every other man, white or black."[117] The following month, during his first debate with Douglas, he repeated that sentiment: "I agree with Judge Douglas he [the Black man] is not my equal in many respects—certainly not in color, perhaps not in moral or intellectual endowment. But in the right to eat the bread, without leave of anybody else, which his own hand earns, *he is my equal and the equal of Judge Douglas, and the equal of every living man.*"[118] On both of those occasions, Lincoln carefully qualified his remarks. As David S. Reynolds observed, he "cunningly surrounded his racist sounding pronouncements with phrases that pointed in a radically abolitionist direction."[119] By stating that African Americans were *perhaps* inferior intellectually and morally, he implied that they were perhaps *not* inferior in those qualities. By his actions, Lincoln demonstrated throughout his presidency and his lifetime his belief in the latter—that Black Americans were not inferior—adeptly using his political capital and cunning to achieve equality in a land that was far less tolerant than he.

Another example of that cunning: in his August 1862 meeting with leaders of Washington's Black community, whom he described as "intelligent," Lincoln did allow that slaves' intellects had been "clouded" by oppression, clearly implying that they might at least equal White people intellectually if they were no longer oppressed.

In private, Lincoln was more blunt in rejecting racist arguments than he was in public. Sometime in the 1850s, he penned an analysis of proslavery logic, warning those who justified enslaving people based on their skin color to "take care," for by "this rule, you are to be slave to the first man you meet, with a fairer skin than your own." He also challenged anyone who maintained that enslaving African Americans was justified because of their supposed intellectual inferiority: "Take care again. By this rule, you are to be slave to the first man you meet, with an intellect superior to your own."[120] As noted in Chapter 1, when asked about his support for Illinois' ban on interracial marriage, Lincoln replied, "The law means nothing. I shall never marry a negress, but I have no objection to any one else doing so. If a white man wants to marry a negro woman, let him do it—*if the negro woman can stand it.*"[121]

The best rebuttal to Gideon Welles's description of Lincoln's racial views—and to critics like Henry Louis Gates who cite Welles—is the evidence adduced in this book describing Lincoln's egalitarian interactions with African Americans.

In 2010, historian Eric Foner wrote that while Lincoln's "racial views changed during the Civil War, he never became a principled egalitarian in the manner of abolitionists such as Frederick Douglass and Wendell Phillips or Radical Republicans like Charles Sumner."[122] And yet, as noted above, Lincoln was less prejudiced (or at least less outspoken) than many abolitionists and Radical Republicans, among them Joshua Giddings, Henry Wilson, Owen Lovejoy, Benjamin F. Wade, Timothy O. Howe, Lyman Trumbull, Ignatius Donnelly, and James A. Garfield. Moreover, as James Oakes noted in 2021, "Lincoln's commitment to the antislavery Constitution implied a corresponding commitment to some standard of racial equality—not the standard of the twenty-first century, but profoundly significant in a nation where virulent racial prejudice was a significant component of mainstream political culture."[123]

Also profoundly significant is the fact, often overlooked, that Lincoln was murdered not because he issued the Emancipation Proclamation (abolishing slavery in most of the Confederacy), nor because he facilitated passage of the Thirteenth Amendment (abolishing slavery throughout the nation), but rather because, on April 11, 1865, he publicly endorsed Black voting rights, enraging one member of his audience—John Wilkes Booth—who turned to a companion and declared, "That means nigger citizenship. Now by God I'll put him through!"[124] He added, "That is the last speech he will ever make."[125] Three days later, Booth assassinated Lincoln, who thus deserves to be considered a martyr to African American citizenship rights as much as Black Americans like Dr. Martin Luther King Jr., Medgar Evers, Jimmie Lee Jackson, and James Earl Chaney, or White Americans like Viola Liuzzo, James Reeb, Michael Schwerner, and Andrew Goodman—and the many others of both races who were murdered while championing the civil rights movement of the twentieth century.[126]

ACKNOWLEDGMENTS

O ver the past thirty-seven years I have been researching the life of Lincoln, I have been the beneficiary of help from many generous friends, fellow scholars, family members, and librarians too numerous to mention by name here. This book was largely written during a sabbatical leave granted by the University of Illinois Springfield, where I am indebted to my colleagues in the History Department, to the research fund of the College of Liberal Arts and Sciences, and to Val Vaden, the patron who established and underwrites the Chancellor Naomi B. Lynn Distinguished Chair in Lincoln Studies, which I have had the honor to hold since 2009.

Lewis E. Lehrman, an exceptionally generous philanthropist and knowledgeable Lincolnian, has been unfailingly supportive for more than two decades. In the Illinois capital, many friends have been kind, most notably Sarah Thomas, John Paul, Mark Johnson, Bruce and Karen Finne, and Dick and Ann Hart. Dick's pioneering scholarship on Springfield's Black community (available on the website of the Abraham Lincoln Association) launched the in-depth study of Lincoln's relations with African Americans.

His work inspired me to undertake this book, the opening chapter of which is based largely on his trailblazing research and writing.

My knowledgeable agent, Don Fehr of the Trident Media Group, helped me navigate the complicated world of modern trade publishing.

At Pegasus Books the staff, which ably assisted me in getting *An American Marriage: The Untold Story of Abraham Lincoln and Mary Todd* into print, has been even more helpful in readying this volume for release. I am especially grateful to the firm's head, Claiborne Hancock, for his willingness to publish books on two of the most controversial subjects in the realm of Lincoln scholarship, knowing full well that they would probably raise hackles in the stormy political and cultural climate of 2021.

Finally, I cannot adequately express my profound gratitude to Lois McDonald, who has enriched my life immeasurably for over three decades, and to my brother Lloyd and to my daughter Jessica. Thanks, thanks to all.

Mystic, Connecticut

ENDNOTES

INTRODUCTION

1   *New York Times* and *New York Herald*, 2 June 1865; manuscript of the eulogy, Frederick Douglass Papers, Library of Congress; Harold Holzer, ed., *President Lincoln Assassinated!! The Firsthand Story of the Murder, Manhunt, Trial, and Mourning* (New York: Library of America, 2015), 310.

2   *The Star of the North* (Bloomsburg, Pennsylvania), 21 December 1864.

3   Lincoln's speech in Chicago, 10 July 1858, in Roy P. Basler et al., eds., *The Collected Works of Abraham Lincoln* (8 vols. plus index; New Brunswick, N.J.: Rutgers University Press, 1953-1955), 2:501–502.

4   Lincoln to Henry L. Pierce and others, Springfield, 6 April 1859, *Collected Works of Abraham Lincoln*, 3:375.

5   Fragment on Slavery [1 April 1854?], *Collected Works of Lincoln*, 2:222.

6   David S. Reynolds, *Abe: Abraham Lincoln in His Times* (New York: Penguin Press, 2020), 124. Reynolds immediately added: "on a personal level he showed compassion towards people of color."

7   Basler, ed., *Collected Works of Lincoln*, 7:259, 5:53. Emphasis added. Democrats complained that the president "classes laboring white men with negroes" and in effect endorses "the new doctrine of 'miscegenation' or

amalgamation." The "most advanced school of abolitionists now take the position that our citizens of Irish birth are inferior to the negro, and that they could be basically improved by the intermixture with the negro. The 'working people' to whom Mr. Lincoln refers, of course, are the Irish, for it was upon them the responsibility of the riot was thrown." West Chester, Pennsylvania. *Jeffersonian*, n.d., copied in the New York *Freeman's Journal & Catholic Register*, 21 May 1864, in Sidney Kaplan, "The Miscegenation Issue in the Election of 1864," *Journal of Negro History* 34 (1949): 318–319.

8   Address to Congress, 4 July 1861, Basler, ed., *Collected Works of Lincoln*, 4:438. Emphasis added.

9   Speech in New Haven, Connecticut, 6 March 1860, *Collected Works of Lincoln*, 4:24.

10 Lincoln to John M. Brockman, Springfield, 25 September 1860, *Collected Works of Lincoln*, 4:121.

11 Lincoln to Isham Reavis, Springfield, 5 November 1855, *Collected Works of Lincoln*, 2:327.

12 Lincoln to William H. Herndon, Washington, 10 July 1848, *Collected Works of Lincoln*, 1:497.

13 Lincoln to George C. Latham, Springfield, 22 July 1860, *Collected Works of Lincoln*, 4:87.

14 Douglass's lecture, "Self-Made Men," *The Frederick Douglass Papers, Series One: Speeches, Debates, and Interviews*, eds. John W. Blassingame et al. (5 vols.; New Haven: Yale University Press, 1979–1992), 5:556.

15 Address before the Wisconsin State Agricultural Society, Milwaukee, 30 September 1859, Basler, ed., *Collected Works of Lincoln*, 3:479.

16 Kenneth J. Winkle, "'Paradox Though It May Seem': Lincoln on Antislavery, Race, and Union, 1837–1860," in Brian R. Dirck, ed., *Lincoln Emancipated: The President and the Politics of Race* (DeKalb: Northern Illinois University Press, 2007), 19.

17 Richard Hart, *Lincoln's Springfield: The Early African American Population of Springfield, Illinois, 1818-1861*, Spring Creek Series (Springfield: the author, 2008), 1. http://abrahamlincolnassociation.org/wp-content/uploads /2019/01/THE-EARLY-BLACK-POPULATION-April-23-2008-am.pdf. See also Hart, "Springfield's African Americans as a Part of the Lincoln Community," *Journal of the Abraham Lincoln Association* 20 (1999): 35–54.

18   Randall Kennedy, *Nigger: The Strange Career of a Troublesome Word* (New York: Pantheon, 2002), 51–52, 54, 95–96, 117; Kennedy, "A Note On The Word 'Nigger,'" *Harpweek*, http://www.abrahamlincolncartoons.info/Sub Pages/Warning.php.

19   John McWhorter, *Nine Nasty Words: English in the Gutter, Then, Now, and Forever* (New York: Avery, 2021), 173.

20   David Sutcliffe, "Gone with the Wind? Evidence for 19th Century African American Speech," *Links and Letters* (1998): 127–145. In 2021, Thuso Mbedu, a Black actress who portrayed Cora in a television series (*The Underground Railroad*) said, "One major thing that shifted my approach to Cora was audio testimonials of formerly enslaved people. . . . What fascinated me was how they sounded. When they speak in movies, they have a very fluent English that we can easily understand. But in the tapes, they spoke a very broken English. What really jarred me was that the English that they spoke is an English that certain Black people speak even today in parts of South Africa." *Wall Street Journal,* 13 May 2021.

CHAPTER 1

1   Arna Bontemps and Robert Lucas, "Lincoln and the Negro," in Brian Dolinar, ed., *The Negro in Illinois: The WPA Papers* (Urbana: University of Illinois Press, 2013), 38. Their essay was written during the New Deal of Franklin Roosevelt and first published in this volume.

2   In 1850, only 146 of the city's 5,106 residents were Black.

3   Richard Hart and Bonnie Paull, *Lincoln's Springfield Neighborhood* (Charleston, S.C.: History Press, 2015), 92.

4   Richard Hart, "Lincoln's Springfield: The Underground Railroad," 2006. https://abrahamlincolnassociation.org/wp-content/uploads/2019/01/SCHS -Underground-Railroad-2012-1.pdf.

5   Hart and Paull, *Lincoln's Springfield Neighborhood,* 94–98. Black Baptists planning to establish schools throughout Illinois with the help of the state objected to the Springfielders' approach. *Illinois State Journal* (Springfield), 22 November 1852. These actions cast doubt on historian Michael Vorenberg's speculation that before "becoming president, Lincoln probably was skeptical of African-Americans' desire for education."

Vorenberg, "Slavery Reparations in Theory and Practice," in Dirck, *Lincoln Emancipated*, 125.

6   Wayne C. Temple, "Mariah (Bartlett) Vance, Daytime Servant to the Lincolns," *For the People: A Newsletter of the Abraham Lincoln Association*, vol. 6 (2004) and vol. 7 (2005); Hart and Paull, *Lincoln's Springfield Neighborhood*, 103–107. Another Black near-neighbor was Jane Pellum, an elderly woman known as "Aunt Jane." The mother-in-law of Jameson Jenkins, she lived with the Jenkins family half a block down the street from the Lincolns, for whom she worked as a laundress.

7   James O. Hall, review of *Lincoln's Unknown Private Life: An Oral History by His Black Housekeeper Mariah Vance, 1850–1860* by Lloyd Ostendorf and Walter Oleksky, *Journal of the Abraham Lincoln Association* 19 (1998): 73–95. https://www.jstor.org/stable/20148965.

8   *Illinois State Journal* (Springfield), 13 July 1903.

9   Jason Emerson, *Giant in the Shadows: The Life of Robert T. Lincoln* (Carbondale: Southern Illinois University Press, 2012), 347, 529n49.

10 *St. Louis Post Dispatch*, 25 November 1894.

11 For biographical sketches of Brown, see Hart and Paull, *Lincoln's Springfield Neighborhood*, 107–108; *History of Sangamon County, Illinois* (Chicago: Inter-State Publishing Company, 1881), 736.

12 Reminiscences of Dr. William G. Ralston as reported by Frank A. Myers, *Evansville Courier and Press*, 19 September 1909, p. 6; Mrs. Ida McFarland, interviewed by Agnes Lynch, *Chicago Tribune*, 8 February 1953, section 3, p. 7; *Illinois State Journal* (Springfield), 4 September 1906, p. 6.

13 W. T. Casey, "History of the Colored People in Sangamon County," in *Directory of Sangamon County's Colored Citizens: A History of the Negro in Sangamon County* (Springfield: Springfield Directory Company, 1926), 15.

14 *Proceedings of the First Convention of the Colored Citizens of the State of Illinois, Convened at the City of Chicago, Thursday, Friday and Saturday, October 6th, 7th and 8th, 1853*, https://omeka.coloredconventions.org /items/show/261.

15 Reminiscences of Dr. William G. Ralston as reported by Frank A. Myers, *Evansville Courier and Press*, 19 September 1909, p. 6; Mrs. Ida McFarland, interviewed by Agnes Lynch, *Chicago Tribune*, 8 February 1953, section 3, p. 7; *Illinois State Journal* (Springfield), 4 September 1906, p. 6.

16 Mrs. Ida McFarland, interviewed by Agnes Lynch, *Chicago Tribune*, 8 February 1953, section 3, p. 7.

17 Reminiscences of Dr. William G. Ralston as reported by Frank A. Myers, *Evansville Courier and Press*, 19 September 1909, p. 6.

18 *Illinois Weekly State Journal* (Springfield), 22 August 1849.

19 Mrs. Phoebe Duncan in Bruce Catton, "Colored Barber Was Lincoln's Confidant," *Evansville Courier and Press*, 12 February 1930, p. 9.

20 John E. Washington, *They Knew Lincoln,* ed. Kate Masur (1942; New York: Oxford University Press, 2018), 183–201; Gossie Harold Hudson, "William Florville, Lincoln's Barber and Friend," *Negro History Bulletin* 37 (1974): 279–281; Lloyd Ostendorf, "The Story of William Florville, Mr. Lincoln's Barber," *Lincoln Herald* 79 (1977): 29–32; John Carroll Power, *Early Settlers of Sangamon County* (1876), 302; *History of Sangamon County, Illinois* (1881), 736; Bontemps and Lucas, "Lincoln and the Negro," 37–39.

21 *Florville v. Allin et al.* (1853) and *Florville v. Stockdale et al.* (1849). See Brian R. Dirck, "Lincoln, the Law, and Race," *Lincoln Lore*, no. 1900 (2012): 10–16.

22 William Florville to Lincoln, Springfield, 27 December 1863, Lincoln Papers, Library of Congress.

23 Bruce Catton, "Colored Barber Was Lincoln's Confidant," *Evansville Courier and Press*, 12 February 1930, p. 9.

24 *Illinois Weekly State Journal* (Springfield), 25 May 1848.

25 *The Impartial Citizen* (Syracuse), 17 September 1851.

26 *Illinois State Journal* (Springfield), 17 January 1851.

27 *Minutes of the Illinois Baptist Pastoral Union of Illinois* (Alton: Telegraph Book and Job Office, 1852), 9.

28 *Illinois State Journal* (Springfield), 18 February 1858. As Richard Hart has noted, these resolutions belie the assertion of Lincoln biographer David Herbert Donald, who claimed that African Americans in Springfield "were not people who could speak out boldly to say that they were as American as any whites, that they had no African roots, and that they did not want to leave the United States." Donald, *Lincoln* (New York: Simon and Schuster, 1995), 16; Hart, "Springfield's African Americans as a Part of the Lincoln Community," *Journal of the Abraham Lincoln Association* 20 (1999): 35–54, http://hdl.handle.net/2027/spo.2629860.0020.

29 Bloomington, Illinois, correspondence by W. J. Davis, 10 March 1863, *Christian Recorder* (Philadelphia), 21 March 1863. In 1887, the *Chicago Tribune* reported that "Elder Davis is well known in Chicago, where he has preached a great deal, being the founder of Bethany Chapel in Third avenue. He is now an elder in Peoria. He was born seventy years ago in Bourbon County, Kentucky, and was manumitted by his master in 1833 and taken to Indiana. He has been preaching for forty-six years, and is a typical colored minister of the old school. He preached in Chicago as early as 1854, and his ministry has been confined to Indiana and Illinois." *Chicago Tribune,* 1 August 1887.

30 See Matthew Norman, "The Other Lincoln-Douglas Debate: The Race Issue in a Comparative Context," *Journal of the Abraham Lincoln Association* 31 (2010): 1–21.

31 Paul Simon, *Lincoln's Preparation for Greatness: The Illinois Legislative Years* (Urbana: University of Illinois Press, 1965), 135; *House Journal, 1839–40,* p. 323 (2 February 1839).

32 Basler, ed., *Collected Works of Lincoln*, 2:264.

33 *The Liberator* (Boston), 13 July 1860; Orville A. Hitchcock and Ota Thomas Reynolds, "Ford Douglass' Fourth of July Oration, 1860," in J. Jeffery Auer, ed., *Antislavery and Disunion, 1858–1861: Studies in the Rhetoric of Compromise and Conflict* (New York: Harper & Row, 1963), 133–151.

34 *Boston Daily Advertiser*, 14 August 1860; speech of 23 September 1860, New Lisbon, Ohio, *Anti-Slavery Bugle*, 6 October 1860.

35 Speech of Trumbull in Chicago, 7 August 1858, *Anamosa* (Iowa) *Eureka*, 3 September 1858.

36 Mark E. Neely, Jr., "Lincoln's Springfield Friends: Friends of the Negro," *Lincoln Lore* no. 1699 (September 1979): 1–3.

37 Winkle, "'Paradox Though It May Seem,'" 18.

38 *New York Independent*, n.d., copied in the San Francisco *Daily Evening Bulletin*, 16 May 1868; "The Repeal Bill: Speech of the Hon. Anson S. Miller, of Winnebago County," *Springfield Sangamo Journal*, 3 April 1845.

39 Speech of 12 June 1857 in Springfield, *New York Herald*, 3 July 1857.

40 *Chicago Tribune*, 24 September 1857.

41 Decatur correspondence, 1 October, *Chicago Tribune*, 2 October 1863.

42 Basler et al., eds., *The Collected Works of Abraham Lincoln* (8 vols. plus index; New Brunswick, N. J.: Rutgers University Press, 1953–1955), 2:546–547. Emphasis added.

43 Reynolds, *Abe: Abraham Lincoln in His Times* (New York: Penguin Press, 2020), 514–515.

44 Speech in Chicago, 10 July 1858, in Basler, ed., *Collected Works of Lincoln*, 2:484–502. This statement casts doubt on Eric Foner's contention that even though Lincoln "may not have embraced racism," nonetheless "he did not condemn it." Eric Foner, *The Fiery Trial: Abraham Lincoln and American Slavery* (New York: W. W. Norton, 2010), 122.

45 David R. Locke in Allen Thorndike Rice, ed., *Reminiscences of Abraham Lincoln by Distinguished Men of His Time* (New York: North American Publishing Company, 1886), 446–447.

46 *Illinois State Register* (Springfield), 27 September 1858.

47 *Ottawa Little Giant*, 22 September 1858, in C. C. Tisler and Aleita G. Tisler, "Lincoln Was Here for Another Go at Douglas" (pamphlet; Jackson, Tennessee: McCowat-Mercer Press, 1958), 52.

48 Basler, ed., *Collected Works of Lincoln*, 3:56 (debate at Freeport, 27 August 1858).

49 *Douglass' Monthly*, March 1859, p. 40; H. Ford Douglas, speech at Framingham, Massachusetts, 4 July 1860, *The Liberator* (Boston), 13 July 1860. See Robert L. Harris, Jr., "H. Ford Douglas: Afro-American Antislavery Emigrationist," *Journal of Negro History* 62 (1977): 225–226.

50 Speech at Framingham, Massachusetts, 4 July 1860, *The Liberator* (Boston), 13 July 1860; *New York Herald*, 8 July 1860; Boston correspondence, 7 July, *New York Tribune*, 9 July 1860.

51 Speech on 23 September 1860, New Lisbon, Ohio, *Anti-Slavery Bugle*, 6 October 1860; John Stauffer, "Fear and Doubt in Cleveland," *New York Times*, 22 December 2010.

52 Wendell Phillips Garrison et al., *William Lloyd Garrison, 1805–1879: The Story of His Life Told by His Children* (4 vols.; New York: Century, 1885–1889), 3:483.

53 Douglas to Frederick Douglass, 8 January 1863, *Douglass' Monthly*, February 1863.

54   Harris, "H. Ford Douglas," 230–234.

55   J. G. Holland, *The Life of Abraham Lincoln* (Springfield, Mass.: G. Bill, 1866), 128.

56   Charles M. Segal, "Lincoln, Benjamin Jonas and the Black Code," *Journal of the Illinois State Historical Society* 46 (1953): 277–282.

57   *The Christian Recorder* (Philadelphia), 6 January 1898. The details of this obituary are verifiable except for this passage.

58   Article by Linda Hanabarger, *Vandalia Leader-Union*, 19 January 2017.

59   Newton N. Newborn, "Judicial Decision Making and the End of Slavery in Illinois," *Journal of the Illinois State Historical Society* 98 (2005): 10. I am grateful to historian Roger Bridges for calling Mary Brown's obituary to my attention, and to genealogist Kathy Lupton for sharing information about Mrs. Brown.

60   Carl Adams, "Lincoln's First Freed Slave: A Review of *Bailey v. Cromwell*, 1841," *Journal of the Illinois State Historical Society* 101 (2008): 235–259; Carl Adams, *Nance: Trials of the First Slave Freed by Abraham Lincoln: A True Story of Mrs. Nance Legins–Costley* (North Pekin, Illinois: n.p., 2016).

61   Illinois Supreme Court, David Bailey, appellant, *v.* William Cromwell et al., administrators of Nathan Cromwell, deceased, appellees, *Bailey v. Cromwell*, 4 Ill. 71, 3 Scam. 71 (1841).

62   For a summary of the case, see Mark E. Steiner, *An Honest Calling: The Law Practice of Abraham Lincoln* (DeKalb: Northern Illinois University Press, 2006), 103-136; "In Re Bryant et al.: Matson for the Use of Coles County, Illinois v. Rutherford," in *The Papers of Abraham Lincoln: Legal Documents and Cases*, ed. Daniel W. Stowell, John A. Lupton, et al. (4 vols.; Charlottesville: University of Virginia Press, 2008), 2:1–43.

63   Albert A. Woldman, *Lawyer Lincoln* (Boston: Houghton, Mifflin, 1937), 56; John J. Duff, *A. Lincoln: Prairie Lawyer* (New York: Holt, Rinehart and Winston, 1960), 144; Paul M. Angle's comment in his edition of Henry C. Whitney, *Life on the Circuit with Lincoln* (Caldwell, Idaho: Caxton, 1940), 315n4.

64   George Sharswood, *A Compend of Lectures on the Aims and Duties of the Profession of Law* (Philadelphia: Johnson, 1854), 26, quoted in Steiner, *An Honest Calling*, 133. Several other legal authorities made the same argument. Ibid., 133–136.

65 Charles R. McKirdy, *Lincoln Apostate: The Matson Slave Trial* (Jackson: University Press of Mississippi, 2011), 96–102.

66 Egbert Viele, "A Trip with Lincoln, Chase, and Stanton," *Scribner's Monthly*, September 1878, 818.

67 Basler, ed., *Collected Works of Lincoln*, 3:29.

68 Orlando B. Ficklin, "Gen. Usher F. Linder," Charleston, Illinois, *Courier*, 15 January 1885, copied in the *Tuscola/Illinois Review*, 7 September 1922.

69 John W. Bunn, statement for Jesse W. Weik, *The Real Lincoln: A Portrait*, ed. Michael Burlingame (Lincoln: University of Nebraska Press, 2002), 198; first inaugural address, Basler, ed., *Collected Works of Lincoln*, 4:264.

70 Kate Masur, *Until Justice Be Done: America's First Civil Rights Movement, from the Revolution to Reconstruction* (New York: W. W. Norton, 2021), 280. Implicit in Lincoln's statement was "an unambiguous endorsement of black citizenship rights that could not be misunderstood," as James Oakes noted. Oakes, *The Crooked Path to Abolition: Abraham Lincoln and the Antislavery Constitution* (New York: W. W. Norton, 2021), 108.

71 They included Marvin Pond, John Randolph Scott, and George Kern.

72 Quarles, *Lincoln and the Negro* (New York: Oxford University Press, 1962), 39, 40.

CHAPTER 2

1 Rosetta Wells in John E. Washington, *They Knew Lincoln* (New York: E. P. Dutton, 1942), 77–78.

2 Keckly interviewed by Smith D. Fry, undated Washington letter, *Lane County Journal* (Dighton, Kansas), 11 July 1901.

3 Washington, *They Knew Lincoln*, 124–125.

4 Ibid., 100–101.

5 William O. Stoddard, *Abraham Lincoln: The True Story of a Great Life* (New York: Fords, Howard, & Hulbert, 1884), 403.

6 Thomas J. McCormack, ed., *Memoirs of Gustave Koerner, 1809–1896* (2 vols.; Cedar Rapids, Iowa: Torch Press, 1909), 2:93–94.

7 Reminiscences of an old settler in Springfield, unidentified newspaper clipping, quoted in a memo in the John J. Duff Papers, box 1, folder 5, Lincoln Presidential Library, Springfield.

8   Mary Lincoln to Mary Brayman, Washington, 17 June 1861, Justin
    G. Turner, Linda Levitt Turner, eds., *Mary Todd Lincoln: Her Life and
    Letters* (New York: Knopf, 1972), 90.

9   *Philadelphia Inquirer*, 22 February 1861.

10 Washington, *They Knew Lincoln*, 128.

11 Audrey Elisa Kerr, *The Paper Bag Principle: Class, Colorism, and Rumor and
    the Case of Black Washington, D.C.* (Knoxville: University of Tennessee
    Press, 2006), 53. For a history of intra-racial discrimination in Washington,
    see ibid., 37–117.

12 Margaret Hunter, "The Persistent Problem of Colorism: Skin Tone, Status,
    and Inequality," *Sociology Compass* 1 (2007): 237–254 (quote on 250).

13 Anna M. Speicher, ed., *The Religious World of Antislavery Women:
    Spirituality in the Lives of Five Abolitionist Lecturers* (New York: Syracuse
    University Press, 2000), 107.

14 Basler, ed., *Collected Works of Lincoln*, 4:277.

15 Lincoln to Welles, Washington, 16 March 1861, *Collected Works of
    Lincoln*, 4:288.

16 Lincoln to Chase, Washington, 29 November 1861, ibid., 5:33.

17 Washington, *They Knew Lincoln*, 131–132.

18 On August 21, 1863, Lincoln also wrote a check for $5 payable to a
    "colored man, with one leg" who, according to biographer Ida Tarbell,
    stopped Lincoln as he was traversing the small park between the White
    House and the War Department and "told him a pitiful story." Ida
    Tarbell, *The Life of Abraham Lincoln* (4 vols.; New York: Lincoln History
    Society, 1924), 3:151; "Lincoln's Bank Checks," *Lincoln Lore* no. 1485
    (November 1961), 1–4.

19 Recommendation, 24 October 1862, Basler, ed., *Collected Works of
    Lincoln*, 5:474.

20 Endorsement, 17 December 1862, on a letter drafted by a staff member to
    John A. Dix, 16 December 1862, Basler, ed., *Collected Works of Lincoln*,
    6:8–9; https://www.christies.com/en/lot/lot-5698208.

21 Washington correspondence, 14 January, *Chicago Tribune*, 19 January 1864.

22 Samuel Wilkeson, "How Mr. Lincoln Indorsed the Negro," *Janesville*
    (Wisconsin) *Gazette*, 23 July 1867.

23 "Shortly after his arrival in the capital, the president referred to the adult Johnson as a 'colored boy,' attaching a belittling racial convention to the man he described as his 'servant.'" Phillip W. Magness and Sebastian Page, "Mr. Lincoln and Mr. Johnson," *New York Times*, 1 February 2012.

24 When a Black man recently sued an employer, alleging that by calling him "boy" the employer showed racial animus, the US Supreme Court, in sending the case back to trial, noted: "The speaker's meaning may depend on various factors including context, tone of voice, local custom and historical usage." R. L. Johnson, "How Racist Is 'Boy'?: It's Always Hard to Say," *The Economist*, 1 November 2010.

25 Washington, *They Knew Lincoln*, 132.

26 David J. Gerleman, "A Good Boy Generally: Abraham Lincoln and Samuel Williams," *Lincoln Editor: The Quarterly Newsletter of the Papers of Abraham Lincoln* 9 (July–September 2009).

27 Lincoln to Salmon P. Chase, Washington, 30 July 1862, Gerleman, "A Good Boy Generally."

28 Samuel Williams to Robert Todd Lincoln, Washington, 28 August 1882, Gerleman, "A Good Boy Generally."

29 Washington, *They Knew Lincoln*, 140–141.

30 Eric S. Yellin, *Racism in the Nation's Service: Government Workers and the Color Line in Woodrow Wilson's America* (Chapel Hill: University of North Carolina Press, 2013), 22.

31 "Black men and women were routinely rejected for federal employment" before Lincoln took office. Jacqueline Jones, *American Work: Four Centuries of Black and White Labor* (New York: W.W. Norton, 1998), 259.

32 "Ethiop" [William J. Wilson] to James McCune Smith, Washington, n.d., New York *Anglo-African*, 5 September 1863, https://civilwardc.org/texts /letters/cww.02507.html.

33 Philip F. Rubio, *There's Always Work at the Post Office: African American Postal Workers and the Fight for Jobs, Justice, and Equality* (Chapel Hill: University of North Carolina Press, 2010), 20.

34 Washington correspondence by Benjamin: Perley Poore, 15 March, *Boston Journal*, 17 March 1868; San Francisco correspondence by

W. H. Yates, a near-relative of Slade, 25 March, *San Francisco Elevator*, 27 March 1868.

35 Natalie Sweet, "A Representative 'of Our People': The Agency of William Slade, Leader in the African American Community and Usher to Abraham Lincoln," *Journal of the Abraham Lincoln Association* 34 (2013): 21–41.

36 Edward D. Neill, *Reminiscences of the Last Year of President Lincoln's Life* (paper presented to the Minnesota Commandery of the Military Order of the Loyal Legion, February 1885), 16; Washington correspondence by Benjamin: Perley Poore, 15 March, *Boston Journal*, 17 March 1868.

37 Washington, *They Knew Lincoln*, 108–111, 235, 107.

38 Ibid., 108–109.

39 San Francisco correspondence by W. H. Yates, 25 March, San Francisco *Elevator*, 27 March 1868.

40 Ibid.; Sweet, "A Representative 'of Our People,'" *passim*.

41 Paul E. Sluby and Stanton L. Wormley Jr., *History of the Columbian Harmony Society and of Harmony Cemetery, Washington D.C.* (Washington: Columbian Harmony Society, 2001), 9, 13, 15.

42 Anna L. Boyden, *Echoes from Hospital and White House: A Record of Mrs. Rebecca R. Pomroy's Experience in War-Times* (Boston: D. Lothrop, 1884), 94–98.

43 Marquis de Chambrun, "Personal Recollections of Mr. Lincoln," *Scribner's Magazine*, January 1893, 28.

44 Washington, *They Knew Lincoln*, 84–87.

45 Richard Wightman Fox, "'A Death–shock to Chivalry, and a Mortal Wound to Caste': The Story of Tad and Abraham Lincoln in Richmond," *Journal of the Abraham Lincoln Association* 33 (2012): 1–19.

46 Charles Carleton Coffin, "Late Scenes in Richmond," *Atlantic Monthly*, June 1865, 754–755.

47 Coffin in Rice, *Reminiscences of Lincoln*, 179–181; Coffin, *Abraham Lincoln* (New York: Harper & brothers, 1893), 193; Richmond correspondence by Coffin in the *Boston Journal*, n.d., *Littell's Living Age*, 85:138 (8 April 1865). New Hampshire-born Charles Carleton Coffin was "an ardent friend of the slaves." According to a biographer, Coffin at the age of twelve "became an ardent abolitionist" and "read the *Liberator, Herald of Freedom, Emancipator* and all the anti-slavery tracts and pamphlets which he could get hold

of. In his bedroom, he had hanging on the wall the picture of a negro in chains. The last thing he saw at night, and the first that met his eyes in the morning, was this picture [of an enslaved Black man], with the words, 'Am I not a man and a brother?'" William Elliott Griffis, *Charles Carleton Coffin: War Correspondent, Traveler, Author, and Statesman* (Boston: Estes and Lauriat, 1898), 35.

48 Richmond correspondence, 6 April 1865, in R. J. M. Blackett, ed., *Thomas Morris Chester, Black Civil War Correspondent: His Dispatches from the Virginia Front* (Baton Rouge: Louisiana State University Press, 1989), 294.

49 David D. Porter, *Incidents and Anecdotes of the Civil War* (New York: D. Appleton, 1885), 295.

50 Coffin, *Lincoln*, 505; Richmond correspondence by Coffin in the Boston *Journal*, n.d., *Littell's Living Age*, 85:138 (8 April 1865).

51 John S. Barnes, "With Lincoln from Washington to Richmond in 1865," *Appleton's Magazine*, May 1907, 748; diary of Lelian Cook, 4 April 1865, Richmond *News Leader*, 3 April 1935, p. 2.

52 W. W. Clemens to his father, Richmond [4 April 1865], transcription, http ://www.civilwarsignals.org/brown/signalmen/williamclemensletters2.pdf, p. 98.

53 Coffin in Rice, ed., *Reminiscences of Lincoln*, 182; Richmond correspondence by Coffin in the *Boston Journal*, n.d., *Littell's Living Age*, 85:138 (8 April 1865).

54 Coffin, "Late Scenes in Richmond," *Atlantic Monthly*, June 1865, 755; Coffin, *Four Years of Fighting: A Volume of Personal Observation with the Army and Navy, from the First Battle of Bull Run to the Fall of Richmond* (Boston: Ticknor and Fields, 1866), 512.

55 Coffin, "Late Scenes in Richmond," *Atlantic Monthly*, June 1865, 755.

56 Charles Carleton Coffin to Thomas Nast, 19 July 1866, reprinted in *The Moorsfield Antiquarian*, vol. 1 (1937): 26–28.

57 Richmond correspondence by Coffin in the *Boston Journal*, n.d., *Littell's Living Age*, 85:138 (8 April 1865).

58 Reminiscences of August Kautz, *Washington National Tribune*, 10 May 1888.

59 Richmond correspondence, 6 April 1865, in Blackett, ed., *Thomas Morris Chester*, 295.

60 Diary of Mrs. Thomas Walker Doswell (Mrs. Francis Anne Sutton), entry for 4 April 1865, library.thinkquest.org/J0113361/diary.htm.

61 Samuel Henry Roberts to Harvey Roberts, Headquarters of the 3rd brigade, 2nd division, 24th Army Corps, Richmond, 16 April 1865, photocopy in the Samuel Henry Roberts Papers, Virginia Historical Society.

62 Shepley, "Incidents of the Capture of Richmond," *Atlantic Monthly* 46 (July 1880): 28.

63 Porter, *Incidents and Anecdotes*, 295.

64 *Richmond News Leader*, 3 April 1935, p. 2.

65 Washington correspondence, 2 November, *Sacramento Daily Union*, 2 December 1864, in Michael Burlingame, ed., *Lincoln Observed: Civil War Dispatches of Noah Brooks* (Baltimore: Johns Hopkins University Press, 1998), 142.

66 Vorenberg, "Slavery Reparations in Theory and Practice," 127.

67 Lincoln to Banks, Washington, 5 August 1863, Basler, ed., *Collected Works of Lincoln,* 6:365.

68 Lincoln to the people of Sangamo County, 9 March 1832, *Collected Works of Lincoln,* 1:8.

69 Horace Porter, *Campaigning with Grant* (New York: Century, 1897), 217–20.

70 Sylvanus Cadwallader, *Three Years with Grant*, ed. Benjamin P. Thomas (New York: Knopf, 1955), 233.

71 Horace Porter to his wife, City Point, 24 June 1864, Porter Papers, Library of Congress; Porter, *Campaigning with Grant*, 219–220.

72 Badeau to Edwin Booth, 27 June 1864, in Ron Chernow, *Grant* (New York: Penguin, 2017), 416.

73 Horace Porter to his wife, City Point, 24 June 1864, Porter Papers, Library of Congress; Porter, *Campaigning with Grant*, 219–220.

74 Coffin, *The Boys of '61; or, Four Years of Fighting* (Boston: Estes and Lauriat, 1885), 313.

75 William O. Stoddard, "White House Sketches No. 7," *New York Citizen*, 29 September 1866, in Stoddard, *Inside the White House in War Times: Memoirs and Reports of Lincoln's Secretary*, ed. Michael Burlingame (1890; Lincoln: University of Nebraska Press, 2000), 173.

76 Vorenberg, "Slavery Reparations in Theory and Practice," 126.

77 As Clarence Lusane, a political scientist at Howard University, noted, "political access to the White House had been extended to the black

community for the first time in U.S. history" during Lincoln's presidency, and that included not only prominent people like Frederick Douglass, Martin Delany, and Sojourner Truth, but also "many lesser-known activists and ordinary African Americans" who "met with him there as well. The significance of these encounters cannot be overstated." The "multiracial space that Lincoln opened would be a critical new element in the ongoing struggle for black freedom and equality." Lusane, *The Black History of the White House* (San Francisco: City Lights Books, 2011), 198.

CHAPTER 3

1   In the 1820s, abolitionist pioneer Benjamin Lundy had included colonization in his multipronged attack on slavery. "Abolitionists who came along later would repudiate colonization, whether voluntary or involuntary, because of the increasingly racist cast of the American Colonization Society. But in Lundy's mind, colonization was part of a larger antiracist project, which was in turn part of a still broader antislavery project." Oakes, *Crooked Path to Abolition*, 61.

2   Lerone Bennett, *Forced Into Glory: Abraham Lincoln's White Dream* (Chicago: Johnson Publishing, 2000), 465, 507, 516; Eric Foner, "The Education of Abraham Lincoln," *New York Times Book Review*, 10 February 2002.

3   See P. J. Staudenraus, *The African Colonization Movement, 1816–1865* (New York: Columbia University Press, 1961); Eric Burin, *Slavery and the Peculiar Solution: A History of the American Colonization Society* (Gainesville: University Press of Florida, 2005); Beverly C. Tomek, *Colonization and its Discontents: Emancipation, Emigration, and Antislavery in Antebellum Pennsylvania* (New York: New York University Press, 2011); Beverly C. Tomek and Matthew J. Hetrick, eds., *New Directions in the Study of African American Recolonization* (Gainesville: University Press of Florida, 2017); Hugh Davis, *Leonard Bacon: New England Reformer and Antislavery Moderate* (Baton Rouge: Louisiana State University Press, 1998).

4   Foner, *Fiery Trial,* 260.

5   John T. Morse, ed., *Dairy of Gideon Welles, Secretary of the Navy under Lincoln and Johnson* (3 vols.; Boston: Houghton Mifflin, 1911), 1:152 (entry

for 26 September 1862). This passage was not in the original diary but added later by Welles.

6   "Lincoln supported colonization because he thought most white Americans were not prepared to accept blacks as equals and fellow citizens, and he saw no other way to solve the problem of slavery." The "burden for Lincoln critics is to show how policies of emancipation and equal citizenship for all blacks could have become public law in the middle of the nineteenth century in any way other than that achieved by Abraham Lincoln." Thomas L. Krannawitter, *Vindicating Lincoln: Defending the Politics of Our Greatest President* (Lanham, Maryland: Rowman & Littlefield, 2008), 35. That burden of proof is not met by the more emphatic critics of Lincoln's colonization policies like Lerone Bennett in *Forced into Glory.* See appendix to this volume.

7   Oakes, *Crooked Path to Abolition*, 108.

8   Springfield correspondence, 4 January 1855, St. Louis *Missouri Republican*, 8 January 1855.

9   Richard J. Hinton, "An Interview with Abraham Lincoln," photocopy of an unidentified clipping in the vertical files of the Abraham Lincoln Presidential Library, Springfield, folder marked "Memoirs," reproduced in *For the People: A Newsletter of the Abraham Lincoln Association*, March 2020, p. 1.

10   Basler, ed., *Collected Works of Lincoln*, 3:356–363.

11   James Finley to Ralph R. Gurley, 14 August 1856, Letters Received, American Colonization Society Papers, Manuscript Division, Library of Congress.

12   Mark E. Steiner, *Lincoln and Citizenship* (Carbondale: Southern Illinois University Press, 2021), 40–45. Michael Lind wrongly asserted that during "the 1830s and 1840s, while he campaigned for tariffs, canals and railroads, and a national bank, he supported colonization." Michael Lind, *What Lincoln Believed: The Values and Convictions of America's Greatest President* (New York: Doubleday, 2004), 114.

13   Basler, ed., *Collected Works of Lincoln*, 2:132.

14   Ibid., 5:520.

15   Ibid., 2:255.

16   Tom W. Shick, *Behold the Promised Land: A History of Afro-American Settler Society in Nineteenth-Century Liberia* (Baltimore: Johns Hopkins University Press, 1980).

17   Basler, ed., *Collected Works of Lincoln*, 2:256.

18   Reynolds, *Abe*, 356.

19   Basler, ed., *Collected Works of Lincoln*, 2:410.

20   Ibid., 2:299.

21   Ibid., 5:48.

22   James D. Richardson, ed., *A Compilation of the Messages and Papers of the Presidents* (New York: Bureau of National Literature, 1897), 3297.

23   Willis Boyd, "Negro Colonization in the National Crisis, 1860–1870" (Ph.D. dissertation, UCLA, 1953), 144.

24   Ira Berlin, et al., eds., *Freedom: A Documentary History of Emancipation 1861–1867, The Wartime Genesis of Free Labor: The Upper South* (Cambridge: Cambridge University Press, 1993), 265.

25   Boston correspondence, 21 April, *London Daily News,* 7 May 1862.

26   *Congressional Globe,* 37th Congress, 2nd session, 1468 (1 April 1862).

27   Basler, ed., *Collected Works of Lincoln*, 5:534–535.

28   V. Jacque Voegeli, "A Rejected Alternative: Union Policy and the Relocation of Southern 'Contrabands' at the Dawn of Emancipation," *Journal of Southern History* 69 (2003): 788.

29   Bruce Tap, "Race, Rhetoric, and Emancipation: The Election of 1862 in Illinois," *Civil War History* 39 (1993): 101–125; Bruce S. Allardice, "'Illinois is Rotten with Traitors!': The Republican Defeat in the 1862 State Election," *Journal of Illinois State Historical Society* 104 (2011): 97–114.

30   Voegeli, "A Rejected Alternative," 765–790.

31   Sheldon H. Harris, *Paul Cuffe: Black America and the African Return* (New York: Simon and Schuster, 1971), 57–60; Daniel Alexander Payne, *Recollections of Seventy Years* (Nashville, Tennessee: Publishing House of the A.M.E. Sunday School Union, 1888), 148.

32   Washington *National Republican*, 30 April 1862.

33   *New York Age*, 22 June 1911.

34   Lincoln to Greeley, Washington, 24 March 1862, Basler, ed., *Collected Works of Lincoln*, 5:169.

35   Michael J. Katz, "Emancipation in the Federal City," *Civil War History* 24 (1978): 250–267.

36   This poison pill amendment was introduced by Kentucky Senator Garrett Davis. William C. Harris, *Lincoln and Congress* (Carbondale: Southern Illinois University Press, 2017), 36.

37   *Baltimore News-American*, n.d., copied in the *Chicago Times*, 18 April 1862.

38   Crisfield to his wife, Washington, 25 April 1862, Crisfield Papers, Maryland Historical Society.

39   Theodore Calvin Pease and James G. Randall, eds., *The Diary of Orville Hickman Browning* (2 vols.; Springfield: Trustees of the Illinois State Historical Library, 1925–1933), 1:541 (entry for 14 April 1862).

40   Basler, ed., *Collected Works of Lincoln*, 5:192.

41   Francis F. Browne, *The Every-Day Life of Abraham Lincoln* (2nd ed.; Chicago: Browne & Howell, 1913), 421.

42   Speech at Freeport, Illinois, 27 August 1858, Basler, ed., *Collected Works of Lincoln*, 3:41–42.

43   Washington correspondence, 16 April 1862, *New York Times*, 17 April 1862; Washington correspondence, 16 April 1862, *Chicago Times*, 22 April 1862.

44   Payne, *Recollections*, 146–148.

45   Washington correspondence by "Sacer," n.d., *Christian Recorder* (Philadelphia), 26 April 1862.

46   Washington correspondence, 16 April 1862, *New York Times*, 17 April 1862; Washington correspondence, 16 April 1862, *Chicago Times*, 22 April 1862.

47   New York *Anglo-African*, n.d., copied in the San Francisco *Pacific Appeal*, 12 July 1862.

48   James M. McPherson, ed., *The Negro's Civil War: How American Negroes Felt and Acted during the War for the Union* (New York: Pantheon Books, 1965), 45; New York *Anglo-African*, 22 March 1862.

49   *Stanford Encyclopedia of Philosophy* (2011), https://plato.stanford.edu/entries /alexander-crummell.

50   Sarah J. Hale, ed., *Liberia; or, Mr. Peyton's Experiments* (New York: Harper & brothers, 1853), 272; *New York Evening Post*, 1 April 1862.

51   Lincoln to Crummell and Johnson, Washington, 5 May 1862, *Boston Herald* [ca. 11 May 1862], photocopy in Phillip W. Magness, "Lincoln and Colonization," https://www.essentialcivilwarcurriculum.com/lincoln-and -colonization.html.

52   These were, according to Johnson, his instructions from the Liberian government. *New York Evening Post*, 1 April 1862.

53   Quarles, *Lincoln and the Negro*, 110.

CHAPTER 4

1   Kate Masur, "The African American Delegation to Abraham Lincoln: A Reappraisal," *Civil War History* 56 (2010): 117–144.

2   The most notable example of such criticism is found in Bennett, *Forced into Glory*. For a philosopher's refutation of Bennet's argument, see Thomas L. Carson, *Lincoln's Ethics* (New York: Cambridge University Press, 2015), 98–106. For more recent criticism of Lincoln's meeting with five leaders of Washington's Black community, see Nikole Hannah-Jones, "America Wasn't a Democracy Until Black Americans Made It One," *New York Times Magazine*, 14 August 2019.

3   Many prominent historians objected to journalist Hannah-Jones's reading of Lincoln's remarks, among her other interpretations of American history. See David North and Thomas Mackaman, eds., *The New York Times' 1619 Project and the Racialist Falsification of History* (Oak Park, Michigan: Mehring Books, 2021); Phillip Magness, *The 1619 Project: A Critique* (n.p.: American Institute for Economic Research, 2020); Peter W. Wood, *1620: A Critical Response to the 1619 Project* (New York: Encounter Books, 2020).

4   Richard J. M. Blackett, *The Captive's Quest for Freedom: Resistance to the 1850 Fugitive Slave Law* (New York: Cambridge University Press, 2017), 107–111.

5   Reminiscences of James Mitchell, Atlanta, Georgia, correspondence, 22 August 1894, *St. Louis Globe-Democrat*, 26 August 1894.

6   Smith to Lincoln, Washington, 5 May 1862, Lincoln Papers, Library of Congress.

7   Mitchell to Lincoln, Washington, 18 May 1862, printed as a pamphlet, *Letter on the Relation of the White and African Races in the United States, Showing the Necessity of the Colonization of the Latter, Addressed to the President of the U.S.* (Washington: Government Printing Office, 1862); Mitchell to Lincoln, Jeffersonville, Indiana, 13 December 1861, Lincoln Papers, Library of Congress.

8   Reminiscences of James Mitchell, Atlanta, Georgia, correspondence, 22 August 1894, *St. Louis Globe-Democrat*, 26 August 1894.

9   Benjamin Quarles, *Black Abolitionists* (New York: Da Capo Press, 1969), 4–8.

10 Washington correspondence, 9 August 1862, New York *Anglo-African*, n.d., copied in the San Francisco *Pacific Appeal*, 13 September 1862.

11 Lincoln to Greeley, Washington, 22 August 1862, Basler, ed., *Collected Works of Lincoln*, 5:388–389.

12 Ibid., 5:534–536.

13 Speed to Lincoln, Louisville, 3 September 1861, Lincoln Papers, Library of Congress.

14 Adams S. Hill to Sydney Howard Gay, Washington, 25 August 1862, Gay Papers, Columbia University.

15 Basler, ed., *Collected Works of Lincoln*, 5:318.

16 Usher to Lincoln, Washington, 2 August 1862, Lincoln Papers, Library of Congress.

17 *Congressional Globe*, 37th Congress, 2nd session, appendix, 98 (11 April 1862).

18 Charles N. Schaeffer to Edward McPherson, Gettysburg, 6 December 1861, McPherson Papers, Library of Congress.

19 McPherson, ed., *Negro's Civil War*, 77.

20 Eli Nichols to John Sherman, New Castle, Ohio, 20 January 1862, John Sherman Papers, Library of Congress.

21 William Davis Gallagher to Chase, St. Louis, 12 February 1862, Chase Papers, Historical Society of Pennsylvania.

22 Senate speech of 18 January 1860, Albert Gallatin Riddle, *The Life of Benjamin F. Wade* (Cleveland: W. W. Williams, 1887), 274–276.

23 Dan R. Tilden to Wade, 27 March 1860, in Robert F. Durden, "The Ambiguous Antislavery Crusade of James S. Pike," *South Carolina Historical Magazine* 56 (1955): 193–194n.

24 Francis P. Blair Sr. to Lincoln, Silver Spring, Maryland, 26 May 1862, Lincoln Papers, Library of Congress.

25 *Congressional Globe*, 37th Congress, 2nd session, 2504 (2 June 1862).

26 Washington correspondence by Frederick Milnes Edge, 16 April 1862, London *Star*, n.d., copied in Edge, *Major-General McClellan and the Campaign on the Yorktown Peninsula* (London: Trubner, 1865), 61.

27 Washington correspondence, 28 September 1862, *Cristian Recorder* (Philadelphia), 4 October 1862, in Jean Lee Cole and Aaron Sheehan-Dean, eds., *Freedom's Witness: The Civil War Correspondence of Henry McNeal Turner* (Morgantown: West Virginia University Press, 2013), 71.

28 Reynolds, *Abe*, 589, 770.

29 *Freedom's Journal* (New York), 14 February 1829, quoted in *The African Repository* 37 (December 1851): 357.

30 Douglass to Samuel Pomeroy, Rochester, 27 August 1862, *New York World*, 3 September 1862. In fact, neither son left the country, for the plan fizzled.

31 Oakes, *Crooked Path to Abolition*, 130.

32 Ibid., 129.

33 Ibid., 107, 110–111.

34 Edward Dicey, *Six Months in the Federal States* (2 vols.; London: Macmillan, 1863), 1:233.

35 Statement of a former slave, the Rev. Mr. Garrison Frazier, Savannah, Georgia, 12 January 1865, *Hartford Courant*, 25 February 1865. When asked if they agreed, eighteen of nineteen of his fellow African American religious leaders said they did.

36 James Redpath, ed., *A Guide to Hayti* (Boston: Haytian Bureau of Emigration, 1861), 172.

37 Martin Delany, *The Condition, Elevation, Emigration, and Destiny of the Colored People of the United States* (1852; n.p.: Outlook Verlag, 2020), 7.

38 Washington *Evening Star*, 27 August 1862.

39 *Springfield* (Massachusetts) *Republican*, 16 August 1862.

40 *The Liberator* (Boston), 15 August 1862.

41 Voegeli, "Rejected Alternative," 771–786.

42 Nicholas Guyatt, "'An Impossible Idea?': The Curious Career of Internal Colonization," *Journal of the Civil War Era* 4 (2014): 245.

43 Garfield to Cox, 25 July 1865, Guyatt, "An Impossible Idea?," 254.

44 In December 1861, the president told Forney: "I want you to sit down and write one of your most careful articles, preparing the American people for the release of Mason and Slidell. I know this is much to ask of you, but it shows my confidence in you, my friend, when I tell you that this course is forced upon us by our peculiar position; and that the good Queen of England is moderating her own angry people, who are as bitter against us as our people are against them. I need say no more." Forney's reminiscence in his weekly paper *Progress: A Mirror for Men and Women* (Philadelphia), 4 September 1884, typed copy, David Rankin Barbee Papers, Georgetown University.

45 Washington correspondence by "Occasional" (John W. Forney), 17 August 1862, *Philadelphia Press*, 18 August 1862.

46 Eugene Berwanger, *The Frontier against Slavery: Western Anti-Negro Prejudice and the Slavery Extension Controversy* (Urbana: University of Illinois Press, 1967), 41; Oakes, *Crooked Path to Abolition*, 127.

47 Springfield correspondence, 4 January, *New York Tribune*, 13 January 1855.

48 Eric Foner, "Lincoln and Colonization," in *Our Lincoln: New Perspectives on Lincoln and His World*, ed. Eric Foner (New York: W.W. Norton, 2008), 166; Steiner, *Lincoln and Citizenship*, 40–45. Allen Guelzo has argued that Lincoln may have been "too passive and acquiescent in the racism around him," but "that is another matter entirely from describing Lincoln as a racist." Though in the 1850s he doubted "that there was much likelihood for civil or political equality for blacks," his "doubts were expressed in terms of the historical circumstances of slavery and the structure of American law, not on some inherent black racial inferiority." Guelzo, "Was Lincoln a Racist?" in Dirck, ed., *Lincoln Emancipated*, xiii, x.

49 Seward to James Shepherd Pike, Washington, 15 February 1864, *Papers Relating to the Foreign Relations of the United States* (8 vols.; Washington Government Printing Office, 1861–1869), 3:310 (emphasis added).

50 Basler, ed., *Collected Works of Lincoln*, 8:332–333.

51 New York *Anglo-African*, n.d., copied in San Francisco *Pacific Appeal*, 20 September 1862.

52 Washington *Daily National Republican*, 15 August 1862.

53 Masur, "African American Delegation," 130–131.

54 *Philadelphia North American*, n.d., copied in the Washington *Daily National Republican*, 18 March 1863; Washington *Evening Star*, 11 April 1863.

55 *Fall River* (Massachusetts) *Daily Evening News*, 20 March 1863.

56 *Washington Critic and Record*, 3 June 1884.

57 Norfolk *Virginian*, 14 June 1869, in Willard B. Gatewood, *Aristocrats of Color: The Black Elite, 1880–1920* (Bloomington: Indiana University Press, 1990), 40.

58 Ibid., 44.

59 *Syracuse Journal*, n.d., copied in *Douglass' Monthly*, September 1862.

60 Paul J. Scheips, "Gabriel Lafond and Ambrose W. Thompson: Neglected Isthmian Promoters," *Hispanic American Historical Review* 36 (1956): 219–228;

Paul J. Scheips, "Lincoln and the Chiriquí Colonization Project," *Journal of Negro History* 38 (1952): 418–453; Sebastian N. Page, "Lincoln and Chiriquí Colonization Revisited," *American Nineteenth Century History* 12 (2011): 289–325; Fredric Bancroft, "Schemes to Colonize Negroes in Central America," in Jacob Cooke, *Frederic Bancroft, Historian* (Norman: University of Oklahoma Press, 1957), 192–227.

61 New York Congressman Charles Baldwin Sedgwick to Gideon Welles, Washington, 7 August 1861, copy, A. W. Thompson Papers, Library of Congress.

62 Ninian W. Edwards to Lincoln, Washington, 10 August 1861, Lincoln Papers, Library of Congress.

63 Charles Roll, *Colonel Dick Thompson: The Persistent Whig* (Indianapolis: Indiana Historical Bureau, 1948), 122–123. Thompson prepared an elaborate, seven-page budget/contract for the Chiriquí project. Undated proposal [1862], Lincoln Papers, Library of Congress.

64 Blair to Lincoln, Silver Spring, Maryland, 16 November 1861, ibid.

65 Chase to Lincoln, Washington, 12 November 1861, ibid.

66 Thompson to Francis P. Blair Sr., Washington, 15 November 1861, Blair-Lee Papers, Princeton University.

67 Lincoln to Chase, Washington, 27 November 1861, Basler, ed., *Collected Works of Abraham Lincoln, First Supplement* (Westport, Conn.: Greenwood Press, 1974), 112.

68 Usher to Richard W. Thompson, Washington, 26 December 1861, Richard W. Thompson Papers, Lincoln Financial Collection, Allen County Public Library, Fort Wayne, Indiana.

69 Smith to Ambrose W. Thompson, Washington, 26 April 1862, Ambrose W. Thompson Papers, Library of Congress.

70 Smith to Lincoln, Washington, 9 and 16 May 1862, copies, ibid.; Edward Jordan to Chase, Washington, 22 March 1862, pamphlet, ibid.; Edward Jordan to A. W. Thompson, Washington, 22 March 1864, copy, ibid.

71 Usher to Lincoln, Washington, 2 August 1862, Lincoln Papers, Library of Congress; Usher to R. W. Thompson, Washington, 25 July 1862, Thompson Papers, Indiana State Library, Indianapolis; Elmo R. Richardson and Alan W. Farley, *John Palmer Usher: Lincoln's Secretary of Interior* (Lawrence: University of Kansas Press, 1960), 21–23.

72 Mitchell to Lincoln, Washington, 1 July 1862, Lincoln Papers, Library of Congress.

73 Basler, ed., *Collected Works of Lincoln,* 5:372.

74 *The American Baptist* (Utica, New York), 19 August 1862.

75 *Douglass' Monthly,* November 1862.

76 Basler, ed., *Collected Works of Lincoln,* 5:371–372.

77 J. C. Davis et al. to Lincoln, August 1862, *An Appeal from the Colored Men of Philadelphia to the President of the United States* (pamphlet, Philadelphia, 1862), 5–6.

78 Thomas Schoonover, "Misconstrued Mission: Expansionism and Black Colonization in Mexico and Central America during the Civil War," *Pacific Historical Review* 49 (1980): 611–614.

79 Beale, ed., *Welles Diary,* 1:150–51 (entry for 26 September 1862); Paul Scheips, "Buchanan and the Chiriquí Naval Station Sites," *Military Affairs* 18 (1954): 64–80.

80 Ambrose W. Thompson to Richard W. Thompson, New York, 6 October 1862, copy, Ambrose W. Thompson Papers, Library of Congress.

81 Washington correspondence by B. F. M., 15 August, *Cincinnati Gazette,* 20 August 1862.

82 A. B. Dickinson to Seward, Leon de Nicaragua, 12 September 1862, *Message of the President of the United States to Two Houses of Congress at the Commencement of the Third Session of the Thirty-seventh Congress* (Washington: Government Printing Office, 1862), 896.

83 Antonio José de Yrisarri to Seward, Brooklyn, 9 September 1862, ibid., 885.

84 James R. Partridge to Seward, Comayagua, Honduras, 26 August 1862, ibid., 891.

85 Schoonover, "Misconstrued Mission," 613–619; Matthew D. Harris, "Struggle for Sovereignty: An African-American Colonization Attempt and Delicate Independence in Mid-Nineteenth Century Central America," (Master's Thesis, West Virginia University, 2020), https://researchrepository .wvu.edu/etd/7600.

86 Sebastian N. Page, "'A Knife Sharp Enough to Divide Us': William H. Seward, Abraham Lincoln, and Black Colonization," *Diplomatic History* 41 (2017): 362–391; Dicey, *Six Months in the Federal States,* 1:233.

87 Address on Colonization to a Deputation of Blacks, 14 August 1862, Basler, ed., *Collected Works of Lincoln*, 5:370–375.

88 W. W. McLain to R. R. Gurley, Washington, 26 August 1862, American Colonization Society Papers, Library of Congress.

89 "The Colored Conventions Project," https://coloredconventions.org.

90 Richard Blackett, "Martin R. Delany and Robert Campbell: Black Americans in Search of an African Colony," *Journal of Negro History* 62 (1977): 1–25; Martin R. Delany et al., "Political Destiny of the Colored Race on the American Continent," appendix 3 in *Report of the Select Committee on Emancipation and Colonization*, 37–59; David M. Dean, *Defender of the Race: James Theodore Holly, Black Nationalist Bishop* (Boston: Lambeth Press, 1979).

91 Alton, Illinois, *Telegraph*, 15 January 1855. For the text of their resolution, see Roger D. Bridges, "Antebellum Struggle for Citizenship," *Journal of the Illinois State Historical Society* 108 (2015): 307.

92 Staudenraus, *African Colonization Movement*, 141.

93 As many as 20,000 African Americans emigrated between 1830 and 1850 and at least another 20,000 did so between 1850 and 1861. Tomek, *Colonization and its Discontents*, 200; James M. McPherson, "Abolitionist and Negro Opposition to Colonization during the Civil War," *Phylon* 26 (1965): 392.

94 Ira Berlin, *Slaves Without Masters: The Free Negro in the Antebellum South* (New York: The New Press, 2007), 356–357.

95 Lott Cary in Marie Tyler-McGraw, *An African Republic: Black and White Virginians in the Making of Liberia* (Chapel Hill: University of North Carolina Press, 2007), 66.

96 Lott Cary, "'Circular Addressed to the Colored Brethren and Friends in America,' An Unpublished Essay by Lott Cary, Sent from Liberia to Virginia, 1827," ed. John Saillant, *Virginia Magazine of History and Biography* 104 (1996): 494.

97 John McKivigan, *Forgotten Firebrand: James Redpath and the Making of Nineteenth-Century America* (Ithaca: Cornell University Press, 2008), 82.

98 Basler, ed., *Collected Works of Lincoln*, 5:520.

99 Washington correspondence, 18 January, *New York Times*, 19 January 1862; *Memorial of Leonard Dugged, George A. Bailey, and 240 Other Free*

Colored Persons of California, Praying Congress to Provide Means for Their Colonization to Some Country in Which Their Color Will Not Be A Badge of Degradation, Miscellaneous Document No. 31, 37th Congress, 2nd session, (16 January 1862), 1–6; Joseph Enoch Williams et al. to the Honorable the Senate and House of Representatives [April 1862], 37A-G21.4, Select Committee on Emancipation, Petitions & Memorials, ser. 467, 37th Congress, RG 233 [D-83].

100 William Seraille, "Afro-American Emigration to Haiti during the American Civil War," *Americas* 35 (1978): 185–200.

101 *Douglass' Monthly*, January 1861.

102 Ibid., March 1861, May 1861; David W. Blight, *Frederick Douglass: Prophet of Freedom* (New York: Simon & Schuster, 2018), 337–339.

103 McKivigan, *Forgotten Firebrand*, 74–75.

104 Ira Berlin et al., eds., *Freedom: A Documentary History of Emancipation 1861–1867, Wartime Genesis of Free Labor: The Upper South* (Cambridge: Cambridge University Press, 1993), 263–264.

105 *Report of the Select House Committee on Emancipation and Colonization*, House Reports no. 148, 37th Congress, 2nd session, issued 16 July 1862 (Washington: Government Printing Office, 1862), 14–16.

106 Purvis to Samuel C. Pomeroy, Philadelphia, 28 August 1862, *New York Tribune*, 30 September 1862.

107 *Douglass' Monthly*, September 1862, 707–708.

108 Douglass to Gerrit Smith, Rochester, 8 September 1862, Smith Papers, Syracuse University.

109 Carson, *Lincoln's Ethics*, 401; McPherson, "Abolitionist and Negro Opposition to Colonization," 391–399; Edna Greene Medford, "Lincoln and Race in Nineteenth-Century Perspective," in *The Living Lincoln*, eds. Thomas A. Horrocks and Harold Holzer (Carbondale: Southern Illinois University Press, 2011), 98–114; Phillip S. Paludan, "Greeley, Colonization, and a 'Deputation of Negroes': Three Considerations on Lincoln and Race," in *Lincoln Emancipated*, ed. Dirck, 43; Michael Vorenberg, "Abraham Lincoln and the Politics of Black Colonization," *Journal of the Abraham Lincoln Association* 14 (1993): 33; Mark E. Neely Jr., "Colonization and the Myth that Lincoln Prepared the People for Emancipation," in *Lincoln's Proclamation: Emancipation*

Reconsidered, eds. William A. Blair and Karen Fisher Younger (Chapel Hill: University of North Carolina Press, 2012), 48.

110 Washington correspondence by "Occasional" (John W. Forney), 17 August 1862, *Philadelphia Press*, 18 August 1862.

111 Washington correspondence, by B. F. M., 15 August, *Cincinnati Gazette*, 20 August 1862.

112 Paludan, "Greeley, Colonization, and a 'Deputation of Negroes,'" 42.

113 Washington correspondence, 25 August, *Christian Recorder* (Philadelphia), 30 August 1862.

114 There are several versions of this speech. See "The Colored Conventions Project," https://coloredconventions.org/garnet-address-1843/full-address.

115 Gregory J. W. Urwin, ed., *Black Flag over Dixie: Racial Atrocities and Reprisals in the Civil War* (Carbondale: Southern Illinois University Press, 2004); Guyatt, "'An Impossible Idea?" 242.

116 Garnet to [Thomas Hamilton], n.p., n.d., New York *Anglo-African*, n.d., copied in the San Francisco *Pacific Appeal*, 11 October 1862. Amazingly, commentators on Lincoln's meeting with the deputation have ignored Garnet's piece. A conspicuous exception is Brian Taylor, "'To Make the Union What It Ought To Be': African Americans, Civil War Military Service, and Citizenship" (Ph.D. dissertation, Georgetown University, 2015), 151–152.

117 Garnet, *The Past and the Present Condition, and the Destiny, of the Colored Race: A Discourse Delivered at the Fifteenth Anniversary of the Female Benevolent Society of Troy, N. Y., Feb. 14, 1848* (Troy: J. C. Kneeland, 1848), 26.

118 *Springfield* (Massachusetts) *Republican*, 22 August 1862. When Mitchell retired from government service, he took his papers with him. Though they may be extant, they have not surfaced. Phillip W. Magness, "James Mitchell and the Mystery of the U.S. Emigration Office Papers," *Journal of the Abraham Lincoln Association* 32 (2011): 50–62.

119 James Mitchell, *Report on Colonization and Emigration* (Washington: Government Printing Office, 1862), 8.

120 Henry Highland Garnet to [Thomas Hamilton], n.p., n.d., New York *Anglo-African*, n.d., copied in the San Francisco *Pacific Appeal*, 11 October 1862.

121 Washington correspondence by Cerebrus, n.d., *Christian Recorder* (Philadelphia), 30 August 1862.

122 W.C.D. to the editor, Newport, R.I., 1 November 1862, ibid., 8 November 1862.

123 Miller, *Lincoln's Virtues: An Ethical Biography* (New York: Knopf, 2002), 364.

124 Basler, ed., *Collected Works of Lincoln*, 2:320–323.

125 Ibid., 2:409.

126 Ibid., 3:304.

127 Ibid., 3:444.

128 T. J. Barnett to S. L. M. Barlow, Washington, 30 November 1862, Barlow Papers, Huntington Library, San Marino, California.

129 Oz Frankel, "The Predicament of Racial Knowledge: Government Studies of the Freedmen during the U.S. Civil War," *Social Research: An International Quarterly* 70 (2003): 45–81.

130 Washington correspondence, 22 February, by Van [D. W. Bartlett], *Springfield* (Massachusetts) *Republican*, 25 February 1865, copied in the Louisville *Courier-Journal*, 5 March 1865. It has been argued that an official report signed by Stephens, Hunter, and Campbell, dated Richmond, 6 February 1865, is first-hand evidence and therefore more reliable than secondhand accounts like those of Bartlett and the *New York Herald*. But that report is also secondhand, for it was written by Stephens, who stated: "Mr. Hunter said something about the inhumanity of leaving so many poor old negroes and young children destitute by encouraging the able-bodied negroes to run away, and asked, what are they, the helpless, to do?" The report goes on to relate a version of the "root hog" story and adds: "Mr. Stephens said he supposed that was the original of 'Root, Hog, or Die,' and a fair indication of the future of the negroes." Augusta, Georgia, *Chronicle and Sentinel*, 7 June 1865.

131 "There is an old farmer out in Illinois who had made his arrangements to raise a large herd of hogs; he informed his neighbors that he had found a way to raise cheap pork. This excited the curiosity of his neighbors, and they asked him how he was going to do it. The farmer replied that he should plant a large field of potatoes, and when they had got their growth, would turn the hogs in and let them dig, thus saving the expense of digging the potatoes and feeding them. 'But,' said his neighbors, 'the frost will come before they are fattened, and in all probability the ground will freeze a foot deep. How do you propose to get around that?' 'Oh,' replied the farmer,

'they will root somewhere anyway, and may as well root away there, even if it is hard work.'" Washington correspondence, 8 February 1865, *New York Herald*, 9 February 1865.

132 Lamon, *Recollections of Abraham Lincoln, 1847–1865*, ed. Dorothy Lamon Teillard (Washington, D.C.: the editor, 1911), 14–15.

133 Basler, ed., *Collected Works of Lincoln,* 3:204–205.

134 Ibid., [October 1858?], 3:204. To show that Lincoln publicly stated that African Americans were intellectually inferior to whites, Michael Lind wrote: "During the Lincoln Douglas debates he suggested that God gave blacks 'but little.'" Lind, *What Lincoln Believed*, 112. But that misconstrues what Lincoln said in his Springfield speech of July 17, 1858: "All I ask for the negro is that if you do not like him, let him alone. If God gave him but little, that little let him enjoy." Lincoln did not say "God gave the negro little" but "IF God gave the negro little." Basler, ed., *Collected Works of Lincoln*, 2:529.

135 "An Act to suppress insurrection, to punish treason and rebellion, to seize and confiscate the property of rebels, and for other purposes, 17 July 1862," *U.S. Statutes at Large*, 37th Congress, 2nd Session, 592. Emphasis added.

136 William H. Seward to Charles Francis Adams, circular of 30 September 1862, reprinted in Mitchell, *Report on Colonization and Emigration*, 29.

137 Reminiscences of James Mitchell, Atlanta, Georgia, correspondence, 22 August, *St. Louis Globe-Democrat*, 26 August 1894.

138 Basler, ed., *Collected Works of Lincoln*, 7:259.

139 Thomas to Lincoln, Washington, 16 August 1862, Lincoln Papers, Library of Congress.

140 Statement of the Danforth B. Nichols, "Return of the Haytian Colonists," Washington correspondence, 25 March 1864, *New York Tribune*, 2 April 1864. In Kock's proposal to Lincoln of October 1, 1862, he pledged to provide the settlers with a "New England Christian minister." Jayme Ruth Spencer, "Abraham Lincoln and Negro Colonization: The Île-à-Vache, Hayti Experience, 1862–1864," MA thesis, College of William and Mary, 1971, Dissertations, Theses, and Masters Projects, Paper 1539624740. https://dx.doi.org/doi:10.21220/s2-k0pj-fp82, 21.

141 Jacob R. S. Van Vleet to Lincoln, Washington, 17 August 1862, Lincoln Papers, Library of Congress.

142 Washington correspondence by Ura, 22 August 1862, *Baltimore Sun*,
23 August 1862; Washington correspondence by H[enry] M[cNeal]
T[urner], 25 August 1862, *Christian Recorder* (Philadelphia), 30 August
1862; Washington *Evening Star*, 23 August 1863.

143 Masur, "African American Delegation to Abraham Lincoln," 137.

144 Ibid., 138–140.

145 Washington correspondence, 21 August, *Baltimore Sun*, 22 August 1862.

146 Henry McNeal Turner, Washington correspondence, 28 October, *Christian
Recorder* (Philadelphia), 1 November 1862, Cole and Sheehan-Dean, eds.,
Freedom's Witness, 82.

147 Washington correspondence, n.d., *Boston Post*, n.d., copied in the St.
Joseph, Michigan, *Herald*, 9 January 1869.

148 Phillip W. Magness and Sebastian N. Page, *Colonization after
Emancipation: Lincoln and the Movement for Black Resettlement* (Columbia:
University of Missouri Press, 2011), 42–46.

149 Menard to Lincoln, New York, 16 September 1863, National Archives,
http://philmagness.com/?page_id=117.

150 *Frank Leslie's Weekly*, 26 December 1868.

151 *The South-Western* (Shreveport, Louisiana), 6 January 1869.

152 J. Willis Menard and eight others to Lincoln, Washington, 27 October
1862, *New York Times*, 2 November 1862.

153 *The Liberator* (Boston), 5 September 1862.

154 Van Vleet to Lincoln, Office of the [Washington] National Republican,
4 October 1862, Lincoln Papers, Library of Congress.

155 Statement of the Danforth B. Nichols, "Return of the Haytian Colonists,"
Washington correspondence, 25 March 1864, *New York Tribune*, 2 April
1864. A Methodist minister employed by the American Missionary
Association, Nichols in 1862 was appointed superintendent of freedmen by
General James Wadsworth, military governor of Washington, thus taking
charge of distributing food, blankets, and clothing to hundreds of refugee
slaves and procuring housing and employment for them. Doane Robinson,
History of South Dakota (2 vols.; Logansport, Indiana: B. F. Bowen, 1904),
2:1046–1047.

156 *Philadelphia Press*, 26 September 1862, in Spencer, "Lincoln and Negro
Colonization," 19. See Elwyn Burns Robinson, "The 'Press': President

Lincoln's Philadelphia Organ," *Pennsylvania Magazine of History and Biography* 65 (1941): 157–170.

157 William Cromwell and Benjamin Tatham, "Condition and Wants of the Colored Refugees," dated New York, December 1862, *New York Tribune*, 9 January 1863. Bates noted in his diary that the two Quakers, escorted by Agriculture Secretary Isaac Newton, had called on him on the night of November 28. Howard K. Beale, ed., *The Diary of Edward Bates, 1859–1866* (Washington: U.S. Government Printing Office, 1933), 267. Lincoln had reportedly offered Tatham the post of commissioner of Indian affairs, but he turned it down as too worldly. John Cox Jr., *Quakerism in the City of New York, 1657–1930* (New York: Privately Printed, 1930), 129.

158 Joseph Crosfield, *Appeal on Behalf of Fugitives from Slavery in America* (London: Edward Newman, 1863), summarized in Willis D. Boyd, "The Île-à-Vache Colonization Venture, 1862–1864," *The Americas* 16 (1959): 49.

159 Report by Albert Howe, summarized in Robert Francis Engs, *Freedom's First Generation: Black Hampton, Virginia, 1861–1890* (New York: Fordham University Press, 2004), 27.

160 Julia Wilbur diary, 17 November 1862, Haverford College, transcription, https://static1.squarespace.com/static/51cdecffe4b04906f65fdecb/t/5 2f29a2ae4b0161345f83a7d/1391630890478/JWilburDiary+- +AlexandriaDiaries.pdf.

161 Julia Wilbur to Lincoln, Alexandria, 7 November 1862, in Paula Tarnapol Whitacre, *A Civil Life in an Uncivil Time: Julia Wilbur's Struggle for Purpose* (Lincoln, Nebraska: Potomac Books, 2017), 91–92. She was assured that the president had seen her letter, which had been forwarded to him by Provost Marshal John C. Wyman via Secretary of War Stanton.

162 Mary Lincoln to her husband, New York, 3 November 1862, *Mary Todd Lincoln: Her Life and Letters,* ed. Justin G. Turner and Linda Levitt Turner (New York: Knopf, 1972), 141.

163 Spencer, "Lincoln and Negro Colonization," 27.

164 Statement of Danforth B. Nichols, "Return of the Haytian Colonists," Washington correspondence, 25 March 1864, *New York Tribune*, 2 April 1864.

165 C. Peter Ripley, ed., *The Black Abolitionist Papers* (5 vols.; Chapel Hill: University of North Carolina Press, 1985–1992), 2:444–445.

166 Amy Murrell Taylor, *Embattled Freedom: Journeys Through the Civil War's Slave Refugee Camps* (Chapel Hill: University of North Carolina Press, 2018), 97–99; "Return of the Haytian Colonists," Washington correspondence, 25 March 1864, *New York Tribune*, 2 April 1864; Frederic Bancroft, "The Île-à-Vache Experiment in Colonization," in Cooke, *Frederic Bancroft*, 230–239; Boyd, "Île-à-Vache Colonization Venture," 45–62; Robert Bray, "Abraham Lincoln & the Colony on Ile a Vache," https://digitalcommons.iwu.edu /eng_scholarship/6/; Spencer, "Lincoln and Negro Colonization."

167 Washington correspondence, 25 March 1864, *New York Tribune*, 2 April 1864.

168 John Eaton, *Grant, Lincoln, and the Freedmen: Reminiscences of the Civil War with Special Reference to the Work for the Contrabands and Freedmen of the Mississippi Valley* (New York: Longmans, Green, 1907), 91–92.

169 Beale, ed., *Bates Diary*, 268 (entry for 5 December 1862).

170 Oakes, *Crooked Path to Abolition*, 129.

171 "Guerre" to the editor, New Bedford, Mass., 18 April 1863, *Christian Recorder* (Philadelphia), 25 April 1863.

172 Magness and Page, *Colonization after Emancipation, passim.*

173 Michael Burlingame and John R. Turner Ettlinger, eds., *Inside Lincoln's White House: The Complete Civil War Diary of John Hay: 1861–1864* (Carbondale: Southern Illinois University Press, 1997), 217 (entry for 1 July 1864).

174 David G. Smith, *On the Edge of Freedom: The Fugitive Slave Issue in South Central Pennsylvania, 1820–1870* (New York: Fordham University Press, 2013), 52.

175 Phillip Magness, "Lincoln and Colonization," https://www.essentialcivil warcurriculum.com/lincoln-and-colonization.html.

176 Reynolds, *Abe*, 924.

177 Scheips, "Lincoln and the Chiriquí Colonization Project," 453.

CHAPTER 5

1 *Philadelphia Evening Telegraph*, 20 October 1866; Magness and Page, *Colonization After Emancipation*, 27.

2 William J. Brown, *The Life of William J. Brown of Providence, R.I., with Personal Recollections of Incidents in Rhode Island* (Durham: University of New Hampshire Press, 2006), 121–124; *Boston Journal*, 5 January 1892.

3   William Coppinger to Daniel L. Collier, Philadelphia, 28 March 1864,
     https://www.fold3.com/image/304952718; Charles Joyce, "Freedmen
     Warriors, Civil Rights Fighters," *Military Images* 34 (2016): 42–49.

4   Phillip W. Magness, "If not Frederick Douglass, who was the first black
     visitor to the White House?" 2013 post, http://philmagness.com/?p=601.

5   J. P. Usher to Lincoln, Washington, 7 March 1864, reporting expenditures
     by the Colonization Office of the Interior Department, Senate Documents,
     vol. 189, 38th Congress, 1st session, miscellaneous document 69, p. 2;
     Lincoln to John Palmer Usher, Washington, 30 January 1863, photocopy
     of a copy, Phillip Magness, "Lincoln and Colonization," https://www
     .essentialcivilwarcurriculum.com/lincoln-and-colonization.html.

6   *New York Tribune,* 20 February 1863.

7   *Providence Evening Bulletin*, 3 November 1881.

8   Edwin S. Redkey, "Black Chaplains in the Union Army," *Civil War History*
     33 (1987): 343.

9   *Philadelphia Evening Telegraph*, 20 October 1866; Philadelphia *National
     Baptist*, 21 November 1872.

10   Franklin B. Guinn, *The Rise and Progress of Shiloh Baptist Church of
     Philadelphia* (Philadelphia: William Watson, 1905), 190. https://archive
     .org/stream/riseprogressofsh00guin/riseprogressofsh00guin_djvu.txt.

11   Charles H. Wesley, "The Struggle for the Recognition of Haiti and Liberia
     as Independent Republics," *Journal of Negro History* 4 (1917): 369–383.

12   Andrew Armstrong to J. Q. Adams, 25 January 1825, in Claude A. Clegg,
     The Price of Liberty: African Americans and the Making of Liberia (Chapel
     Hill: University of North Carolina Press, 2004), 45.

13   Thomas Hart Benton, *Thirty Years' View; or, A History of the Working of
     the American Government for Thirty Years, from 1820 to 1850* (2 vols.; New
     York: D. Appleton, 1854–56), 2:69.

14   Speech in Congress, 2 June 1862, in Cox, *Eight Years in Congress, from 1857
     to 1865* (New York: D. Appleton, 1865), 161.

15   Washington correspondence by Caroline Eliot Kasson, 9 March, Des
     Moines *Iowa State Register*, 18 March 1863, in "An Iowa Woman in
     Washington, D.C., 1861–1865," *Iowa Journal of History* 52 (1954): 77;
     Washington *Court Journal,* n.d, copied in the Columbus *Ohio Statesman*,
     28 March 1863; Washington correspondence, n.d., St. Louis *Missouri*

Republican, n.d., copied in the *Detroit Free Press,* 25 March 1863. The hair of both reportedly had "a decided disposition to kinkiness."

16 Washington correspondence by Caroline Eliot Kasson, 9 March, Des Moines *Iowa State Register*, 18 March 1863, in "An Iowa Woman in Washington, D.C., 1861–1865," 77.

17 Washington correspondence, n.d., St. Louis *Missouri Republican*, n.d., copied in the *Detroit Free Press,* 25 March 1863; Washington correspondence, n.d., St. Paul *Weekly Pioneer and Democrat*, 3 April 1863. The remarks of this gentleman were reported in thick Black dialect, which I have rendered in standard English.

18 Edward Gilbert, speech delivered on 11 June 1863 in New York, *New York Times*, 12 June 1863.

19 Jane Grey Swisshelm in the *Chicago Journal*, 29 March 1863, copied in the *Milwaukee Sentinel,* 13 April 1863. It is not clear whether March 29 is the date of the Washington correspondence by Swisshelm or the date of the article's publication.

20 Washington correspondence, n.d., *Christian Recorder* (Philadelphia), 28 March 1863.

21 Washington *National Republican*, 18 March 1863, copied in *Douglass' Monthly*, June 1863.

22 "Guerre" to the editor, New Bedford, Mass., 18 April 1863, *Christian Recorder* (Philadelphia), 25 April 1863.

23 Washington correspondence, n.d., *Christian Recorder* (Philadelphia), 28 March 1863.

24 Ibid.

25 Correspondence by J[ames] W. C. P[ennington], Poughkeepsie, New York, 8 April 1863, New York *Anglo-African*, 18 April 1863.

26 Poughkeepsie, New York, *Daily Eagle*, 8 April 1863, copied ibid.

27 "Walkabout: The Gloucester Family of Brooklyn," Suzanne Spellen (using the pen name Montrose), *Brownstoner: Brooklyn Real Estate*, 9 and 11 October 2012.

28 Report by Observer, Washington *National Republican*, 2 June 1863.

29 Washington correspondence, 31 May, *New York Tribune*, 1 June 1863.

30 At a meeting in New York on June 11, the committee reported on their White House conversations. I have conflated three similar accounts of

Lincoln's words as reported at that meeting: *New York Times, New York World, New York Herald*, 12 June 1863. Much of the account of Lincoln's remarks was given by Col. James Fairman.

31 Lincoln to Sumner, Washington, 1 June 1863, Basler, ed., *Collected Works of Lincoln*, 6:233–234.

32 *Rochester Union*, 23 July 1863, copied in the *Washington Daily National Intelligencer*, 27 July 1863.

33 William Whiting to Edward Gilbert, Washington, 18 July 1863, *The Liberator* (Boston), 31 July 1863.

34 Frémont to Charles Sumner, New York, 9 June 1863, Lincoln Papers, Library of Congress; Edward Gilbert to Edwin Stanton, New York, 12 October 1863, in Ira Berlin et al., eds., *Freedom: A Documentary History of Emancipation 1861–1867: The Black Military Experience* (New York: Cambridge University Press, 1982), 106.

35 Jacob Thomas, letter to the editor, Troy, 2 September 1863, *Buffalo Morning Express*, 22 October 1863.

36 Berlin, ed., *Black Military Experience*, 105–107.

37 *Washington National Intelligencer*, 27 August 1863; Washington *Evening Star*, 26 August 1863.

38 *Washington Chronicle* and *Washington Evening Union*, 26 August 1863; Lincoln to whom it may concern, Washington, 21 August 1863, Basler, ed., *Collected Works of Lincoln,* 6:401.

39 Redkey, "Black Chaplains," 332.

40 Richard K. MacMaster, "Henry Highland Garnet and the African Civilization Society," *Journal of Presbyterian History* 48 (1970): 95–112; William M. Brewer, "Henry Highland Garnet," *Journal of Negro History* 13 (1928): 36–52.

41 *New York Tribune*, 28 October 1863.

42 Edythe Ann Quinn, *Freedom Journey: Black Civil War Soldiers and the Hills Community, Westchester County, New York* (Albany: State University of New York Press, 2015), 94–95; Memphis *Public Ledger*, 13 July 1874.

43 *Knoxville Journal and Tribune*, 29 October 1886.

44 Kenneth E. Mann, "Richard Harvey Cain: Congressman, Minister and Champion of Civil Rights," *Negro History Bulletin* 35 (1972): 64–66;

Ronald L. Lewis, "Cultural Pluralism and Black Reconstruction: The Public Career of Richard H. Cain," *Crisis* 85 (February 1978): 57–60.

45 "Princeton Seminary and Slavery: A Report of the Historical Audit Committee," 41. https://slavery.ptsem.edu/wp-content/uploads/2018/10/Princeton-Seminary-and-Slavery-Report.pdf.

46 Eric K. Washington, *Boss of the Grips: The Life of James H. Williams and the Red Caps of Grand Central Terminal* (New York: Liveright, 2019), 17–20.

47 Blair L. M. Kelley, *Right to Ride: Streetcar Boycotts and African American Citizenship in the Era of Plessy v. Ferguson* (Chapel Hill: University of North Carolina Press, 2010), 29–30.

48 *New York Sun*, 4 February 1876.

49 Ibid., 1 December 1871.

50 New York correspondence, 25 July 1884, *Boston Globe*, 26 July 1884.

51 *New York Evening Post*, 12 November 1863; Phillip W. Magness, "The British Honduras Colony: Black Emigrationist Support for Colonization in the Lincoln Presidency," *Slavery & Abolition* 34 (2013): 39–60.

52 Washington correspondence, 20 March 1863, *New York World*, 21 March 1863.

53 Charles Russell Lowell to John Murray Forbes, Centreville, 13 September 1863, and to Josephine Lowell, Washington, 3 August [1863], Edward W. Emerson, *Life and Letters of Charles Russell Lowell* (Boston: Houghton, Mifflin, 1907), 296, 290.

54 Basler, ed., *Collected Works of Lincoln*, 5:421.

55 Reynolds, *Abe*, 809.

56 Order of retaliation, 30 July 1863, Basler, ed., *Collected Works of Lincoln,* 6:357.

57 *Weekly Anglo-African*, 17 August 1863, in Donald Yacovone, "The Pay Crisis and the 'Lincoln Despotism,'" in Martin H. Blatt, Thomas J. Brown, and Donald Yacovone, eds., *Hope & Glory: Essays on the Legacy of the Fifty-Fourth Massachusetts Regiment* (Amherst: University of Massachusetts in association with the Massachusetts Historical Society, 2001), 45.

58 Douglass to Stearns, Rochester, 1 August 1863, in Douglass, *Life and Times of Frederick Douglass* (Hartford: Park, 1882), 418–419.

59 Charles E. Heller, *Portrait of an Abolitionist: A Biography of George Luther Stearns, 1809–1867* (Westport, Connecticut: Greenwood Press, 1996), 156–57.

60 Douglass, *Life and Times*, 412.

61 Douglass's speech of 4 December 1863, in John W. Blassingame et al., eds., *The Frederick Douglass Papers, Series One: Speeches, Debates, and Interviews* (5 vols.; New Haven: Yale University Press, 1979–1992), 3:606–608.

62 Douglass, *Life and Times*, 422.

63 Blassingame et al., eds., *Douglass Papers, Series One*, 3:606; Douglass to George Luther Stearns, Philadelphia, 12 August 1863, copy, Records of the Free Military School for Command of Colored Regiments, Historical Society of Pennsylvania.

64 Blassingame et al., eds., *Douglass Papers, Series One*, 3:606.

65 Speech of 13 January 1864, *New York Times*, 14 January 1864.

66 *Life and Times of Douglass*, 422–23.

67 Blassingame et al., eds., *Douglass Papers, Series One*, 3:606.

68 Rice, ed., *Reminiscences of Lincoln*, 187–188.

69 Douglass, *Life and Times*, 423–424.

70 Rice, ed., *Reminiscences of Lincoln*, 188.

71 Douglass, *Life and Times*, 424.

72 Douglass to George Luther Stearns, Philadelphia, 12 August 1863, copy, Records of the Free Military School for Command of Colored Regiments, Historical Society of Pennsylvania.

73 Blassingame et al., eds., *Douglass Papers, Series One*, 3:606.

74 Douglass, *Life and Times*, 425.

75 Berlin, ed., *Black Military Experience*, 360–368.

76 John Cimprich, *Fort Pillow: A Civil War Massacre and Public Memory* (Baton Rouge: Louisiana University Press, 2005).

77 Basler, ed., *Collected Works of Lincoln*, 7:303.

78 Usher's lecture, "Lincoln and His Times," *Salt Lake Weekly Tribune* (Salt Lake City, Utah), 27 May 1882; Lincoln's address at Sanitary Fair, Baltimore, 18 April 1864, and Lincoln to Stanton, Washington, 17 May 1864, Basler, ed., *Collected Works of Lincoln*, 7:302–303, 345.

79 Lincoln to Stanton, Washington, 17 May 1864, Basler, ed., *Collected Works of Lincoln*, 7:345–346.

80 Reynolds, *Abe*, 809.

81 Douglass, *Life and Times*, 436; Rice, ed., *Reminiscences of Lincoln*, 196.

CHAPTER 6

1 After a few months, the president replaced Butler with Nathaniel P. Banks.

2 Bates to Salmon P. Chase, Washington, 29 November 1862, issued as a pamphlet, *Opinion of Attorney General Bates on Citizenship* (Washington: Government Printing Office, 1862), 6, 8, 26–27.

3 *The Congregationalist* (Boston), 2 January 1863.

4 Oakes, *Crooked Path to Abolition*, 118–120; 124–125; Elizabeth Stordeur Pryor, *Colored Travelers: Mobility and the Fight for Citizenship before the Civil War* (Chapel Hill: University of North Carolina Press, 2016), 124–125. In 1861, Seward had anticipated this practice by issuing a passport to Henry Highland Garnet.

5 *L'Union* (New Orleans), 11 February 1864, in David C. Rankin, "The Origins of Negro Leadership in New Orleans during Reconstruction," in Howard M. Rabinowitz, ed., *Southern Black Leaders of the Reconstruction Era* (Urbana: University of Illinois Press, 1982), 170.

6 *New Orleans Tribune*, 4 August 1864, ibid., 224.

7 *L'Union* (New Orleans), 11 February 1864, ibid., 170.

8 New Orleans correspondence, 4 November, *Buffalo Commercial Advertiser*, 21 November 1863.

9 The text can be found in *Appleton's Annual Cyclopaedia and Register of Important Events for the Year 1863* (New York: D. Appleton, 1864), 591–592.

10 For a reproduction of that document and its signatures, along with a transcription of the text and all the names of the signers, see Jari Honora, "Cast Your Eyes Upon a Loyal Population: Lincoln and Louisiana's Free People of Color," *La Créole, A Journal of Creole History and Genealogy* 2 (2009): 4–16.

11 New Orleans correspondence, 9 February 1864, *New York Tribune*, 10 February 1864, copied in the New York *Anglo-African*, 27 February 1864.

12 *New Orleans Tribune*, 9 February 1864, in Donald E. Everett, "Demands of the New Orleans Free Colored Population for Political Equality, 1862–1865," *Louisiana Historical Quarterly* 38 (1955): 48.

13 David C. Rankin, "The Forgotten People: Free People of Color in New Orleans, 1850–1870" (Ph.D. dissertation, Johns Hopkins University, 1976), 216–217.

14 New Orleans *Daily Picayune*, 16 July 1859.

15 Plumly to William Lloyd Garrison, New Orleans, 20 October 1864, *The Liberator* (Boston), 11 November 1864; David Rankin, "The Politics of Caste: Free Colored Leadership in New Orleans during the Civil War," in Robert R. MacDonald, John R. Kemp, and Edward F. Haas, eds., Louisiana's Black Heritage (New Orleans: Louisiana State Museum 1979), 133.

16 On February 10, Thomas J. Durant wrote Lincoln introducing Roudanez and Bertonneau. Lincoln Papers, Library of Congress.

17 New Orleans correspondence, 21 February 1864, *New York Tribune*, n.d., copied in the *Vermont Phoenix* (Brattleboro), 18 March 1864.

18 Washington correspondence, 5 March 1864, *Ohio State Journal* (Columbus), copied in the *Cincinnati Commercial*, 15 March 1864.

19 Ibid.

20 James McKaye, *The Mastership and its Fruits: The Emancipated Slave Face to Face with His Old Master; A Supplemental Report to Hon. Edwin M. Stanton, Secretary of War* (New York: Loyal Publication Society, 1864), 5.

21 "To Sugar Planters," advertisement by Roudanez, New Orleans *Times-Picayune*, 7 February 1854.

22 William P. Connor, "Reconstruction Rebels: The New Orleans Tribune in Post-War Louisiana," *Louisiana History* 21 (1980): 159–181.

23 James A. Joseph, *Remaking America: How the Benevolent Traditions of Many Cultures Are Transforming Our National Life* (San Francisco: Jossey-Bass, 1995), 90.

24 James G. Hollandsworth Jr., *The Louisiana Native Guards: The Black Military Experience During the Civil War* (Baton Rouge: Louisiana State University Press, 1995).

25 Berlin, ed., *Black Military Experience*, 313.

26 Bertonneau to Captain Wickham Hoffmann, 2 March 1863, in Holdsworth, *Louisiana Native Guards*, 73.

27 New York correspondence by James McKaye, 1 March 1864, New York *Anglo-African*, 19 March 1864; Bertonneau's service records, National Archives, accessed on the fold3 website. https://www.fold3.com/memorial /653669085/arnold-bertonneau-civil-war-stories.

28 Not on March 12, the date cited by almost all sources except contemporary newspapers. The *New York Evening Post* on 4 March 1864 reported that the

meeting took place the preceding day. Other papers reported that it took place the following day.

29 Petition addendum, 10 March 1864, *The Liberator* (Boston), 1 April 1864.

30 Ibid.

31 Reminiscences of John W. Forney in a lecture delivered in November 1865 before the Ladies' Soldiers' Aid Society of Weldon, Pennsylvania, *New York Evening Post*, 30 November 1865.

32 Washington correspondence, 5 March 1864, *Ohio State Journal* (Columbus), 9 March 1864.

33 *New York Evening Post*, 4 March 1864.

34 Washington correspondence, 4 March 1864, *Cleveland Daily Leader*, 5 March 1864.

35 Chase to Durant, Washington, 28 December 1863, John Niven et al, eds., *The Salmon P. Chase papers* (5 vols.; Kent, Ohio: Kent State University Press, 1993–1998), 4:230. See also Chase to Lyman D. Stickney, Washington, 29 December 1863, in LaWanda Cox, *Lincoln and Black Freedom: A Study in Presidential Leadership* (Columbia: University of South Carolina Press, 1981), 80.

36 Lincoln's December 16 endorsement on John L. Riddell to Lincoln, 15 December 1863, Basler, ed., *Collected Works of Lincoln*, 7:71.

37 Lincoln to Hahn, Washington, 13 March 1864, Basler, ed., ibid., 7:243.

38 James G. Blaine, *Twenty Years of Congress: From Lincoln to Garfield* (2 vols.; Norwich, Conn.: Henry Bill, 1884–86), 2:40.

39 Washington correspondence by Agate [Whitelaw Reid], 23 June, *Cincinnati Gazette*, 24 June, copied in the Washington *Daily National Republican*, 28 June 1865.

40 Herman Belz, "Origins of Negro Suffrage During the Civil War," *Southern Studies* 17 (1978): 115–130; Robert J. Cook, "The Fight for Black Suffrage in the War of the Rebellion," *The American Civil War: Explorations and Reconsiderations*, ed. Susan-Mary Grant and Brian Holden Reid (New York: Longman, 2000), 217–238.

41 Cox, *Lincoln and Black Freedom,* 66–78 and *passim.*

42 George S. Denison to Chase, New Orleans, 8 October 1864, Chase Papers, Library of Congress.

43 *New Orleans Daily True Delta*, 18 November 1864, in Rankin, "Politics of Caste," 134.

44 *New York Times*, 23 June 1865.

45 *The Liberator* (Boston), 12 May 1865.

46 Kelley to S.N.T., n.p., n.d., *New Orleans Tribune*, 23 May 1865, in Cox, *Lincoln and Black Freedom*, 118.

47 Brown to the editors of the *St. Louis Globe-Democrat*, Washington, 22 December 1864, reproduced as a pamphlet, "Freedom and Franchise Inseparable: Letter of the Hon. B. Gratz Brown" (Washington: Gibson Brothers, 1864), 4.

48 *Congressional Globe*, 38th Congress, 2nd session, 300 (17 January 1865).

49 McKim to Garrison, Washington, 5 May 1864, in Wendell Phillips Garrison, *William Lloyd Garrison, 1805–1879: The Story of His Life Told by His Children* (4 vols.; Boston: Houghton Mifflin, 1894), 4:122.

50 Cox, *Lincoln and Black Freedom*, 121–129.

51 Stoddard, *Inside the White House in War Times*, ed. Burlingame, 139; Stoddard, *Abraham Lincoln and Andrew Johnson* (New York: F.A. Stokes, 1888), 40.

52 *Boston Daily Advertiser*, 13 April 1864, copied in the *National Anti-Slavery Standard* (New York), 23 April 1864.

53 Blassingame et al., eds., *Douglass Papers, Series One*, 4:2.

54 Everett, "Demands of the New Orleans Free Colored Population," 60–62.

55 James G. Hollandsworth, Jr., *An Absolute Massacre: The New Orleans Race Riot of July 30, 1866* (Baton Rouge: Louisiana State University Press, 2001), 107; Bertonneau's testimony, 4 August 1866, House Executive Documents, 39th Congress, 2nd session, vol. 10, no. 68, p. 130.

56 Donald E. DeVore and Joseph Logsdon, *Crescent City Schools: Public Education in New Orleans, 1841–1991* (Lafayette: Center for Louisiana Studies, University of Southwestern Louisiana 1991), 89.

57 New Orleans *Daily Picayune*, 3 January 1868.

58 Melissa Daggett, *Spiritualism in Nineteenth-Century New Orleans: The Life and Times of Henry Louis Rey* (Jackson: University Press of Mississippi, 2017), 81.

59 *Ouachita Telegraph* (Monroe, Louisiana), 28 February 1879; Roger A. Fischer, *The Segregation Struggle in Louisiana, 1862–1877* (Urbana: University of Illinois Press, 1974), 141; Louis R. Harlan, "Desegregation in New Orleans Public Schools during Reconstruction," *American Historical Review* 64 (1962): 663–675.

60 Vorenberg, "Slavery Reparations in Theory and Practice," 126.

61 David S. Cecelski, *The Fire of Freedom: Abraham Galloway and the Slaves' Civil War* (Chapel Hill: University of North Carolina Press, 2012), 115–127. The delegation's members were, in addition to Galloway, Clinton D. Pierson, John R. Good, Isaac K. Felton, Edward H. Hill, and Jarvis M. Williams.

62 Edward Kinsley in Cecelski, *Fire of Freedom*, xv.

63 John Richard Dennett, *The South As It Is: 1865–1866* (New York: Viking, 1965), 151–152.

64 *North Carolina Times* (New Bern), 21 May 1864.

65 New Bern, North Carolina correspondence by "Reporter," 15 June 1864, New York *Anglo-African*, 2 July 1864.

66 *North Carolina Times* (New Bern), 21 May 1864.

67 Weymouth T. Jordan Jr. and Gerald W. Thomas, "Massacre at Plymouth: April 20, 1864," *North Carolina Historical Review* (1995): 125–197.

68 "Caroline Johnson," four-page handwritten manuscript, described and partially reproduced, offered for sale by Swann Auction Galleries, March 2020, https://www.invaluable.com/auction-lot/lincoln-abraham -story-of-caroline-johnson-a-freed-146-c-5f5423fab6#.

69 F. B. Carpenter, *Six Months at the White House with Abraham Lincoln* (New York: Hurd and Houghton, 1866), 200–202; Washington correspondence by "Sojourner," 5 April 1864, *Newark Daily Advertiser*, 6 April 1864; letter to the editor by "Mrs. C," [Philadelphia], 6 March 1865, *National Antislavery Standard* (New York), 11 March 1865. According to the account by Mrs. C (a Quaker woman), Mrs. Johnson desired to express her gratitude to the president by making a gift for him. She did so and wanted her minister, James Hamilton, to present it. Her friend Mrs. C insisted that Mrs. Johnson make the presentation in conjunction with Hamilton. Mrs. C wrote: "She concluded to do so, and asked for an introductory letter to the President, which was given her. Isaac Newton, who is at the head of the Agricultural Department, and the President's wife, were written to, and the answer was, that 'she would be received.'"

70 Benjamin Brown French, *Witness to the Young Republic: A Yankee's Journal, 1828–1870*, ed. Donald B. Cole and John J. McDonough (Hanover, NH: University Press of New England, 1989), 448 (entry for 6 April 1864).

71   Lincoln to Stanton, Washington, 11 April 1864, Basler, ed., *Collected Works of Lincoln,* 7:297.

72   *New York Herald,* 18 July 1855.

73   R. J. M. Blackett, *The Slave's Quest for Freedom: Fugitive Slaves, the 1850 Fugitive Slave Law, and the Politics of Slavery* (Cambridge: Cambridge University Press, 2018), 115–125. (quote on 115); Howard H. Bell, "The Negro Emigration Movement, 1849–1854: A Phase of Negro Nationalism," *Phylon Quarterly* 20 (1959): 132–142.

74   Gabriel Coakley to Benjamin Brown French, Washington, 27 June 1864, and French to Coakley, Washington, 30 June 1864, both reproduced in D. I. Murphy, "Lincoln: Foe of Bigotry," *America,* 11 February 1928, 432–433; Morris J. MacGregor, *The Emergence of a Black Catholic Community: St. Augustine's in Washington* (Washington: Catholic University of America Press, 1999), 3–5, 36–39; Basler, ed., *Collected Works of Lincoln*, 7:419: Benjamin Quarles, *The Negro in the Civil War* (New York: Russell & Russell, 1953), 253; Washington correspondence, 8 July 1864, New York *Anglo-African*, 23 July 1864.

75   Carpenter, *Six Months at the White House,* 196.

76   William E. Doster, *Lincoln and Episodes of the Civil War* (New York: G. P. Putnam's Sons, 1915), 241 (diary entry for 4 July 1864).

77   Michael Burlingame and John R. Turner Ettlinger, eds., *Inside Lincoln's White House: The Complete Civil War Diary of John Hay* (Carbondale: Southern Illinois University Press, 1997), 220 (entry for 5 July 1864).

78   *Albany Argus,* n.d., copied in the *Louisville Daily Democrat,* 16 August 1864. Similarly, a Washington paper observed that "[i]n our recollection, that space has never been used for such a purpose." Washington *National Intelligencer*, 6 July 1864.

79   *Pittsfield* (Massachusetts) *Sun,* 27 July 1864.

80   *North Branch Democrat* (Tunkhannock, Pennsylvania), 20 July 1864.

81   *Dayton Daily Empire,* 29 July 1864.

82   *Plymouth* (Indiana) *Democrat,* 28 July 1864.

83   Washington *Evening Star,* 3 August 1864.

84   Ibid., 5 August 1864. J. R. Pierre, the superintendent of the Third Colored Baptist Sabbath School, had written to Lincoln on July 23. B. B. French replied two days later, indicating that the president's approval was necessary.

85 *Washington Constitutional Union*, n.d., copied in the Columbus *Ohio Statesman*, 17 August 1864.

86 Georgetown, D.C., *Evening Union*, 5 August 1864.

87 *Boston Evening Transcript*, 8 September 1864.

88 Baltimore correspondence, 31 March 1867, *New York Times*, 1 April 1867.

89 *Baltimore Sun*, 1 April 1867.

90 Basler, ed., *Collected Works of Lincoln*, 7:542; Washington *National Intelligencer*, Washington *National Republican*, 7 September 1864; A. W. W[ayman] to the editor, Baltimore, 4 October 1864, *Christian Recorder* (Philadelphia), 15 October 1864.

91 Ira Berlin et al., eds., *Freedom: A Documentary History of Emancipation, 1861–1867*, ser. 1, vol. 3, *The Wartime Genesis of Free Labor: The Lower South* (New York: Cambridge University Press, 1990), 61.

92 Eaton, *Grant, Lincoln, and the Freedmen*, 173; Douglass's speech on 13 January, *New York Times*, 14 January 1864.

93 Lincoln to Charles D. Robinson, Washington, 17 August 1864, draft, Basler, ed., *Collected Works of Lincoln*, 7:500.

94 Douglass to Theodore Tilton, Rochester, 15 October 1864, in Philip S. Foner, ed., *The Life and Writings of Frederick Douglass* (4 vols.; New York: International Publishers, 1950), 3:423.

95 *Life and Times of Douglass*, 435.

96 Rice, ed., *Reminiscences of Lincoln*, 190.

97 Douglass, eulogy for Lincoln, 1 June 1865, manuscript, Douglass Papers, Library of Congress; *Life and Times of Douglass*, 425.

98 Douglass, "The Assassination and Its Lesson," speech delivered in Brooklyn, 29 January 1866, *Brooklyn Daily Eagle*, 30 January 1866.

99 Douglass to Lincoln, Rochester, 29 August 1864, Lincoln Papers, Library of Congress.

100 Douglass to Theodore Tilton, Rochester, 15 November 1864, in Foner, ed., *Life and Writings of Douglass*, 3:422–424.

101 Ira Berlin, "Who Freed the Slaves? Emancipation and Its Meaning," in *Union and Emancipation: Essays on Politics and Race in the Civil War Era*, ed. David W. Blight and Brooks D. Simpson (Kent: Kent State University Press, 1997), 107–121; Vincent Harding, *There is a River: The Black Struggle for Freedom in America* (New York: Harcourt, Brace,

Jovanovich, 1981); Ira Berlin et al., eds., *Freedom: A Documentary History of Emancipation 1861–1867: The Destruction of Slavery* (New York: Cambridge University Press, 1985), 1–56; Robert Engs, "The Great American Slave Rebellion," paper delivered to the Civil War Institute at Gettysburg College, 27 June 1991; Barbara J. Fields, "Who Freed the Slaves?" in *The Civil War: An Illustrated History* ed. Geoffrey Ward (New York: Knopf, 2009), 178–181. Fields argued that the goal of preserving the Union was "too shallow to be worth the sacrifice of a single human life." Ibid., 178.

102 Neely, "Lincoln and the Theory of Self-Emancipation," in *The Continuing Civil War: Essays in Honor of the Civil War Round Table of Chicago*, ed. John Y. Simon and Barbara Hughett (n.p.: Morningside, 1992), 51, 57–58.

103 James McPherson, *Drawn with the Sword: Reflections on the American Civil War* (New York: Oxford University Press, 1996), 206–207.

104 Lincoln said this to D. H. Chamberlain on April 6, 1865. Chamberlain to the editor, New York, 22 September 1883, *New York Tribune*, 4 November 1883.

105 Douglass to Lincoln, Rochester, 29 August 1864, *New York Times*, 16 February 2002.

106 Douglass, "The Assassination and Its Lessons," speech delivered in Brooklyn, 29 January 1866, *Brooklyn Daily Eagle*, 30 January 1866.

107 Eaton, *Grant, Lincoln, and the Freedmen*, 175–176.

108 Eulogy for Lincoln, 1 June 1865, manuscript, Douglass Papers, Library of Congress.

109 "The Assassination and Its Lessons," delivered in Brooklyn, 29 January 1866, *Brooklyn Daily Eagle*, 30 January 1866.

110 Speech given in Boston, 24 October 1865, *The Liberator* (Boston), 27 October 1865.

111 Eulogy for Lincoln, 1 June 1865, manuscript, Douglass Papers, Library of Congress.

112 Rice, ed., *Reminiscences of Lincoln*, 193.

113 *Ibid.*

114 Reminiscences of John E. Roll, *Chicago Times-Herald*, 25 August 1895.

115 Lincoln to Mrs. O. H. Browning, Springfield, 1 April 1838, Basler, ed., *Collected Works of Lincoln*, 1:118.

116 For a discussion of the impact of Lincoln's early years on his views toward slavery, see Michael Burlingame, *The Inner World of Abraham Lincoln* (Urbana: University of Illinois Press, 1994), 20–56.

CHAPTER 7

1   Deborah Davis, *Guest of Honor: Booker T. Washington, Theodore Roosevelt, and the White House Dinner That Shocked a Nation* (New York: Atria Books, 2012).

2   That subject has been misrepresented in the historical literature. Nell Irvin Painter mistakenly wrote that "[t]hroughout Lincoln's two administrations, such receptions remained off limits to blacks." Painter, *Sojourner Truth: A Life, A Symbol* (New York: W.W. Norton, 1996), 203. In his biography of U. S. Grant, Ron Chernow asserted that during his subject's administration, Black callers were offered "unprecedented" access to the White House. Ron Chernow, *Grant* (New York: Penguin, 2017), 684. But in fact, as Don E. Fehrenbacher observed, Lincoln "opened the White House to black visitors in a way that set aside all precedent." Don E. Fehrenbacher, "Only His Stepchildren," in Fehrenbacher, *Lincoln in Text and Context: Collected Essays* (Stanford: Stanford University Press, 1987), 107. Historian Kate Masur has adduced evidence supporting Fehrenbacher's contention. Masur, "Color Was a Bar to the Entrance: African American Activism and the Question of Social Equality in Lincoln's White House," *American Quarterly* 69 (2017): 1–22. While Professor Masur's well-documented work is a welcome corrective, she has elsewhere erroneously maintained that Lincoln "evidently did not take a strong stand for admitting them [Blacks] to more 'social' occasions, such as public receptions [and] New Year's Day levees." Masur, *Example for All the Land: Emancipation and the Struggle over Equality in Washington, D.C.* (Chapel Hill: University of North Carolina Press, 2010), 104.

3   *Life and Times of Douglass*, 443–445.

4   Speech to Union League of Brooklyn, 13 February 1894, John W. Blassingame et al., eds., *The Frederick Douglass Papers, Series One, Speeches, Debates, and Interviews* (5 vols.; New Haven: Yale University Press, 1979–1992), 5:544–45; Rice, ed., *Reminiscences of Abraham Lincoln*, 192–193.

5   Julia Wilbur diary, 5 March 1865, Quaker and Special Collections, Haverford College, transcription, https://www.alexandriava.gov/uploaded Files/historic/info/civilwar/JuliaWilburDiary1865.pdf.

6   Keckley, *Behind the Scenes,* 160.

7   Washington correspondence, 4 March 1865, *New York Herald,* 5 March 1865.

8   *Washington Chronicle,* 5 March 1865, copied in the *Boston Daily Advertiser,* 6 March 1865.

9   Washington correspondence, n.d., *New York News,* n.d., copied in the *Cincinnati Enquirer,* 10 March 1865.

10 Washington correspondence, 5 March 1865, *New York Evening Express,* 7 March 1865.

11 *Ohio Statesman* (Columbus), 17 March 1865.

12 Blassingame, ed., *Speeches of Douglass, Series One,* 5:544–545; Masur, "Color Was a Bar to the Entrance," 1–22. Cf. the statement in Douglass's autobiography: "no colored persons had ever ventured to present themselves on such occasions." *Life and Times of Douglass,* 444.

13 Anderson Abbott, "Civil War Memoirs from Dr. Anderson Abbott," in the Abbott Collection, Metropolitan Toronto Reference Library, Catherine Slaney, *Family Secrets: Crossing the Colour Line* (Toronto: Natural Heritage Books, 2003), 202. That attaché could have been Demosthenes Bruno, secretary of the legation and assistant chargé d'affaires.

14 *Life and Times of Douglass,* 445.

15 French, *Witness to the Young Republic,* 496.

16 Washington *Evening Star,* 1 January 1866.

17 Boston *Commonwealth,* n.d., copied in the Washington *National Republican,* 8 January 1866.

18 Washington correspondence by "Potomac," 2 January 1866, *Baltimore Sun,* 3 January 1866.

19 Washington *Evening Star,* 2 January 1866; Washington correspondence, 1 January 1866, *New York Herald,* 2 January 1866; *Boston American Traveler,* 6 January 1866; Washington correspondence, 1 January 1866, *Boston Daily Advertiser,* 2 January 1866; Washington correspondence, 1 January 1866, *Philadelphia Inquirer,* 2 January 1866; *Washington National Intelligencer,* 2 January 1866.

20 In January, Johnson was reported to have stopped participating in formal receptions. *Pittsburgh Daily Commercial,* 12 January 1866.

21 *Pall Mall Gazette* (London), n.d., copied in the *London Guardian,* 2 March 1866.

22 According to a historian of the Executive Mansion, "in the last quarter
of the nineteenth century, as a policy, blacks were not admitted to the
receptions." William Seale, *The President's House: A History* (2 vols.;
Baltimore: Johns Hopkins University Press, 2008), 2:653. That policy
continued at least through Theodore Roosevelt's presidency (1901–1909).
Ibid., 1:315, 2:709.

23 *New York Observer*, 4 January 1866.

24 Washington correspondence, 3 January 1864, *Newark Daily Advertiser*,
5 January 1864.

25 Quarles, *Lincoln and the Negro* (New York: Oxford University Press,
1962), 47.

26 Les Wallace, "Charles Lenox Remond: The Lost Prince of Abolitionism,"
Negro History Bulletin 40 (1977): 696–701.

27 *Convention of the Colored Citizens of Massachusetts,* 1 August 1858, New
Bedford, https://omeka.coloredconventions.org/items/show/264.

28 Diary of Julia Wilbur, Quaker and Special Collections, Haverford College
(entry for 3 January 1864). The night of January 1, Remond spoke at
the Israel Bethel Church in Washington. Julia Wilbur had met with
him the preceding week.

29 Undated entry in the diary of C. Edwards Lester, in Lester, *Life and Public
Services of Charles Sumner* (New York: United States Publishing, 1874), 391.

30 Washington correspondence, n.d., *London Morning Star*, n.d., copied in the
New York *Anglo-African*, 23 January 1864; Henry Johnson to the editor,
Washington, 6 January 1864, ibid., 31 January 1864.

31 *Washington Chronicle*, 2 January 1864, copied in *The Liberator* (Boston),
22 January 1864.

32 *Belfast* (Maine) *Republican Journal*, 8 January 1864.

33 *Plymouth* (Indiana) *Democrat*, 14 January 1864.

34 *Huntington* (Indiana) *Democrat*, 7 January 1864.

35 Washington correspondence, n.d., *Greencastle* (Indiana) *Press*, 13 January
1864, copied in the *Sullivan* (Indiana) *Democrat*, 21 January 1864.

36 *Detroit Free Press*, 27 February 1864.

37 Statement of Iowa Senator James Grimes, 25 February 1864, *Congressional
Globe*, 38th Congress, 1st session, 817–818, quoting a letter from a
knowledgeable judge.

38 "The Case of Private George Taylor," *Washington Daily Morning Chronicle,* 3 March 1864.

39 Augusta to Captain C. W. Clappington, Washington, 1 February 1864, in the Washington correspondence by "Castine" [Noah Brooks], 11 February, *Sacramento Weekly Union,* 19 March 1864.

40 "Opening of the Street-Cars to Colored Persons," *The Works of Charles Sumner* (15 vols.; Boston: Lee and Shepard, 1870–1883), 7:111–117.

41 Augusta to Lincoln, Toronto, 7 January 1863, Berlin, ed., *Black Military Experience,* 354.

42 Ibid., 354n.

43 Letter of 30 March 1863, Berlin, ed., *Black Military Experience,* 355n.

44 Savannah, Georgia, correspondence, n.d. *Cincinnati Commercial,* n.d., copied in the *Cleveland Daily Leader,* 27 November 1865.

45 Washington correspondence, n.d., *New York Evening Post,* n.d., copied in the *Cleveland Daily Leader,* 8 May 1863.

46 M. Dalyce Newby, *Anderson Ruffin Abbott: First Afro-Canadian Doctor* (Markham, Ontario: Fitzhenry & Whiteside, 1998), 59–60.

47 *Chicago Post,* n.d., copied in the *Rock Island* (Illinois) *Argus,* 11 May 1863.

48 *Baltimore Clipper,* 2 May, copied in *The Liberator* (Boston), 8 May 1863; A. T. Augusta to the editor, Washington, 15 May 1863, *Christian Recorder* (Philadelphia), 30 May 1863.

49 Washington correspondence, n.d., *National Anti-Slavery Standard* (New York), n.d., copied in the *Monmouth Democrat* (Freehold, New Jersey), 14 May 1863.

50 Julia Wilbur diary, 5 March 1865, Quaker and Special Collections, Haverford College, transcription, https://www.alexandriava.gov /uploadedFiles/historic/info/civilwar/JuliaWilburDiary1865.pdf.

51 Protest by J. B. McPherson et al., Camp near Bryantown, Maryland, February 1864, in Ric Murphy and Timothy Stephens, *Section 27 and Freedman's Village in Arlington National Cemetery: The African American History of America's Most Hallowed Ground* (Jefferson, North Carolina: McFarland, 2020), 143.

52 *Dayton Daily Empire,* 4 February 1864. The quotations marks around "gentleman is received" passage refers to Frederick Douglass's description of how the president greeted him in August 1863.

53 *New Haven Columbian Register,* 12 March 1864.

54 Washington correspondence, 24 February 1864, *Baltimore Sun,*
    25 February 1864.

55 "Civil War Memoirs from Dr. Anderson Abbott," in Slaney, *Family Secrets,*
    202.

56 William M. Thayer, *Character and Public Services of Abraham Lincoln,*
    President of the United States (Boston: Dinsmoor, 1864), 22.

57 William O. Stoddard, "White House Sketches, no. 7," *New York Citizen,*
    29 September 1866, in Stoddard, *Inside the White House in War Times,* ed.
    Burlingame, 172.

58 "Civil War Memoirs from Dr. Anderson Abbott," in Slaney, *Family Secrets,* 202.

59 Washington correspondence, 24 March 1864, *Chicago Times,* n.d., copied
    in the Indianapolis *Indiana State Sentinel,* 4 April 1864.

60 Ford Risley, "The President's Editor: John W. Forney of the *Press* and
    Morning Chronicle," American Journalism 26 (2009): 63–85.

61 Washington correspondence, n.d., *Missouri Republican* (St. Louis),
    7 January 1865, copied in the *Milwaukee Daily News,* 16 January 1865.

62 Diary of Julia Wilbur, Quaker and Special Collections, Haverford College
    (entry for 2 January 1865), transcription, https://www.alexandriava.gov
    /uploadedFiles/historic/info/civilwar/JuliaWilburDiary1865.pdf.

63 Washington correspondence by "Puritan," 18 February 1865, *Boston
    Recorder,* 24 February 1865.

64 *Washington National Intelligencer,* 3 January 1865. Benjamin Brown French
    noted in his journal that he was on duty at the White House that day,
    introducing the guests "such as desired it" to the First Lady, who withdrew
    at about 2 p.m. French, *Witness to the Young Republic,* 462 (entry for
    2 January 1865).

65 Washington correspondence by H. R. G., 3 January 1865, *New York
    Independent,* n.d., copied in the *Boston Traveler,* 14 January 1865. That
    abolitionist paper was unlikely to have quoted Black dialect in an attempt
    to belittle those African Americans.

66 *Illinois State Register* (Springfield), 8 January 1865.

67 *Milwaukee Daily News,* 16 January 1865.

68 Washington correspondence by "an old pen," 12 February 1865, New York
    Anglo-African, 25 February 1865.

69   Fred Tomkins, *Jewels in Ebony* (London: British and Foreign Freedmen's
     Aid Society, [1865]), 1. "The receptions of Mrs. Lincoln and Mrs. Sprague
     yesterday [February 25] were the largest of any given this winter."
     Washington correspondence, 26 February 1865, *Philadelphia Inquirer,*
     27 February 1865.

70   Julia Wilbur Small Diary, entry for 25 February 1865, Quaker and Special
     Collections, Haverford College, transcription, https://www.alexandriava
     .gov/uploadedFiles/historic/info/civilwar/JuliaWilburDiary1865.pdf.

71   Tomkins, *Jewels in Ebony,* 2. There is no evidence that Sojourner Truth
     met more than once with Lincoln. Carlton Mabee, *Sojourner Truth: Slave,
     Prophet, Legend* (New York: New York University Press, 1993), 124.

72   Sojourner Truth to Rowland Johnson, 17 November, *National Anti-Slavery
     Standard* (New York), 17 December 1864 and same to same, *The Liberator*
     (Boston), 24 December 1864.

73   Lucy Colman, Washington correspondence, n.d., *Rochester Express,*
     n.d., copied in *The Liberator* (Boston), 18 November 1864. In her 1891
     reminiscences, Colman described Lincoln's reception of the women
     as much less cordial. Colman's later unflattering account of Lincoln's
     treatment of Sojourner Truth is dubious on its face, making Lincoln out to
     be racially insensitive and tactless, as well as contemptuous of abolitionists,
     in a way that is inconsistent with all the evidence adduced in this book as
     well as her 1864 dispatch. Lucy N. Colman, *Reminiscences* (Buffalo:
     H. L. Green, 1891), 66–67.

74   Henry Louis Gates Jr. and Donald Yacovone, eds., *Lincoln on Race and
     Slavery* (Princeton: Princeton University Press, 2009), lxi; Margaret
     Washington, *Sojourner Truth's America* (Urbana: University of Illinois
     Press, 2009), 315.

75   Seale, *The President's House,* 2:653.

76   Philippe R. Girard, "Trading Races: Joseph and Marie Bunel, a
     Diplomat and a Merchant in Revolutionary Saint-Domingue and
     Philadelphia," *Journal of the Early Republic* 30 (2010): 351–376. According
     to Girard, many historians have misidentified Joseph Bunel as a mulatto.

77   *Life and Times of Douglass,* 446–447.

78   Douglass, "The Assassination and Its Lesson," speech delivered in
     Brooklyn, 29 January 1866, *Brooklyn Daily Eagle,* 30 January 1866.

Historian James Oakes plausibly speculated that "there is every reason to believe that Lincoln invited Douglass to the Soldiers' Home because he enjoyed Douglas's company as much as he valued Douglass's opinion." Oakes, *The Radical and the Republican: Frederick Douglass, Abraham Lincoln, and the Triumph of Antislavery Politics* (New York: W.W. Norton, 2007), 238.

Historian Kate Masur has criticized the Lincolns for enforcing the color line, but that seems hardly fair to the president. After all, he regretted that Sojourner Truth had been turned away from Mrs. Lincoln's reception on February 25 and vowed that it would not happen again. He overruled the guards who attempted to block Frederick Douglass on March 4. Through the *Washington Chronicle*, he heartily invited all Washingtonians, *regardless of color*, to attend the 1865 New Year's Day reception.

In January 1866, the Washington correspondent Benjamin Perley Poore reviewed the history of White House receptions and concluded thus: "the she-secessionists hereabouts last year were startled by the announcement that 'niggers were permitted to enter the White House.' The good and just heart of Abraham Lincoln prompted him to receive representatives of every class then fighting for the Union, nor was he above shaking black hands, for hands of that color then carried the stars and stripes, or used musket or sabre in its defense. This, too, when cowardly white men remained at home, folding their white hands peacefully." Washington *National Republican*, 6 January 1866.

CHAPTER 8

1   Joel Schor, *Henry Highland Garnet: A Voice of Black Radicalism in the Nineteenth Century* (Westport, Connecticut: Greenwood Press, 1977), 205–209; Earl Ofari Hutchinson, *Let Your Motto Be Resistance: The Life and Thought of Henry Highland Garnet* (Boston: Beacon Press, 1972), 187–203.

2   Washington *Evening Star*, 4 March 1865.

3   Washington correspondence, 7 March 1865, *London Times*, 15 March 1865.

4   *Washington Chronicle*, 2 March 1865, copied in the *Cleveland Plain Dealer*, 6 March 1865.

5   Washington correspondence, 7 March 1865, *New York Herald*, 8 March 1865.

6   *Cleveland Plain Dealer*, 6 March 1865.

7   *New York World*, 4 March 1865.

8 Delany, *The Condition, Elevation, Emigration, and Destiny of the Colored People of the United States, Politically Considered* (Philadelphia: the author, 1852), 25.

9 Delany to Douglass, Buffalo N.Y., 7 August 1862, *Douglass' Monthly*, September 1862.

10 Delany to Stanton, Chicago, 15 December 1863, Ripley, ed., *Black Abolitionist Papers*, 5:261–262.

11 *New York Citizen*, n.d., copied in the *Chicago Tribune*, 11 August 1865.

12 *Pittsburgh Dispatch*, n.d., copied in the *Cleveland Leader*, 10 March 1865; Frank [Frances] A. Rollin, *Life and Public Services of Martin R. Delany* (Boston: Lee and Shepard, 1868), 19.

13 Delany to Douglass, New York, 10 July 1852, *Frederick Douglass' Paper*, 23 July 1852.

14 Ron Soodalter, "'My Soul Is Vexed Within Me So': The Rise and Fall of Martin Delany," *History Net*, March 2019, https://www.historynet.com /soul-vexed-within.htm.

15 *Douglass' Monthly*, August 1862.

16 William Wells Brown, "The Colored People of Canada" (1861), in Ripley, ed., *Black Abolitionist Papers*, 2:472.

17 *Christian Recorder* (Philadelphia), 5 February 1885.

18 Robert E. Fleming, "Black, White, and Mulatto in Martin R. Delaney's Blake," *Negro History Bulletin*, 36 (1973): 37–39.

19 Rollin, *Life and Public Services of Delany*, 166.

20 Lincoln to Johnson, Washington, 26 March 1863, Basler, ed., *Collected Works of Lincoln*, 6:149.

21 *Washington Chronicle*, 1 March 1865, copied in the *Philadelphia Press*, 3 March 1865.

22 *Pittsburgh Dispatch*, n.d., copied in the *Cleveland Leader*, 10 March 1865.

23 Payne, *Recollections of Seventy Years*, 160.

24 Delany to the editor, Charleston, 20 April 1865, New York *Anglo-African*, n.d., copied in *The Christian Recorder* (Philadelphia), 20 May 1865.

25 *Pittsburgh Courier*, 25 July 1936.

26 Victor Ullman, *Martin R. Delany: The Beginnings of Black Nationalism* (Boston: Beacon Press, 1971); Theodore Draper, "The Father of American Black Nationalism," *New York Review of Books*, 12 March 1970, 33–41.

27 Reynolds, *Abe*, 821, 825.

CHAPTER 9

1   Eulogy for Lincoln, 1 June 1865, manuscript, Douglass Papers, Library of Congress; *New York Times* and *New York Tribune*, 2 June 1865. I have combined the manuscript with the newspaper accounts, which differ slightly from that document. The reporters may have misrepresented what Douglass said, but it is more likely that Douglass departed from the prepared text spontaneously.

2   Blight, *Frederick Douglass*, 731, 8.

3   Washington correspondence, 2 November 1864, *Sacramento Daily Union*, 2 December 1864, in Michael Burlingame, ed., *Lincoln Observed: Civil War Dispatches of Noah Brooks* (Baltimore: Johns Hopkins University Press, 1998), 142.

4   Oakes, *The Radical and the Republican*, 279.

5   Ibid., 195.

6   Rice, ed., *Reminiscences of Lincoln*, 193.

7   Speech to the Republican National League, February 1883, in Blassingame, ed., *Frederick Douglas Papers*, 5:340–344.

8   Speech in Brooklyn, 12 February 1893, ibid., 5:536–537.

APPENDIX

1   Reynolds, *Abe*, 775.

2   Quarles, *Lincoln and the Negro*, 36, 194, 204.

3   Miller, *Lincoln's Virtues*, 240; Basler, "Lincoln, Blacks, and Women," in Cullom Davis et al., eds., *The Public and the Private Lincoln: Contemporary Perspectives* (Carbondale: Southern Illinois University Press, 1979), 48. Eric Foner made a similar point: "Lincoln's personal dealing with blacks did not reveal prejudice." Foner, *Fiery Trial*, 12.

4   Miller, *Lincoln's Virtues*, 367.

5   Oakes, *Crooked Path to Abolition*, 111; Reynolds, *Abe*, 802–803, 929.

6   John M. Rozett, "Racism and Republican Emergence in Illinois, 1848–1860: A Re-Evaluation of Republican Negrophobia," *Civil War History* 22 (1976): 114.

7   W. M. Chambers to Lincoln, Charleston, 22 July 1858, and Thomas A. Marshall to Lincoln, Charleston, 2 June 1858, Lincoln Papers, Library of Congress.

8   Basler, ed., *Collected Works of Lincoln*, 2:501.

9   Thomas A. Marshall to Lincoln, Charleston, 22 July 1858, Lincoln Papers, Library of Congress.

10   David Davis to Lincoln, Bloomington, 3 August 1858, ibid. See also David Davis to O. M. Hatch, Springfield and Bloomington, 18 August 1858, *For the People: A Newsletter of the Abraham Lincoln Association* 4, no. 3 (Autumn 2002): 6–7, and Willard King, *Lincoln's Manager: David Davis* (Cambridge: Harvard University Press, 1960), 124–125.

11   Basler, ed., *Collected Works of Lincoln*, 3:145–146.

12   Oakes, *Crooked Path to Abolition*, 123.

13   Don E. Fehrenbacher, "Only His Stepchildren: Lincoln and the Negro," *Civil War History* 20 (1974): 304–305.

14   Paludan, "Greeley, Colonization, and a 'Deputation of Negroes," 46.

15   Douglass, "What Shall Be Done with the Slaves If Emancipated?" *Douglass' Monthly*, January 1862.

16   Donald, *Lincoln*, 221.

17   McPherson, *The War That Forged a Nation: Why the Civil War Still Matters* (New York: Oxford University Press, 2015), 117.

18   Reynolds, *Abe*, 775.

19   Donald, *Lincoln*, 633. Donald did note that "Lincoln fortunately escaped the more virulent strains of racism. Unlike many of his fellow Republicans, he never spoke of African-Americans as hideous or physically inferior; he never declared that they were innately inferior mentally or incapable of intellectual development; he never described them as indolent or incapable of sustained work; he never discussed their supposed licentious nature or immorality."

20   On Northern Negrophobia, see Leon Litwack, *North of Slavery: The Negro in the Free States, 1790–1860* (Chicago: University of Chicago Press, 1961); Lorman Ratner, *Powder Keg: Northern Opposition to the Antislavery Movement, 1831–1840* (New York: Basic Books, 1968); George M. Fredrickson, *The Black Image in the White Mind: The Debate on Afro-American Character and Destiny, 1817–1914* (1971; Middletown, Connecticut: Wesleyan University Press, 1987), 140–164; James A. Rawley, *Race and Politics: "Bleeding Kansas" and the Coming of the Civil War* (Philadelphia: J. B. Lippincott, 1969), 65–67; Eric Foner, "Racial Attitudes of the New York Free Soilers," *New York History* 46 (1965): 311–29; Eric

Foner, "Politics and Prejudice: The Free Soil Party and the Negro, 1849–1852," *Journal of Negro History* 50 (1965): 239–56; James D. Bilotta, *Race and the Rise of the Republican Party, 1848–1865* (New York: Peter Lang, 1992); Eugene H. Berwanger, "Negrophobia in Northern Pro-Slavery and Antislavery Thought," *Phylon* 33 (1972): 266–275, and *The Frontier against Slavery: Western Anti-Negro Prejudice and the Slavery Extension Controversy* (Urbana: University of Illinois Press, 1967); Voegeli, *Free but Not Equal*; Robert F. Durden, "Ambiguities in the Antislavery Crusade of the Republican Party," in Martin B. Duberman, ed., *The Antislavery Vanguard; New Essays on the Abolitionists* (Princeton, N.J.: Princeton University Press, 1965), 362–94; Foner, *Free Soil, Free Labor, Free Men*, 60–61, 266–267.

21   Miller, *Lincoln's Virtues*, 361. "Critics of Lincoln on race compare him unfavorably to a list of abolitionists and anti-slavery politicians, almost all of whom come from New England or from pockets of New England migration like the Western Reserve [of Ohio] or the burnt-over district in upstate New York, or from places of comparative enlightenment in the east." Ibid.

22   On Midwestern Republicans' racism, see Voegeli, *Free but Not Equal*, 160–182.

23   *Congressional Globe*, 35th Congress, 2nd session, 346 (12 January 1859).

24   Speech in Congress, 5 April 1860, in Lovejoy, *His Brother's Blood: Speeches and Writings, 1838–1864,* ed. William F. Moore and Jane Ann Moore (Urbana: University of Illinois Press, 2004), 193.

25   Lovejoy, speech in Chicago, 15 October 1860, ibid., 240.

26   Lovejoy, speech in Congress, 21 February 1859, ibid., 177.

27   Oakes, *Crooked Path to Abolition*, 107.

28   *Congressional Globe*, 36th Congress, 1st session, 58–59 (8 December 1859).

29   Unidentified clipping attached to a letter from Charles Taintor Jr. to Trumbull, Jackson, Michigan, December 1859, Trumbull Family Papers, Lincoln Presidential Library, Springfield.

30   Speech of Lyman Trumbull in Chicago, 7 August 1858, *National Era* (Washington), 2 September 1858.

31   *Congressional Globe*, 31st Congress, 1st session, part 1, p. 136 (10 January 1850).

32   Allan Peskin, *Garfield: A Biography* (Kent, Ohio: Kent State University Press, 1978), 253.

33 Robert Dixon Sawrey, *Dubious Victory: The Reconstruction Debate in Ohio* (Lexington: University Press of Kentucky, 1992), 37.

34 Peskin, *Garfield*, 304.

35 Howe to William P. Fessenden, 28 August 1864, Howe Papers, Historical Society of Wisconsin, quoted in Hans L. Trefousse, *The Radical Republicans: Lincoln's Vanguard for Racial Justice* (New York: Alfred A. Knopf, 1969), 31.

36 *Congressional Globe*, 38th Congress, 1st session, 2038–39 (2 May 1864).

37 *Chicago Tribune*, 12 August 1861.

38 George M. Fredrickson, *Big Enough to be Inconsistent: Abraham Lincoln Confronts Slavery and Race* (Cambridge: Harvard University Press, 2008), 41. Cf. ibid., ix.

39 As James Oakes put it, for Lincoln "the entire issue" of racial equality "was a distraction. He wanted questions about race moved off the table, and he needed a strategy to get rid of them." Oakes, *The Radical and the Republican*, 117–118.

40 David R. Locke in Rice, ed., *Reminiscences of Lincoln*, 446–447. Emphasis in the original.

41 Voegeli, *Free but Not Equal*, 8, 179.

42 Nathaniel Paul, speech to the Albany Anti-Slavery Convention, 1 March 1838, *Friend of Man* (Utica, NY), 14 March 1838.

43 Hans L. Trefousse, *Benjamin Franklin Wade, Radical Republican from Ohio* (New York: Twayne Publishers, 1963), 118, 187; Wade to his wife, Washington, 9 March 1873, Wade Papers, Library of Congress. See also Hans L. Trefousse, "Ben Wade and the Negro," *Ohio Historical Quarterly* 68 (1959): 166–167.

44 Oakes, *The Radical and the Republican*, 113.

45 Elizabeth Brown Pryor, "Brief Encounter: A New York Cavalryman's Striking Conversation with Abraham Lincoln," *Journal of the Abraham Lincoln Association* 30 (2009): 1–24.

46 Sumner, *Collected Works*, 20:41; Reynolds, *Abe*, 774.

47 Carwardine, *Lincoln's Sense of Humor* (Carbondale: Southern Illinois University Press, 2017), 77, 84–85.

48 Reynolds, *Abe*, 802. Locke "launched a wholesale assault on racial prejudice that energized Lincoln's political battles and contributed to his evolving views on race." Ibid., 772.

49 Ibid., 236–237.

50 McMahon to Lincoln, Harmbrook, Pennsylvania, 5 August 1864, Nicolay Papers, Library of Congress.

51 Nicolay to McMahon, Washington, 6 August 1864, Basler, ed., *Collected Works of Lincoln*, 7:482.

52 In 1857, he wrote to legal clients: "There is no longer any difficult question of *jurisdiction* in the Federal courts; they have jurisdiction in all possible causes, except such as might redound to the benefit of a 'nigger' in some way." Lincoln to Newton Deming and George P. Strong, Springfield, 25 May 1857, ibid., 2:396.

53 *New York Tribune*, 7 March 1854.

54 Douglas's speech at Springfield, 17 July 1858, in Paul M. Angle, ed., *Created Equal? The Complete Lincoln-Douglas Debates of 1858* (Chicago: University of Chicago Press, 1958), 62–65, and in the *Indiana State Sentinel* (Indianapolis), 22 July 1858.

55 See Walter B. Stevens, *A Reporter's Lincoln*, ed. Michael Burlingame (1916; Lincoln: University of Nebraska Press, 1998), 85.

56 *Quincy Whig*, 26 August 1858.

57 Morris, Illinois, correspondence by J. W. N., 21 August 1858, *Belmont Chronicle and Farmers, Mechanics, and Manufacturers Advocate* (St. Clairsville, Ohio), 2 September 1858.

58 Stevens, *A Reporter's Lincoln*, ed. Burlingame, 75.

59 Ibid., 85.

60 Hillsboro correspondence, 2 August, *Chicago Press and Tribune*, 7 August 1858.

61 Alton correspondence, 15 October, *New York Tribune* (semi-weekly ed.), 26 October 1858, in Edwin Erle Sparks, ed., *The Lincoln-Douglas Debates of 1858* (Collections of the Illinois State Historical Library, vol. 3; Lincoln Series, vol. 1; Springfield: Illinois State Historical Library, 1908), 504.

62 Basler, ed., *Collected Works of Lincoln*, 3:91.

63 Washington correspondence, 31 January 1854, *New York Times*, 2 February 1854.

64 Waters to Lemuel Waters, Washington, 12 August 1862, Lucien P. Waters Papers, New-York Historical Society, in Pryor, "Brief Encounter," 22. The reference to "darkies" occurs in a letter Waters wrote to his parents in 1862. Ibid., 7.

65 Samuel G. Buckingham, *The Life of William A. Buckingham, the War Governor of Connecticut* (Springfield: W. F. Adams, 1894), 262–63.

66 William D. Kelley, *Lincoln and Stanton* (New York: Putnam's, 1885), 86; Michael Burlingame and John R. Turner Ettlinger, eds., *Inside Lincoln's White House: The Complete Civil War Diary of John Hay* (Carbondale: Southern Illinois University Press, 1997), 216 (entry for 1 July 1864).

67 Garrison to Oliver Johnson, 9 September 1862, Walter M. Merrill, ed., *The Letters of William Lloyd Garrison* (6 vols.; Cambridge: Belknap Press of Harvard University Press, 1971–1981), 5:112.

68 Northampton *Free Press*, n.d., copied in the Boston *Commonwealth*, 20 September 1862.

69 James B. Newcomer to Henry S. Lane, Reading, Pennsylvania, 11 July 1862, typed copy, Lane Papers, Indiana University; Mark Grimsley, *The Hard Hand of War: Union Military Policy toward Southern Civilians, 1861–1865* (Cambridge: Cambridge University Press, 1995), 67–95; Silvana R. Siddali, *From Property to Person: Slavery and the Confiscation Acts, 1861–1862* (Baton Rouge: Louisiana State University Press, 2005), 167–191.

70 Elizabeth Todd Grimsley, "Six Months in the White House," *Journal of the Illinois State Historical Society* 19 (1926–27): 60.

71 Sumner told this to Adams Hill. Hill to Sydney Howard Gay, Washington, 9 July 1862, Sydney Howard Gay Papers, Columbia University.

72 Moncure Daniel Conway, "A Southern Abolitionist's Memories of Mr. Lincoln," London *Fortnightly Review*, June 1865, in Rufus Rockwell Wilson, ed., *Intimate Memories of Lincoln* (Elmira, N.Y.: Primavera Press, 1945), 182.

73 Remarks made on 20 June 1862, Basler, ed., *Collected Works of Lincoln*, 5:278–279; William D. Kelley to the editor of the *New York Tribune*, Philadelphia, 23 September 1885, in Kelley, *Lincoln and Stanton: A Study of the War Administration of 1861 and 1862* (New York: G. P. Putnam's Sons, 1885), 83–85; Kelley in Rice, ed., *Reminiscences of Lincoln*, 281–283; Memorial of the Religious Society of Progressive Friends to Lincoln, 7 June 1862, Lincoln Papers, Library of Congress; *New York Journal of Commerce*, n.d., copied in the *National Anti-Slavery Standard* (New York), 5 July 1862.

74 Washington correspondence, 18 August 1862, *New York Examiner*,
    21 August 1862, in Michael Burlingame, ed., *Dispatches from Lincoln's
    White House: The Anonymous Civil War Journalism of Presidential Secretary
    William O. Stoddard* (Lincoln: University of Nebraska Press, 2002), 95.

75 On Lincoln's temper, see Burlingame, *Inner World of Lincoln*, 147–235.

76 Burlingame, ed., *Lincoln Observed*, 211; Mary Lincoln, interview with
    William H. Herndon, September 1866, in Douglas L. Wilson and Rodney
    O. Davis, eds., *Herndon's Informants: Letters, Interviews, and Statements
    about Abraham Lincoln* (Urbana: University of Illinois Press, 1998), 361.

77 Henry Samuel, "My Interview with Lincoln," typescript, 8 March 1889,
    Abraham Lincoln Presidential Library Springfield.

78 Gates, ed., *Lincoln on Race and Slavery*, lxi.

79 https://www.yourdictionary.com/cuffee.

80 Pierce, "The Freedmen at Port Royal," in *Enfranchisement and Citizenship:
    Addresses and Papers by Edward L. Pierce*, ed. A. W. Stevens (Boston:
    Roberts Brothers, 1896), 87; Pierce to William H. Herndon, Milton,
    Massachusetts, 15 September 1889, Wilson and Davis, eds., *Herndon's
    Informants,* 677.

81 Barbara A. White, *Visits with Lincoln: Abolitionists Meet the President at the
    White House* (Lanham, Maryland: Lexington Books, 2011), xi.

82 Phillips's lecture at the Smithsonian, 14 March, *New York Tribune*,
    18 March 1862; Washington *Evening Star*, 15 March 1862.

83 Moncure D. Conway to his wife Ellen, Boston, 8 March 1862, Conway
    Papers, Columbia University.

84 Wendell Phillips's speech in Boston, 18 April 1862, *New York Tribune*,
    19 April 1862; Phillips to his wife Ann, en route from Milwaukee to
    Madison, Wisconsin, 31 March 1862, Phillips Papers, Harvard University.
    Emphasis in original.

85 Washington correspondence, 26 January 1863, *Boston Evening Journal*,
    28 January 1863. Among the callers were Wendell Phillips, Moncure
    Conway, Oakes Ames, George Luther Stearns, and Frank Bird. Frank
    Preston Stearns, *The Life and Public Services of George Luther Stearns*
    (Philadelphia: J. B. Lippincott, 1907), 277.

86 Moncure D. Conway, *Autobiography: Memories and Experiences* (2 vols.;
    Boston: Houghton Mifflin, 1904), 1:379.

87 Conway journal, 5 February 1863, in John d'Entremont, *Southern Emancipator: Moncure Conway, the American Years, 1832–1865* (New York: Oxford University Press, 1987), 91–92.

88 Victor B. Howard, *Religion and the Radical Republican Movement, 1860–1870* (Lexington: University Press of Kentucky, 1990), 57.

89 Stearns, *Life of Stearns*, 280.

90 Garrison to his wife, Philadelphia, 11 June 1864, Merrill, ed., *Garrison Letters*, 5:212.

91 Wendell Phillips Garrison, *William Lloyd Garrison, 1805–1879: The Story of His Life Told by His Children* (4 vols.; New-York: Century, 1885–1889), 4:117.

92 William Garrison to his wife, 27 June 1864, Garrison Family Papers, Smith College, in Harriet Hyman Alonso, *Growing Up Abolitionist: The Story of the Garrison Children* (Amherst: University of Massachusetts Press, 2002), 218.

93 *The Liberator* (Boston), 20 May 1864.

94 *New York Times*, 7 February 1864; Henry Mayer, *All On Fire: William Lloyd Garrison and the Abolition of Slavery* (New York: St. Martin's, 1998), 562, 563.

95 *The Liberator* (Boston), 18 March 1864.

96 Merrill, ed., *Garrison Letters*, 5:180.

97 Garrison to Lincoln, Boston, 13 February 1865, Lincoln Papers, Library of Congress.

98 *The Liberator* (Boston), n.d., copied in the *National Anti-Slavery Standard* (New York), 8 October 1864.

99 Frederick Douglass to Theodore Tilton, Rochester, 15 October 1864, Philip S. Foner, ed., *The Life and Writings of Frederick Douglass* (4 vols.; New York: International Publishers, 1950–55), 3:424; *The Liberator* (Boston), 23 February 1864.

100 J. W. C. Pennington to Robert Hamilton, New York, 9 June 1864, *Anglo-African* (New York), 25 June 1864, in Ripley, ed., *Black Abolitionist Papers*, 5:277.

101 New York *Anglo-African*, 22 July 1864.

102 Ibid., 24 September 1864. Emphasis in original.

103 Martin B. Pasternak, *Rise Now and Fly to Arms: The Life of Henry Highland Garnet* (New York: Garland, 1995), 119.

104 *Weekly Pacific Appeal* (San Francisco), 9 January 1864.

105 Thomas Carson, *Lincoln's Ethics* (New York: Cambridge University Press, 2015), 335–375.

106 Phillip Shaw Paludan conceded that "Lincoln and true racists of the time used the N-word," but insisted "it makes some difference whether it is used thoughtlessly or in malice." Lincoln "never used the word with malice." His "occasional 'racist' remarks revealed everything from the instinctual bias of a childhood in proslavery territory to the careful efforts of a subtle politician to achieve a radical goal by wrapping it in conservative bunting." Paludan, "Greeley, Colonization, and a 'Deputation of Negroes,'" 31, 42.

107 David R. Locke in Rice, ed., *Reminiscences of Lincoln,* 446–447. Emphasis in the original.

108 Carson, *Lincoln's Ethics*, 396.

109 Gates, ed., *Lincoln on Race and Slavery,* xxii.

110 Unidentified newspaper clipping, ca. December 1866, reproduced in *For the People: A Newsletter of the Abraham Lincoln Association*, March 2020, p. 1.

111 Gates, *Lincoln on Race and Slavery*, xxxix–xli; Welles, "The Administration of Abraham Lincoln," *Galaxy* (October 1877), 440.

112 Morse, ed., *Welles Diary,* 2:374.

113 Manuscript of a speech, ca. December 1865, Douglass Papers, Library of Congress.

114 Douglass, "The Assassination and Its Lesson," speech delivered in Brooklyn, 29 January 1866, *Brooklyn Daily Eagle*, 30 January 1866.

115 Hodes, *Mourning Lincoln* (New Haven: Yale University Press, 2015), 273.

116 Carson, *Lincoln's Ethics*, 370.

117 Basler, ed., *Collected Works of Lincoln,* 2:520.

118 Ibid., 3:16.

119 Reynolds, *Abe,* 356.

120 Basler, ed., *Collected Works of Lincoln,* 2:222–223.

121 David R. Locke in Rice, ed., *Reminiscences of Lincoln*, 446–447. Emphasis in the original.

122 Foner, *Fiery Trial,* xviii.

123 Oakes, *Crooked Path*, 113.

124 Booth told this to David Herold, who in turn told it to his attorney, Frederick Stone, who then told Louis J. Weichman. Louis J. Weichman, *A*

True History of the Assassination of Abraham Lincoln and of the Conspiracy of 1865 (New York: Knopf, 1975), 148. Herold's attorney also told this to George Alfred Townsend. Townsend, *Katy of Catoctin, or, The Chain-Breakers: A National Romance* (New York: D. Appleton, 1886), 490n.

125 Booth said this to Lewis Powell, one of Booth's co-conspirators, who in turn told it to Thomas T. Eckert. Eckert's testimony, 30 May 1867, "Impeachment of the President," House Report no. 7, 40th Congress, 1st session (1867): 674.

126 See the compilation of civil rights martyrs compiled by the Southern Poverty Law Center, https://www.splcenter.org/what-we-do/civil-rights-memorial/civil-rights-martyrs.

INDEX